FAST COMPANY's
GREATEST HITS

Um̃
7 Apr 2009

FAST COMPANY's

GREATEST HITS

TEN YEARS OF THE

MOST INNOVATIVE IDEAS

IN BUSINESS

Edited by **MARK N. VAMOS** and **DAVID LIDSKY**

with a Foreword by JIM COLLINS

PORTFOLIO

PORTFOLIO
Published by the Penguin Group
Penguin Group (USA) Inc., 375 Hudson Street, New York, New York 10014, U.S.A. · Penguin Group
(Canada), 90 Eglinton Avenue East, Suite 700, Toronto, Ontario, Canada M4P 2Y3 (a division of
Pearson Penguin Canada Inc.) · Penguin Books Ltd, 80 Strand, London WC2R 0RL, England ·
Penguin Ireland, 25 St. Stephen's Green, Dublin 2, Ireland (a division of Penguin Books Ltd) ·
Penguin Books Australia Ltd, 250 Camberwell Road, Camberwell, Victoria 3124, Australia (a division of
Pearson Australia Group Pty Ltd) · Penguin Books India Pvt Ltd, 11 Community Centre,
Panchsheel Park, New Delhi - 110 017, India · Penguin Group (NZ), Cnr Airborne and Rosedale
Roads, Albany, Auckland 1310, New Zealand (a division of Pearson New Zealand Ltd) · Penguin
Books (South Africa) (Pty) Ltd, 24 Sturdee Avenue, Rosebank, Johannesburg 2196, South Africa

Penguin Books Ltd, Registered Offices:
80 Strand, London WC2R 0RL, England

First published in 2006 by Portfolio,
a member of Penguin Group (USA) Inc.

1   3   5   7   9   10   8   6   4   2

Copyright © Fast Company, a publication of Mansueto Ventures LLC, 2006
Foreword copyright © Jim Collins, 2006
All rights reserved

"Built to Flip" by Jim Collins. Copyright © Jim Collins, 2000.
Reprinted by permission of the author.

"How to Give Feedback" by Seth Godin. Copyright © Seth Godin, 2004.
Reprinted by permission of the author.

"In Search of Courage" by John McCain. Copyright © John McCain, 2004.
Portions of this work were adapted from *Why Courage Matters: The Way to a Braver Life* by
John McCain with Mark Salter (Random House, 2004). Used with permission.

LIBRARY OF CONGRESS CATALOGING IN PUBLICATION DATA
Fast company's greatest hits : ten years of the most innovative ideas in business / edited
by Mark N. Vamos and David Lidsky ; with a foreword by Jim Collins.
    p. cm.
ISBN 1-59184-118-6
1. Business.   2. Management.   3. Entrepreneurship.   I. Vamos, Mark N.
II. Lidsky, David.   III. Fast company.
HF1008.F37 2006
658.4'063—dc22   2006043474

Printed in the United States of America
Set in Minion
Designed by Helene Berinsky

To our readers—past, present, and future

CONTENTS

theoretically replace. A self-service kiosk may look simple as it alters how we check in at the airport. Just wait until it reinvents your job.

ACKNOWLEDGMENTS

The authors would like to thank

Alan Webber and Bill Taylor for having the genius to start *Fast Company*;

Joe Mansueto for being our wise and encouraging owner;

Adrian Zackheim for having the idea to do this story collection;

John A. Byrne for wanting to do it;

John Koten for greenlighting this project;

Will Weisser for his sage counsel and patience;

Keith H. Hammonds, Linda Tischler, Bill Breen, Charles Fishman, Dean Markadakis, Chuck Salter, and Heath Row, for their suggestions and input;

and Jim Collins for lending his insight and support.

And finally, David Lidsky would like to thank his darling wife, Carol Vinzant, for her immeasurable support, for listening to him talk incessantly about this project for a year, and for the many nights and weekends he spent reading eight-year-old magazine articles.

FOREWORD

In the early 1990s, Alan Webber was at the top of his game—well-compensated, admired, editorial director and managing editor of the *Harvard Business Review*—and miserable. He'd become entrapped by the curse of competence, successful in a job that he no longer enjoyed. The longer he stayed, the more successful he became. The more successful he became, the greater the cost of giving up his job. The greater the cost of giving up his job, the more his own success became a prison.

Meanwhile, Webber's colleague Bill Taylor, who had previously worked with consumer advocate Ralph Nader, had already quit his editing job at *HBR*. "I felt myself drawn to the creative intensity—the raw animal spirit—coming from places like Silicon Valley and Asia," reflected Taylor. "And I wanted to create a magazine that would be its voice."

Spurred on by Taylor, Webber considered his options. He could stay in his job, successful and unhappy. Or he could join Taylor, and if he failed—well, what's the worst that could happen? He could always get another job. Sure, once you've had a taste of freedom, it's hard to work for someone else; but it's not like you're going to *die*. "I had to give it a try. If I didn't go then, I'd never go, and I'd wonder for the rest of my life," recalls Webber. "There was a part of me that said, 'Your whole life has been a preparation for this moment.'"

Bill Taylor and Alan Webber perceived three big trends:

Trend No. 1: digitalization. Powerful devices would make computing both more personal and more social.

Trend No. 2: globalization. Russians, Americans, Chinese, Brazilians—people from everywhere—would embrace and share the best ideas, independent of national origin.

Trend No. 3: democratization. Baby-boomers hitting their fifties would accelerate the diffusion of power in society.

Taylor and Webber believed that no magazine had taken the lead in these trends, and they founded *Fast Company.* Yet their genius came not in reporting on these trends, but in the magazine's mission *to shape the conversation,* and thereby shape a generation, much the way *Rolling Stone* did with the rock 'n' roll counterculture. "Every great magazine serves a noble purpose," reflects Bill Taylor. "We wanted to be about how people—and business at its best—can make a positive impact on the world."

And so, in November 1995, *Fast Company* hit the newsstands, seeking to ignite conversations that would have a catalytic impact. People discovered the magazine and became passionate about its message. The freshness of hearing a successful CEO say, "Everything I thought I knew about leadership is wrong," or exploring, in "Free Agent Nation," the growing movement of people abandoning their jobs to carve their own paths caused people to read and reflect, and—most important—discuss. They ripped out pages and passed them around; they pasted text into e-mails and sent links; they met and talked in groups, and reconnected on the Web site. *Fast Company* did something rare in publishing: it created a *community* of readers.

Then something quite unfortunate happened: the Internet bubble. At the end of 1995, the NASDAQ stock index closed at just above 1,000. In the next five years, it multiplied more than four times, with some dot-com IPOs posting first-day price increases of more than 300 percent. Of course, the bubble was destined to burst—but not before it would corrupt the whole idea of the new economy. *Fast Company* achieved the success it wished for: it experienced explosive growth and Webber and Taylor and their backers were able to sell the magazine at an Internet valuation in 2000. Since then, the magazine's financial fortunes have mirrored the aftereffects of the bubble, further reinforcing the notion that *Fast Company* was nothing more than a mouthpiece of the dot-com era—an unfortunate mischaracterization that I hope this book helps to erase.

I entered *Fast Company*'s story in 1999, with a call from Alan Webber. "I'm sitting here watching what's happening, and I'm thinking, 'Did I blink and miss something?' " he said. "We used to talk about building companies, changing lives, having an impact, creating a better workplace, realizing potential—and now all people want to talk about is flipping companies, getting rich, and cashing out." Alan asked if I would pen an essay, which became "Built to Flip," published in March 2000. Together, we crafted an all-out attack on the "It's OK to work just for money, so long as it's a *lot* of money—and, oh, by the way, I'm entitled to be rich" mentality that infected the late 1990s. Like a Zen master with a bamboo stick, Alan wanted to whack people on the head and say, "Wake up! You're missing the whole point!"

The point—that we should think about life, work, and the connection between the two—needs to be resuscitated. Sifting through the best articles from *Fast Company*'s first ten years, I see an underlying order to the chaos, captured in five basic premises that—while the bubble has come and gone—remain relevant:

Premise No. 1: Work is not a means to an end; it is an end in itself. If you create work you are deeply passionate about—because you love to do it and you believe in what it can contribute—the very act of work can become a source of sanctuary and meaning.

Premise No. 2: If your competitive scorecard is money, you will always lose. There are two ways to be wealthy. One is to have a huge amount of money. The other is to have simple needs. What is your answer to "How much is enough?" As professor Michael Ray of Stanford taught: comparison is the primary sin of modern life.

Premise No. 3: Business is a mechanism for social change—for good and ill. If you build a great enterprise, it will have an impact—on its people, on its customers, on the communities it touches. The question is: will that impact be positive? How will the world be better off, beyond wealth creation?

Premise No. 4: Entrepreneurship is a life concept, not just a business concept. There are two approaches to life. One is to buy the "paint-by-numbers kit" and stay within the lines. The other is to start with a blank canvas and try to paint a masterpiece. You can be an entrepreneur without starting a company, by creating a path uniquely designed to you.

Premise No. 5: Performance is the fundamental requirement. Good intentions mean nothing without great performance. Businesses must deliver results. Nonprofits must deliver on mission. People must deliver on responsibilities. There is no room for those who simply cannot perform.

Reading the articles collected in this wonderful book is like listening in on a series of fascinating conversations with some of the best minds and creative thinkers of a generation. And not just about business. "We wanted to do for this new era what *Fortune* did for the industrial era," explains Webber. "I remember coming across an early issue of *Fortune* from 1930—volume 1, issue no. 2—and there was an article by Ernest Hemingway on the economics of bullfighting. And I realized something *Fortune* realized in 1930: a great business magazine is about life, about society, about economics, about human stuff good and bad—about the types of things Ernest Hemingway would write about. We wanted to be the business magazine that if Hemingway were around today, he would want to write for us."

I suspect Hemingway would have loved to write for *Fast Company* because of one underlying ethos: passion. Running through the best of the magazine like a red thread is the idea that nothing great ever happens without passion. My favorite *Fast Company* writers are passionate—passionate about ideas, passionate about their work, passionate about correcting the wrongs in the world, passionate about a cause, passionate about values, passionate about performance. Some of these are businesspeople, but they are just as likely to be Senator John McCain in his article about courage, Major Tony Burgess and how he "fell in love with leading" in "Grassroots Leadership: U.S. Military Academy," or coach John Smith and his systematic approach to helping 100-meter runners shave a hundredth of a second in "Stop Time." Just like a Hemingway story, these articles can be enjoyed as much today as when first published. Read. Absorb. Reflect. Enjoy. Renew.

But above all, follow the underlying message: If you're not deeply passionate about what you're doing, then it's time to change. We live short and die long, in the words of Dr. Walter M. Bortz, and the urgency of getting on with what we are meant to do with this one short life increases with each passing day.

Jim Collins
Boulder, Colorado
December 1, 2005

Jim Collins is the author of *Good to Great: Why Some Companies Make the Leap . . . And Others Don't* and coauthor of *Built to Last: Successful Habits of Visionary Companies.* A recipient of the Distinguished Teaching Award while a faculty member at the Stanford University Graduate School of Business, Jim now works from his management-research laboratory in Boulder, Colorado. More of Jim Collins's work can be found at www.jimcollins.com.

INTRODUCTION

In its first few years, *Fast Company* captured an extraordinary period in our national life. It was a time of optimism about where business could take us, of exuberance and impatience about getting there, and of passion about taking the voyage.

But now, in this manifestly less exuberant era, I'm often asked about *Fast Company*'s current role in the business world. My answer is simple: Times change. The power of great ideas doesn't.

As the remarkable stories in this collection make clear, *Fast Company* has always been about ideas—insights into how to become a better leader or worker, how to harness the power of design, how to manage career and worklife, how to solve a scientific mystery or meet an organizational challenge, how to overcome obstacles and cope with failure.

What we do, and what we have always done, is seek out the folks who are putting those ideas to work. There is no more compelling, no more useful story in business journalism than the chronicle of imaginative people taking risks to accomplish something new and worthwhile. Their goal may be to create a must-have gadget, cure a deadly disease, revive a struggling company, or reinvent an entire industry. But they're all using imagination, brains, and skill to do something better, and we focus on them because their stories are dramatic, inspiring, and instructive.

Innovation—which is ideas put to work—remains the most precious commodity in business. And that's as true now as it was when *Fast Company* launched. Whether it results in a wholly new thing (think iPod) or a new business model (think JetBlue), innovation works magic. Without it, people and organizations remain trapped in trench warfare, fighting a grinding battle to compete on cost or marginal features.

Innovation is what lets us leap out of the trenches. It's how real winners are made, how real money is earned, how things of beauty and usefulness are created, how consumers' lives are enriched and society made better, and how America must compete in this world.

If you're in a business that hungers for useful ideas to stay ahead of fast-moving technology, changing consumer patterns, and rising competition (and who isn't?), you'll find the stories that *Fast Company* became known for in its first decade, and will remain known for in its second, more compelling than ever.

A few words about how we created this collection. We both enjoyed and dreaded the process of sifting through 10 years of *Fast Company*—100 issues in all—to find the best articles in the history of the magazine. That's a lot of magazines!

Fortunately, they made for great reading. Richly detailed, well-told stories have been a hallmark of the magazine since its inception. But we figured that, like the monthly magazine, this book should be useful as well as entertaining. So it was important to pick pieces that still have relevance today. They had to be great reads, but the ideas underpinning the stories still had to resonate in 2006 as much as they did when first published. We also asked our writers and longtime contributors to give us their favorites. Most of them, a humble lot, argued that we should *not* include one of their stories. And we looked to reader feedback over the years to discover the articles that had the most impact.

We hope we've included all of your favorites, but we know we may have left out one or two pieces you tore out and have been passing around to colleagues for years. Sorry. But we hope this book helps you rediscover some old favorites you've forgotten—or find some new ones.

—Mark N. Vamos
Editor, *Fast Company*

FAST COMPANY's
GREATEST HITS

Handbook of the Business Revolution

From: Issue 01 | November 1995 |
By: Alan M. Webber and William C. Taylor

The founding editors outline how the business world is changing and why
next-generation business leaders need a magazine—and a community—to
help them lead the charge for change.

Something is happening and it affects us all. A global revolution is changing business, and business is changing the world. With unsettling speed,
two forces are converging: a new generation of business leaders is rewriting
the rules of business, and a new breed of fast companies is challenging the
corporate status quo.

That convergence overturns 50 years of received wisdom on the fundamentals of work and competition. No part of business is immune. The
structure of the company is changing; relationships between companies are
changing; the nature of work is changing; the definition of success is changing. The result is a revolution as far-reaching as the Industrial Revolution.

We are just beginning to comprehend this new world even as we create
it. This much we know: we live and work in a time of unparalleled opportunity and unprecedented uncertainty. An economy driven by technology and
innovation makes old borders obsolete. Smart people working in smart
companies have the ability to create their own futures—and also hold the
responsibility for the consequences. The possibilities are unlimited—and
unlimited possibilities carry equal measures of hope and fear.

Fast Company aims to be the handbook of the business revolution. We
will chronicle the changes under way in how companies create and compete, highlight the new practices shaping how work gets done, showcase

teams who are inventing the future and reinventing business. Most of all, we will equip the people exploring this uncharted territory with the tools, techniques, models, and mind-sets they need.

Fast Company is where best practice meets big ideas; new talent meets innovative tools; the emerging business community meets the emerging conversation about the future of business.

Here's What We've Set Out To Do:

- Accurately, honestly, and entertainingly identify the knowledge workers, management innovators, and idea merchants leading the business revolution. Our new community is waiting to emerge and converge. We mean to have serious fun. All we need is the meeting ground.

- Create the language of the revolution: a new business vocabulary that captures and expresses our common experiences, the common language we use to talk to each other.

- Identify the values of the revolution and the people who are building companies that embody them: a commitment to merge economic growth with social justice, democratic participation with tough-minded execution, explosive technological innovation with old-fashioned individual commitment.

- Debunk old myths and discover new legends—before they're celebrified beyond recognition. A new community needs its own legitimate heroes and heroines, its models and mentors. At the same time, it's open season on pretenders, phonies, and purveyors of business snake oil.

- Start conversations, stimulate debates, provoke arguments, create healthy tension. *Fast Company* will be the first—not the last—word in cutting-edge business thinking. If you find something to apply in your work, something to talk about with your colleagues, something to help reframe a problem, something to disagree with, then *Fast Company* is succeeding.

One last thing. Throughout the magazine you will find opportunities for follow-up and feedback with our editors, authors, and the people and companies we write about. We hope you take advantage of those opportunities. When you reconnect with us to share your ideas, reactions, insights, and innovations, the community of change grows.

The revolution spreads.

THE LAST WORD

I am damn proud to be a charter subscriber. You have a long way to go before even a fraction of the people in business see how radically the world is changing. Too bad for young professionals like me. There's nothing like watching opportunities go by while someone is holding you down, bound and gagged.

Keep up the perspective and attitude. At least I know that other people are feeling and thinking the same things I am. It's great inspiration to see that some people are riding the business revolution to great personal and professional achievement. Maybe someday it will be me. For now I must follow my annual-review partner's advice: "There's no place for mavericks in this business. If you want to succeed, you have to run with the herd." I gave her the premiere issue of Fast Company. *I'll let you know what she says.*

Name Withheld

Everything I Thought I Knew About Leadership Is Wrong

From: Issue 02 | April/May 1996 | By: Mort Meyerson

What makes a modern leader? Mort Meyerson, who had a great run atop Electronic Data Systems in the 1980s, chronicles his epiphany that modern success looks far different. He details the revolution in his thinking that occurred when he became CEO of Perot Systems in the 1990s. The arrogance and micromanaging that had marked his first CEO gig had to go. So did the demand he made of everyone who worked for him that they sacrifice everything at the altar of financial rewards. Meyerson embraces values beyond profits, and realizes that treating employees and customers well can lead to greater gains than the alternative. Meyerson doesn't have all the answers, but he knows the questions to ask: To get rich, do you have to be miserable? And, to be successful, do you have to punish your customers? Work through those questions, as Meyerson does, and the result is a revelation about what it truly means to be a great boss.

In 1992 Ross Perot asked me if I would join Perot Systems as CEO. It had been five years since he and I had left EDS. I told him I would do it—with the disclaimer that I didn't know much about the current shape of the business. Ross told me, "Just follow your nose."

That's what I did. It took me six months. I visited with all the associates of Perot Systems and all of our customers. Then I went back to Ross and told him, "Everything I thought I knew about leadership is wrong."

All the reasons he'd asked me to rejoin him for were wrong. The people who had signed on, thinking we'd re-create a new and improved EDS at

Perot Systems, had expectations that were wrong. They would have to either change or leave.

It was a traumatic meeting. Not that he got mad. It was just a mouthful to tell somebody.

I was telling him that everything had changed. Technology, customers, the environment around customers, the market—all had changed. The people in the organization and what they wanted from their work had changed.

Organizations must change radically: we are at the beginning of a revolutionary time in business. Not just an evolutionary time. Not a year-to-year change. A fundamental revolution. Many companies that have enjoyed decades of fabulous success will find themselves out of business in the next five years if they don't make revolutionary changes.

Of course, many of these changes are about technology. They're also about the fundamentals of business and people, and they raise elemental questions: How does this business revolution affect the organization? What does it mean to the people in the organization? What changes do we have to make in the way we communicate?

And most important: What is the new definition of leadership?

I can't offer absolute answers to these questions. But I do know from my own experience that the leadership techniques that applied 20 years ago don't apply anymore.

My intense self-examination left me wrestling with two questions:

To get rich, do you have to be miserable?

To be successful, do you have to punish your customers?

To answer these questions, I would have to look deeply into myself, reinvent my concept of leadership. And in the process, we'd all have to reinvent Perot Systems.

To Get Rich, Do You Have to Be Miserable?

In purely financial terms, my seven years running EDS had been unbelievably successful. When I left, I was very proud of the people, the company, and our achievements. From the day I started as president in 1979 to the day I left in 1986, EDS never had a single quarter where we lost money. We never even had a quarter where we were flat—every quarter we grew like gangbusters. That kind of economic performance made a lot of our people very rich. I used to take enormous pride in the fact that I was instrumental in getting a lot of equity into the hands of the people at EDS.

What I realized after I left was that I had also made a lot of people very unhappy. Our people paid a high price for their economic success. Eighty-hour weeks were the norm. We shifted people from project to project and simply expected them to make the move, no questions asked. We called our assignments "death marches"—without a trace of irony. You were expected to do whatever it took to get the job done. In terms of priorities, work was in first place; family, community, other obligations all came after.

None of that happened by accident. I had helped design EDS to operate this way, using the compensation system to motivate people: I tied their pay to profit-and-loss performance. If you ran your project very profitably, you were richly rewarded. If you didn't, you weren't. I routinely spent an extraordinary amount of my time on compensation and rewards—roughly 15%. I did it because I knew that compensation mattered most.

The system worked; that is, we got exactly what we wanted. We asked people to put financial performance before everything else, and they did. They drove themselves to do whatever was necessary to create those results—even if it meant too much personal sacrifice or doing things that weren't really in the best interests of customers. Sometimes they did things that produced positive financial results in the short term but weren't in the company's long-term interest. That's a charge you'd usually apply to a CEO—but I've never heard it said about individuals down to the lowest ranks of a company. Yet my pay-for-performance approach effectively encouraged that behavior from all of our people.

When I came to Perot Systems, what I saw in my six months of listening inside the company convinced me that we were about to make the same mistake. The emphasis on profit-and-loss to the exclusion of other values was creating a culture of destructive contention. We were about 1,500 people, with revenues of roughly $170 million. Our people were committed to growing the company—but we risked becoming a company where the best people in the industry wouldn't want to work.

For example, I listened to some of our senior leaders talk about how they handled people on teams who didn't perform. I heard talk of "drive-by shootings" to "take out" nonperformers; then they'd "drag the body around" to make an example out of them. They may have meant it only as a way of talking, but I saw it as more: abusive language that would influence behavior. Left unchallenged, these expressions would pollute the company's culture.

The first moment of truth came when we held a three-day off-site meeting in Phoenix, Arizona, with the top 12 leaders in the company. We had to decide the fundamental purpose and character of Perot Systems: Were we here only to create a successful Initial Public Offering (IPO)? Or were we here to build a great company? And if it was the latter, were we bold enough to review everything we'd done—and then reinvent the company?

We decided that, as much as we wanted to do the IPO, we had to build a great company. And we concluded that this wasn't just "feel good" talk—it was a serious business proposition. We had to launch a transformation of Perot Systems. It was a decisive moment, but none of us truly knew what we had begun.

We convened meetings of the top 100 people in the company and asked them long lists of questions: How did they feel about the company culture? What was their evaluation of our top executives? What were their feelings about our customer relations? The answers were a laundry list of horrifying bad news. Our people were angry, frustrated, irritated, deeply unhappy. If our company were entered in a 100-yard dash, I concluded, we were beginning the race from 50 yards behind the starting line.

We set up teams to address these concerns and then reconvened the top 100 to ask them, again, how they felt. We got the same answers. We initiated a companywide program to teach us how to disagree with each other without tearing each other down. I attended the seminars three times; all our company leaders in the United States and Europe participated; and we extended it down into the ranks, so that today two-thirds of the entire company has been through the course.

During these seminars, we identified people who were abusive. We coached them and took them through a personal reinvention process to show them new ways of leading. These were high-ranking company officials who had generated significant business, met or exceeded their financial goals—but simply mistreated their people. Not all of them could convert. Those who couldn't change, we asked to leave. We gave them fair and extended compensation; we didn't strong-arm them out the door; and we tried to keep communications open with them. We simply told them that this wasn't a company that was right for them.

In all, several dozen people, ranking from project leader on up, left Perot Systems. This one difficult step made us a better place and a better competitor. Our people looked at what we'd said and then at how we'd handled those who'd left and saw that we walked our talk: we did ask them to leave, and we didn't treat them abusively in turn.

We involved top leaders and associates throughout the company in a discussion of our values and work styles. Finally, after nearly a year of internal conversation, we arrived at statements that we could all agree on. All of these efforts—the emotionally charged meetings, the constructive contention seminars, the drafting of our company values—produced a genuine transformation. We started to behave like a company whose people not only focused on day-to-day business and economic performance, but also concerned themselves with the well-being of the people on their teams and the concerns of their customers. We were becoming a company where the larger issues of life were as important as the demands of profit-and-loss performance.

My approach to compensation also changed. We still tell people we'll give them everything we can in the way of financial rewards. In fact, more than 60% of our company is owned by the people who run the company. So if we go public someday, we'll still make a lot of our people very rich.

But we will have done it without having first made them miserable— by offering them another dimension they can't get in most other high-performance companies: a human organization. If any of our people have an interest outside the company, we will encourage and support them; if they have needs outside the company, we will recognize them.

For example, rather than contributing corporate money to charities, we encourage our people to contribute their own time to a cause they believe in. Very simply, we don't believe in "write a check to charity." Instead we have an office that helps our employees carry out their own contributions to the community—helping at a senior center or an orphanage, or teaching English-as-a-second-language in the afternoon at a local school.

Inside the company we apply the same set of values. Business-the-old-way told people to leave their personal problems at home. Now we make it clear that personal issues are our issues as well. Not long ago, one of our sales executives had a child born with a hole in its heart. Through e-mail, I knew about that child within four hours of its birth. Within eight hours we had a specialist working with the infant. The child will now be able to lead a normal life. Our company made that happen because it was the right thing. It's not the only kind of thing we should do—but it does represent what we should be, the kind of feeling our company should create.

To Be Successful, Do You Have to Punish Your Customers?

I had the same kind of question about our customers as I did about our people. Looking back on my years at EDS, I was absolutely convinced that we produced real value for our customers that exceeded what we charged them. But I also had to acknowledge that all too often, our relations with customers were unnecessarily strained and difficult.

Of course we delivered what we promised. But there were two problems: we made sure we won virtually every negotiation that decided what would be delivered; and our tone was often paternalistic, almost condescending. Customers felt like they were outgunned at every turn. Too often we made them feel incompetent or just plain stupid—after all, they had called us to bail them out of trouble, hadn't they? I left EDS thinking not that our aims had been wrong or dishonorable, but that the way we had pursued them—in truth, the spirit with which I had led the company—had ultimately diminished both our own organization and our relations with customers.

It wasn't until I had been out of EDS for a year, consulting to several other companies, that I began to get a clear line of sight on this question. As a consultant, I watched other vendors sell their products, many of which were the same ones I had sold. This time, I listened to their presentations with the ears of the purchaser. And what had sounded good when I was on the pitching side didn't sound so authentic from the receiving side. It sounded arrogant, rigid, and high-handed.

I had to acknowledge that at EDS I had encouraged that attitude—it was a reflection of my own approach to leadership. To be a leader at EDS, you had to be tougher, smarter, sharper. You had to prove that you could make money. You had to prove that you could win at negotiations every time. I used to pride myself on my negotiating skill. I made sure I swept the table clean of every loose penny that was around. It never occurred to me that winning big could be a negative thing. At the time it felt great: business is a competitive sport, and I just cleaned the table!

But you can overplay that hand. A company culture that isn't satisfied with winning but also needs to dominate, that isn't content with getting great results but also has to eliminate everything in its path is fundamentally destructive—and ultimately self-destructive. After I left EDS, I learned that sometimes it's better to leave something on the table. Sometimes you do better if you leave people with alternatives. You do better if your customer or your competitor doesn't feel taken advantage of. You do better, in fact, if your customer feels like your partner.

Here again, at Perot Systems, I turned to the compensation system to help us live the lesson. We use 360-degree evaluations for our people—asking boss, peers, and subordinates to participate—and always include input from our customers. We also ask our customers to give us report cards—and then we temper bonuses based on customer ratings of how well we support their needs.

But the lesson really struck home when I went to Switzerland recently to put the finishing touches on our strategic alliance with Swiss Bank Corp. It's the biggest deal in the history of our company, a hybrid relationship that goes beyond the bank simply outsourcing its information technology. We are partners. They have an option to own shares in Perot Systems; we have a stake in their information technology subsidiary in Switzerland; together we agreed to a 25-year relationship that transfers management of Swiss Bank's corporatewide information technology infrastructure to Perot Systems.

To brief their own people on this relationship, the top leaders of the bank called a meeting. My only role was to be introduced and say a few words. Almost all of the meeting was conducted in German; finally, at the end, to introduce me, they switched to English. In this first public introduction, what they chose to talk about was our values and our approach to partnering.

At the end of the introduction, the senior Swiss Bank executive took out a Perot Systems card with our values and said, "Five years from now, when we look back at our partnership, we should use these values to judge how well we've done." That one introduction convinced me that what we're trying to do is very powerful and knows no cultural bounds.

The Three Jobs of the Leader

We should never lose sight of the fact that we're in business to create a first-class organization and to survive. That's what businesses are supposed to do.

At the same time, we need a more expansive definition of victory. There's a much larger calling in business today than was allowed by the old definitions of winning and losing. One hundred years from now, we'll know we were on the right track if there are more organizations where people are doing great work for their customers and creating value for their shareholders. And raising their children, nurturing their families, and taking an interest in their communities. And feeling proud of the contributions they make. These are things you can't measure when winning and losing are only financial metrics.

It's taken me a while to learn these things. When I returned to Perot Systems, my first job as a leader was to create a new understanding of myself. I had to accept the shattering of my own self-confidence. I couldn't lead anymore, at least not in the way I always had. There was a time during that first year at Perot Systems when I would go home and look in the mirror and say to myself, "You don't get it. Maybe you ought to get out of this business. You're like a highly specialized trained beast that evolved during one period and now you can't adjust to the new environment."

I told myself I was having the same experience as a caterpillar entering a cocoon. The caterpillar doesn't know that he'll come out as a butterfly. All he knows is that he's alone, it's dark, and it's a little scary. I came out the other end of the experience with a new understanding of leadership. I don't have to know everything. I don't have to have all the customer contacts. I don't have to make all the decisions. In fact, in the new world of business, it can't be me, it shouldn't be me, and my job is to prevent it from being me.

In my early days at Perot Systems, people came to me and asked for "the plan." When I told them I don't know the plan, they got angry with me. All I would say was, I don't know the plan. If that disqualifies me from being a leader, then you'd better go get another leader. We're either going to figure out the company's future together or we're not going to do it at all.

I made it clear that there were a whole set of things that I couldn't do—and that for the good of Perot Systems I wouldn't do. I couldn't get us into businesses or out of businesses. I couldn't set the company's strategy, delineate the company's tactics, or write the field orders for our competitive battles. I couldn't decide what products to launch. I couldn't be that kind of leader. I could do that in the old days at EDS because the competition was stable and I had overpowering knowledge. If I tried to do that today, I'd make every wrong move in the book. The way to be a leader today is different. I no longer call the shots. I'm not the decision maker.

So what is my job as a leader? The essence of leadership today is to make sure that the organization knows itself. There are certain durable principles that underlie an organization. The leader should embody those values. They're fundamental. But they have nothing to do with business strategy, tactics, or market share. They have to do with human relationships and the obligation of the organization to its individual members and its customers. For example, our most controversial value—the one that was narrowly approved—speaks to our commitment to the community. It was also the one I argued most heatedly for. And today, it's one our entire organization supports fervently.

The second job of the leader is to pick the right people to be part of the organization and to create an environment where those people can succeed. That means encouraging others to help develop the strategy and grow the philosophy of the company. It means more collaboration and teamwork among people at every level of the company. I am now a coach, not an executive. When people ask me for a decision, I pick up a mirror, hold it up for them to look into, and tell them: Look to yourselves and look to the team, don't look to me.

The third job of the leader is to be accessible. I want to be open to people in a broad range of their experiences in life if they need it, and I want to be accessible for two-way communication that's honest, open, and direct. During my years at EDS I communicated the way most CEOs do: I showed up on stage every six months and delivered a pep rally speech. I wrote memos that went to the top dozen people in the company and had meetings with them every two weeks.

Today I travel with my laptop and get e-mail from all over the company. I get thousands of messages per month, some of them trivial, many important. Everyone in Perot Systems knows they can e-mail me and I'll read it—me, not my secretary. Electronic mail is the single most important tool I have to break through the old organization and the old mind-set. E-mail says that I'm accessible to anyone in our company in real time, anywhere. I am an instant participant in any part of the organization. No more dictating memos that get scrubbed before their formal distribution to the corporate hierarchy. Now, when I hear about a win in a hotly contested competition, within an hour of the victory I'm sending out congratulatory e-mails to our team members around the world. The impact from that kind of direct communication is enormous.

And I'm accessible on issues and concerns that transcend the traditional boundaries of work and the company. Not long ago, for example, I got an e-mail message from one of our new senior associates. The news was urgent: his father-in-law had just been diagnosed as having cancer and he was going off the Net for the next two days. I e-mailed back immediately that the company would stand behind him any way we could. The next day I got another e-mail message: it was worse than they had thought; they were in a small Texas town, and they didn't know who to go to for help. I e-mailed back with the name of a doctor at Southwestern Medical School who referred them to the best help they could find.

Today I tell the people in Perot Systems that this is the path that we have chosen. It's the path we'll all be on for the rest of our lives. It has no destination. There is no sense of arrival. It's a continuous process.

In a world where the lines between companies, industries, and even nations get blurred, a leader builds an effective organization around values and work style. And a leader learns to define success in business as both producing financial strength and generating a team of people who support and nurture each other.

THE LAST WORD

My partner found your article in Fast Company *and left it for me with a note that read, "There is someone else out there who's discovered what we already know." I found it to be one of the most reassuring articles on management in a long time.*

Back in 1980 my partner and I formed an ad agency based on the belief that we could not only produce great work and make our clients successful, but that we could also treat the people who worked for us like real, living, breathing human beings. That's tough in this crazy, demanding industry.

We developed our values based on the belief that stretching and supporting each other was a good thing, that people want positive reinforcement, that people want leadership to clear the way so they can be successful, not the other way around.

It's like being on a roller coaster. Some people will get scared and want to get off. Some people will be exhilarated and can't get enough. But the ride is always interesting. And the result is we have grown a group of people who will do just about anything for our company and customers.

Thanks for your words of encouragement and your story.

David C. Hukari
Chairman
Priscaro & Hukari Advertising
San Mateo, California

Wide Awake on the New Night Shift

From: Issue 04 | August/September 1996 | By: Ana Marie Cox

Your competition, and even your team, may be spread across the globe. Deadline pressure dictates a constant rush to produce faster than ever. This is the 24-hour world in which we live. In this piece, Ana Marie Cox, best known today as Wonkette, the blogger-turned-novelist, captured the new up-all-night culture of creative workers. Cox knew well of what she wrote. She may have a day job now, but at the time she wrote this, Cox spent many a late night producing essays for the cutting-edge proto-blog Suck.com.

It's 3 A.M.—do you know where your employees are? If you're Andrew Sather, 24-year-old founder and president of Adjacency, a Madison, Wisconsin, new-media design firm, the answer is yes—they're at work. But probably not at their desks.

They're scattered around the company's soaring loft space—located in a postindustrial-chic renovated Greyhound terminal—playing pool or tossing a Frisbee over the heads of those few stalwarts still glued to their workstations. The aggressive beat of Wu-Tang Clan is punctuated by the slap of a hockey puck and the whoosh of Rollerblades coming from the firm's "recreation room" across the hall.

The 21 programmers, artists, and marketers—not one over the age of 26—are revving up to launch the latest in a line of style-setting Web sites, this time for Rollerblade. It's the second night in a row at the office for Sather. He's fresh from a two-hour snooze on one of the company's three hotel-quality rollaway beds. After a caffeine infusion and a piece of Power-Bar ("astronaut energy bread"), Sather cranks up the music and sits down to his computer to review the site.

This is not some postgraduate fraternity reunion. Nor is Adjacency un-usual in making "all-night" part of the workday. But, in contrast to their cousins on the assembly line, hospital rounds, or third shift at Kinko's, this cadre of entrepreneurs, software engineers, and designers is kept awake by the unprecedented challenges and opportunities of competing in the net-work economy. Survival on Net time means leveraging talent and technol-ogy, intensity and collaboration to deliver excellent results—fast.

Meet the new night shift. Peter Sapienza, 30, a market research analyst at Patagonia, the Ventura, California–based adventure gear company, works through the night about once every two weeks. Robert von Geoben, 33, un-til recently graphic arts manager at Geffen/ DGC Records, says, "Working with HTML is like building with a blindfold on. You get addicted to the process of working. You find yourself thinking, 'Just fix this last bug, put in this last link.' All of a sudden—it's dawn."

To many on the new night shift, the all-nighter is a symbol of the new work ethic: they're willing to sacrifice sleep for fast cycle time, but they de-mand fun and flexibility in exchange. Patagonia's Sapienza explains, "Our definition of work and leisure has changed. People are searching for more fun out of work, more adventure. They expect that work is going to satisfy other needs, so they're willing to give more."

To some, night work is built into the job description. Craig Kanarick, 29, is one of the principals at Razorfish, a bleeding-edge multimedia design firm in New York. Kanarick spends his days in meetings, then leads the night shift in designing Web sites—putting virtual scent strips into www.ralphlaurenfragrance.com or recarbonating www.pepsimax.com. He says, "Managing during the day, I don't start my own work until seven."

Razorfish, which has more than 50 sites to its credit, doesn't encourage marathon work sessions, but does provide support for the inevitable all-nighter—including gourmet spreads and limousine service home. "We don't want to put in a shower because people will start to live here," says Ka-narick. "But when people are here all night, we want to make sure that they're going to be productive."

Adjacency, which was catapulted out of Sather's basement on the power of contracts with such high-profile companies as Specialized, Land Rover, and Motorola, has crossed Razorfish's boundaries: the showers are coming. Rollaways and several couches are already in place; the in-line skating rink is installed; and there are plans for a new work/play space with a conference table on wheels to make way for pickup basketball games.

In fact, Adjacency has all-nighters down to a science. Sather has even classified the two main types, each with its own work pattern, mode of relaxation, food, and sound track. The first, the "inadvertent all-nighter," is a flow-inspired work groove. "You don't go home to prepare for this," Sather says. "It's an extended day that sneaks up on you because you're doing great work, you're in the zone, and then you look at the clock, and it's 4 A.M. and you say, 'Hell, I'll just keep going.' "

And then there is the other kind—the more common "iron-willed, bleary-eyed, comin'-at-you-with-a-fury all-nighter," says Sather. "You know from the moment you walk in that you're going to have an all-nighter. These communal all-nighters are what make companies go. They're all about collaboration. They build a sense of loyalty, family, and common purpose. You want everyone to peak together."

And they have a recognizable rhythm. Adjacency's art director, Bernie DeChant, describes it: "The night starts out crazy. At midnight people get restless—they know they're going to be here all night. At two, it gets mellow, and at three, the music gets really loud. We might play pool or skate—that's when the second wind comes around."

THE LAST WORD

I read Ana Marie Cox's article on all-nighters with recognition and disgust. I've been through the not-so-new rite of passage that companies use to exploit people who are talented, young, and career-obsessed. Big Six firms like Arthur Andersen, consulting firms like EDS, and software companies like Microsoft control the souls of unsuspecting recruits promising fame, fortune, and glory— in exchange for their time, personality, and dignity.

Some of us have discovered that six-figure incomes and the power rush of managing hundreds of people aren't more important than a decent relationship with our spouse, daily interaction with our children, and time to develop our personal talents. What I hope Ms. Cox realizes—and what I'd wished she'd added to her article—is that a large percentage of the people running around the office at 3 A.M. are either too young to have a family; hate going home to the family they have; enjoying the only social life they are capable of realizing;

or allowing greed to determine where they spend their time and how they treat their families.

I used to be a victim of the "big lie" that included pulling all-nighters and performing other acts of corporate servitude. Today, at 35, I own a company that's fast-paced and technology-centric. We compete successfully all over the world. However, people at my company work from 8:30 to 5:30 and have weekends off. The only people knocking around our offices at 3 A.M. are the cleaning people. The rest of us are at home, in bed with our spouses, and down the hall from our sleeping children—who are happy that we are at home.

Scott Kinnaird
Managing Partner
Kinnaird Technical Resources
Edmond, Oklahoma

Starwave Takes the Web . . . (Seriously)

From: Issue 05 | October/November 1996 | By: Michael S. Malone

---

When you think about the Internet and its development, you can consider both how far we've come and how many issues are still unresolved. This fascinating piece could have been written today, given its deft analysis of the issues facing companies trying to build a Web business. When Michael S. Malone dropped in on Starwave, the Paul Allen–backed start-up was the hottest producer of online content, creating and operating such ground-breaking blockbuster sites as ESPN.com. What he found was a group of people who knew the right questions to ask about how to succeed online— and were smart enough to answer them. Many of the problems they were trying to solve a decade ago still bedevil people—everything from how you make money online to how to bring about convergence. The approaches that the Starwave gang tried to apply to these problems continue to edify our own explorations into what is still, when you think about it, "new media."

The first wave on the Web was spun out of romance. All of a sudden there was a new space, uncharted, open, free—cyberspace—with few require-ments and fewer rules. It was open to exploration and self-expression, and an unspoken etiquette was all that was needed to maintain order among its members. It was Web-stock.

The second wave on the Web was spun out of greed. All of a sudden anything with "net" or "web" in its name could attract venture capital or go public; in the last 18 months, investors have thrown something like $3.5 bil-lion at the Web. The Web was a place you went if you wanted to cash in and cash out—fast. It was Web-rush.

Now we are into the third wave on the Web—and it is spun out of a newfound seriousness of purpose. All of a sudden, the bubble has popped and there's talk of a shakeout—the heady IPOs and sky-high stock market multiples look like a passing phase in the Web's evolution rather than a permanent destination. Now it's time for a long, hard look at what it takes to build a serious company on the Web. It's Web-business.

On the outskirts of Seattle, the men and women of Starwave Corp. are betting that the third wave will be their wave—and they are taking the Web very seriously. Backed by billionaire Paul Allen, boasting a collection of the best and brightest talent from the converging worlds of publishing, broadcasting, entertainment, and software, and offering a stable of some of the Web's most successful programming, Starwave is making a serious bid to be considered the Web's first real company.

This isn't a romantic fantasy, and it certainly isn't a get-rich-quick scheme. In fact, in the course of building a serious company, Starwave has lost serious money.

Starwave's model isn't the only one for doing business on the Web. Jeff Bezos, founder and CEO of Seattle-based Amazon.com, has thought long and hard about the business of Web business. He chose not to enter Starwave's market—multimedia content—and to conquer another front in the Net revolution, electronic commerce. In two years, Bezos has built the world's largest online bookstore—and a business model that more and more companies want to emulate.

Building a Web site is easy. Building a Web business is anything but. A close look at the challenges facing Starwave reveals the still-emerging shape of business on the Web. The company's challenges suggest the nature and scale of what lies ahead for any group of ambitious, committed pioneers who set out to create a defining company on the Web.

Challenge Number One

HOW FAR CAN EGOLESS LEADERSHIP AND PATIENT CAPITAL TAKE YOU?

If you want to know CEO Mike Slade's idea of running Starwave, look at the two magazines on the coffee table in his office: *Nation's Business* and *MAD* magazine. That's the dichotomy—call it casual intensity—that runs through all of Starwave right to its CEO.

Starwave is headquartered in an anonymous office building next to a drab Seattle freeway. It isn't until you get off the elevator and enter the open and bright reception area that you get the feeling you've arrived someplace a little . . . different.

On this day, a crew from Ziff-Davis TV is visiting the company, gathering up its gear beneath a bizarre mural spatter-painted directly onto the wall by noted illustrator Ralph Steadman. The slightly ominous painting shows, amidst Steadman's trademark swirls and drools, a weird buglike creature trapped in a pond. It bears the title, "Thus Spokane Methuselaa."

Slade, 39, wears khakis and a knit shirt, and his hair is thick and spiky—the look of a man just back from two sets of tennis and a quick shower. But once he starts talking, the words come spilling out in a flood that barely leaves room for questions.

Ask to see Slade's business plan for Starwave and he laughs: "Which one?" Since he joined the company in February 1993, Slade has generated more business plans built on more financial models than most CEOs do in their entire lives. The reason for the proliferation is simple. There is no single plan or model for doing business on the Web because there is no business—yet.

"Opening a site on the Web is kind of like opening a restaurant in SoHo or Greenwich Village," he says. "You can do whatever you want. You own the building. You can decorate it. You don't have to adhere to building codes. On the other hand, there might be a couple of homeless people sleeping outside the door when you wake up in the morning."

If that sounds like a skeptic rather than a cheerleader, listen to what Slade says about making money on the Web. "If you're a venture capitalist investing in Web site number 677," he warns, "the best strategy you can have is to sell it to an even bigger fool."

Slade has come by his skepticism the old-fashioned way—he's earned it. Under Slade's leadership, Starwave has gone from 8 people to more than 280, including 55 top-flight software engineers. It has created some of the best-known and most-visited programming on the Web : ESPNET SportsZone, Mr. Showbiz, Outside Online, Family Planet. It has also reportedly spent something on the order of $60 million. The only way Slade and his colleagues can make sense of all this red ink is to treat the entire Web as an R&D laboratory.

"What we have right now is a kind of access schizophrenia," says Slade.

"There's a lot of sound and fury targeted at people who aren't especially good customers while everybody waits for the real customers to catch up."

Slade has a big advantage in this R&D waiting game. Sitting behind him is Starwave's main investor, Microsoft cofounder Paul Allen. Having access to Allen's patient money has enabled the company to develop a long-term strategy that's otherwise impossible in a hyperpaced, Web-based IPO market that expects a company to go public within 18 months of its founding.

"Paul understands that you have to seek risk—that a new medium plus big risk equals a big reward. And because of that he's allowed us to run this company like the new media operation of a big company rather than like a start-up," says Slade.

Allen has also given Slade the chance to change his mind—and the company's fundamental direction. When Slade joined Starwave, the company had no content or product focus—it was trying to make something happen in interactive media, possibly as a tools company, possibly as a content company. Slade focused Starwave on opportunities in sports, entertainment, kids, and families—and identified a three-pronged strategy of online services, CD-ROMs, and broadcast. Then, one year later, Starwave did a sharp turn onto the Net. The credit for the strategy, says Allen, goes to Slade.

"It was Mike who really restarted this company," Allen says. "He was excited about Net-based vehicles for things like sports and family information. I was anticipating the birth of something—we placed our bets in a number of different areas, not knowing exactly which would mature. It turned out to be the instantiation of those opportunities Mike had identified."

Most start-ups wouldn't have survived such a wrenching reinvention. But Slade could afford to take his time and get it right—and that freedom has made him an uncommonly egoless executive. "It's been quite an education," he says. "When I joined Starwave, I viewed it as a software-company type of management challenge. As I've gotten educated, mostly by the people I've hired, I've realized that Starwave is really a next-generation media company."

The promise of new media has always been about convergence: the digitization of everything that makes possible a combining of text, graphics, video, audio—delivered through another convergence that combines television and computing. If Slade's experience is any indication, convergence is still at the heart of new media—but not technological convergence. What really matters is human convergence: melding talents from a wide variety of existing media—every medium, in fact, that predates the Web, from radio to film—and existing industries, from software to entertainment.

The management challenge associated with convergence, he says, is to blend people's experiences into a shared vision. "Try asking a Hollywood person and a Microsoft employee to define 'development,' " Slade suggests. "Or try to get publishing people to think about interactive media instead of linear media. It's like night and day. Managing expectations and uncertainty is a basic job description."

But if the management challenge is new, Slade sees the competitive challenge as not particularly different from other media. "In theory," he says, "the Web is this big, wide-open field where a thousand flowers can bloom and anyone can prosper. That's bull. The Web is already dominated by big, well-funded media entities that are seeking to 'aggregate' and 'brand' and 'lock out' competitors. The marketing challenges are the same as in any other type of media. In most large categories on the Web there will be only one, two, or three winners. So the race to get ahead or to catch up is furious."

It's a race Slade enjoys running. "This is the coolest and funnest thing I've seen since the Apple Macintosh," he says. "We're a proud bunch. We try to do things in a super-excellent, super-high-quality, blow-away-the-competition manner. That's not always the right approach, but when it works, it shows."

Challenge Number Two

CAN YOUR TECHNOLOGY KEEP PACE—OR EVEN BETTER, SET THE PACE?

If Mike Slade is an egoless leader, Patrick Naughton, Starwave's senior vice president of technology, is an angry young man. Eight years ago, when he joined Sun Microsystems as a brash young programmer, he took great pride in his status as an outsider. But now he's 31 and widely accorded the status that goes with being one of the most gifted programmers in the world. So he bristles at being left outside—and today, he's bristling at three old friends from Sun.

In their presentations at a recent conference on Java—the wildly popular programming language for the Web that Naughton had a big role in inventing—Sun's CEO (and Naughton's longtime hockey teammate) Scott McNealy, cofounder and Vice President for Research Bill Joy, and chief scientist of JavaSoft James Gosling (another friend) managed never to mention Naughton's name. To Naughton it's a slight with epic meaning, a conscious effort to rewrite the history of Java now that Naughton has left Sun. "It's like 1984," he says, "and I've gone down the memory hole."

Naughton has a genuine claim as a founding father of Java. In 1990, a 25-year-old Naughton told McNealy he was quitting Sun to join Steve Jobs at NeXT. Sun was hopeless when it came to software and user interfaces, he complained, and he wanted to go to a company that knew what it was doing. McNealy asked Naughton to write a memo outlining his indictment. The CEO forwarded the e-mail up and down the management chain; the electronic conversations it sparked created the research project that became Java.

Naughton left Sun in the fall of 1994, but he has far from disappeared. Indeed, his decision to join Starwave is generally considered one of the company's biggest coups. His programming skills give the company a major weapon in an uncertain competition where technology both defines the medium and continually reinvents it. Naughton and his engineers are scrambling to figure out ways to create distinctive Web experiences. Why would someone of Naughton's reputation join a startup to design clever screen presentations of NBA box scores?

"Well," he says with typical intensity, "one answer is that you don't get to do a Java—that is, to revolutionize the way a million programmers work—more than a couple of times in your life. We created Java precisely because we felt that Sun had lost track of its customers. We wanted to build software that would allow consumers to have a satisfying experience again. That's always been my goal. I try to bring all my experiences to bear to make my work invisible, to create a Starwave experience for consumers that's so positive that they come away saying, 'That's really cool.' "

One of those "experiences" is Starwave TV, and it's already in prototype. Imagine that you could watch the NBA finals on your computer, see footage of, say, Dennis Rodman going up for a rebound, touch the cursor to his moving figure—and instantly call up his entire career statistics. "Just think of Bloomberg TV and make it SportsZone on the PC," says Naughton.

The prospect of reinventing the technological experience of the Net is enough of a challenge to keep Patrick Naughton at Starwave—at least for now. "For the next two years," he says, "technology is going to be vitally important here. Desire is still ahead of development. People want stuff we haven't written software for." Then he adds, with typical self-assurance, "But we're already finishing the architectures, so I can tell you that the Web of 1997 will look radically different than it does now."

Challenge Number Three

CAN YOU ASSEMBLE A TEAM OF UNPARALLELED EDITORIAL TALENTS—WHO ARE WILLING TO OBSOLETE THEIR PROVEN SKILLS IN PURSUIT OF AN UNPROVEN NEW BUSINESS?

If Mike Slade is the heart of Starwave, then Senior Vice President Tom Phillips is its soul.

Tall and angular, with a frame that practically vibrates with nervous tension, topped by a thick shock of black hair, Phillips hardly looks the part. And, at age 41, he already holds the distinction of being one of the oldest people at Starwave. But alone among the people at the company, perhaps in the whole world of the commercial Web, Phillips knows what it means to ride the zeitgeist, to feel both the exhilaration and the decompression of the ride. As a founder of *Spy* magazine—one of the defining publications of the 1980s—he has seen what it's like to be in the hottest enterprise in your medium, what it takes to hold such an emotional business together, and what it feels like when the air goes out of the balloon.

He also knows what building a creative, on-the-pulse-of-the-times company is ultimately all about: finding and recruiting those few people with the rare combination of great talent in their current career and a willingness to throw away that success to take a flier on something totally new, dangerously unproven—and potentially spectacular.

What Phillips has been trying to create with his eclectic team is the workplace equivalent of a thriving new community. In addition to hiring talent, he explains, he's been looking to avoid "prospectors" and bring in "homesteaders." Prospectors are strictly focused on the short term. Their goal is to make the quick strike—if it doesn't happen fast, they tend to grow bored and move on. Homesteaders, on the other hand, are people who leave their successful careers, looking for that one big adventure in which they can stake out their claim, regain control over their lives, and settle down in a safe place for their families. It's only partly in jest that Phillips's wife, an aspiring novelist, calls herself a "pioneer wife."

As homey as all this sounds, and as clever as Phillips's categories are, the problem Starwave faces is the same that confronts most start-from-scratch communities: Is it a new town they all share, or just a random collection of neighborhoods? The answer may determine whether Starwave becomes the first big Web company, or instead remains a series of loosely linked Web projects. At the moment, the company's various editorial departments are very much next-door neighbors but operate in separate realities: these homesteaders are a far cry from collaborating to build one town they can all inhabit.

"It's important to have diversity in our services, but at the same time tying them all together is problematic," Phillips acknowledges. "Especially when they're all competing for engineering and advertising resources. When it comes to building a corporate culture, sharing learning, that sort of thing, we're not there yet."

Challenge Number Four

HOW DO YOU PRODUCE AS MUCH ORIGINAL MATERIAL AS POSSIBLE—AND
LEVERAGE RELATIONSHIPS WITH BRAND-NAME PARTNERS FOR THE REST?

"I think you can accurately describe this as bedlam," says Susan Mulcahy, editor-in-chief and publisher of Mr. Showbiz, as she walks through its offices and gestures at the posters and Hollywood detritus.

In cultural terms, no one has come as far to Starwave as Mulcahy. Witness a short inventory of items in her office : a copy of a 1952 *New Yorker* cover, a postcard of the St. Regis Hotel bar, a Henry Alford column about walking around Manhattan in pajamas, a metal desk-spike from the *New York Post* city room, Norma Shearer and Rudolph Valentino paper dolls, a cheesy Mexican comic book (*Páginas Intimas*), and a 1950s plastic doll from New Jersey.

This office, combined with her languid-yet-nervous style emblematic of a proto–New York City magazine editor, makes Mulcahy seem like a rare orchid lost in the Olympic rain forest. In fact, however, Mulcahy's journey to Starwave was shorter—in miles—than almost any other recruit's.

When she agreed to develop an online entertainment service for Starwave in 1994, Mulcahy was burned out from the New York scene and living in a trailer in Joseph, a small town in eastern Oregon. "I was tired of the downsizing, the chronic kvetching, and the overwhelming sense of going nowhere," she says. So she had lit out for Oregon and a self-created life, struggling to make a living writing articles and screenplays.

When Phillips first contacted her, Mulcahy had never so much as gone online. So she bought a 2400-baud modem and signed up with America Online. "A few days later," she recalls, "I called him up and said, 'Why is anybody interested in this? It takes an hour to get a page.' " But Phillips was insistent, and six months later, Mulcahy moved north—"partly because I wanted to eat again," she laughs.

The service she created and now directs, Mr. Showbiz, offers perhaps the best view into the challenges facing Starwave both externally, as it tries to build a business on the Web, and internally, as it struggles to coordinate its various operations. Mr. Showbiz has more than 20,000 users per day, generating about 600,000 visits and 12 million hits per month. Those numbers make Mr. Showbiz a hit by Web standards—but they're just a fraction of the traffic at the mighty SportsZone. As a result, Mr. Showbiz commands ad rates of only $4,500 per month, about a third of the rates charged by its neighbor down the hall.

Moreover, unlike SportsZone or Outside Online, Mr. Showbiz has yet to find a strategic partner—which puts a lot of pressure on the staff to generate original material and to create a powerful enough Web presence on its own to become a brand. Add to that the ongoing education of a print journalist to the technological and editorial demands of the Web, and you begin to appreciate the pressure on Mulcahy and her group to make Mr. Showbiz come to life.

Mulcahy and her team of well-schooled magazine writers have had to contend with a fundamental redefinition of the nature of the product. Writing for print and writing for the Web, it turns out, are two different things. "I won't say that the Web totally changes the nature of writing," she says. "But it will transform the nature of feature writing. For one thing, you have to think visually. It's not just that you need pictures with your story; it's also mechanical things. You can't put all the visual elements of the story in the first few paragraphs. And the Web doesn't allow you to write stories that go on forever. The fact is that people just don't want to read much online. So you have all of this apparent freedom, where you don't have to worry about column inches, but in the end you've still got to keep your copy short and to the point."

At this point, what happens with Mr. Showbiz may be the best test of Starwave's ability to create a brand. For Mulcahy, the challenge is worth it. "Look," she says, calling from her old trailer in Joseph, to which she still retires to work on her novel during her rare days off, "I can go back to New York and get a magazine job anytime. But nobody's going to offer me a chance to create a whole new magazine in a whole new medium. At Starwave I've got that chance."

Then she adds one final thought. "I do wish we had a hell of a lot more advertising."

Challenge Number Five

CAN YOU MAINTAIN YOUR EDITORIAL INTEGRITY—WHEN "INTEGRITY" IS STILL UNDEFINED?

It's a nonobvious question, and a nontrivial problem: how do you define integrity in a medium with no publishing tradition, no boundary between advertising and editorial, and an insatiable appetite for advertising revenues? It is precisely this question that worries ESPNET SportsZone's Mitch Gelman.

In a company filled with distinguished veterans, the soft-spoken Gelman, SportsZone's editor, is among the most distinguished of all. The author of a critically acclaimed book about his life as a cub reporter, *Crime Scene* (Random House, 1992), he also shared a Pulitzer Prize in 1991 for his work at *New York Newsday*. Credentials like these usually mean a lifetime sinecure at a fat daily newspaper. But last summer, Gelman's paper died beneath him. Around the same time, he saw an article in *Sports Illustrated* about the new world of sports online.

"I realized that I was seeing the creation of a whole new industry, the next wave of journalism," says Gelman. "It reminded me of all those newspaper reporters coming home from World War II and going into this new medium called television. I wanted to be part of the adventure."

He signed on with the right explorers. SportsZone's numbers are staggering—one of the most tantalizing hints of the Web's promise as a mass medium. Gelman's site contains 60,000 pages of material, 6,000 photos, 2,500 audio clips, and 1,000 video clips. This massive content draws huge numbers of visitors. SportsZone averages 7.5 million hits per day; it generated almost 12 million hits per day during the Summer Olympics. Its fans are almost exclusively male (95%), young (82% are under 35 years old), and affluent for their age, with an average household income of $55,000 per year.

All of which translates into serious advertising: sponsors pay up to $100,000 for a three-month advertising presence on the site. SportsZone is one of the leading generators of revenue on the Web and reportedly produces roughly 80% of Starwave's estimated $7 million in total revenues.

But as SportsZone attracts more readers and its readers attract more advertisers, tough questions inevitably emerge. Ask online editors how they think about their services and they invariably draw parallels between themselves and the newspaper business. Ask these same editors about the all-too-cozy links to advertisers that appear on their Web pages, and suddenly they redefine themselves as part of the entertainment industry and compare their offerings to television infomercials.

But what happens when editorial copy becomes just a hook to pull the user into the virtual mall? Is that really the same thing as ads in the newspaper or commercials on network television? Or does the Web, by its very nature, produce a different kind of experience that erases the demarcation between editorial and ads? Where are the standards governing such matters?

"I think about it all the time," Gelman says. "This is a business and we have to make a profit. But advertisers come to where the users are—and though this business is slightly different from print journalism, the one thing we have in common is credibility. If we do anything that jeopardizes that, we will lose those users, and then we'll lose our advertisers."

Good ethics equals good business. It is a conclusion that other industries have taken years to reach. Many still haven't. Will the Web world one day come to the same conclusion? "The rules of the game?" Gelman quips. "We have to figure them out first."

And yet . . . there is something wonderfully perverse about the Web. It rewards a kind of cranky honesty while eviscerating the insincere and calculating, no matter how slick the presentation. In this cyberreality, companies that answer the siren call of selling out to advertisers may exchange short-term gain for long-term oblivion.

Meanwhile, attitudes like Mitch Gelman's, which might seem an anachronistic remnant of another medium and another time, may prove to be the defining difference between success and failure for companies like Starwave. For one thing, Gelman takes seriously his role as mentor to the new generation of reporters enrolling in the new medium. "We can learn from them how to do this business, and we can teach them what to do in terms of accuracy and ethical standards," he says.

And that suggests one final convergence. Beyond technology and people, success on the Web will also depend on a convergence of philosophies between those pursuing technology and those chasing commerce, between the desire to break barriers with the new medium and the need to retain lessons learned by its predecessors. Defining how business should be conducted on the Web may be the first requirement to defining what it means to be the first Web-based business.

THE LAST WORD

This article just grates on old wounds for me. I've seen this same enthusiasm, the same mantras, and the same lifestyle with start-ups on track to something meaningful and those who were hopelessly clueless regarding real profitability and sustainability. I still have a streak that favors important and productive change, genuine innovation, and sustainable fundamentals, but you have to offer me more than youthful exuberance and insights born of 18 months of single-task experience.

Don Jarrell
Via the Internet

The Brand Called You

From: Issue 10 | August/September 1997 | By: Tom Peters

Brands dominate our lives. We're all, directly or indirectly, in the business of creating them for our companies, and we're all subject to every product's efforts to communicate what it's all about. Many of us go so far as to derive parts of our identity from our affiliation with particular brands. Wearing a T-shirt from a skateboarding company, carrying a Starbucks cup, or donning those telltale white iPod headphones all say something about who we are and what we believe in. Tom Peters knows this and makes a provocative exhortation in this essay: the competition between individuals for prime gigs is no different than the battles companies wage for market share. You need to apply to your own achievements the principles that they use to brand their products. It's been a controversial idea since it was first published, all the more so because the market for talent has gone global. But until you read it yourself, you can't decide how to position the brand called You.

It's a new brand world.

That cross-trainer you're wearing—one look at the distinctive swoosh on the side tells everyone who's got you branded. That coffee travel mug you're carrying—ah, you're a Starbucks woman! Your T-shirt with the distinctive Champion "C" on the sleeve, the blue jeans with the prominent Levi's rivets, the watch with the hey-this-certifies-I-made-it icon on the face, your fountain pen with the maker's symbol crafted into the end. . . .

You're branded, branded, branded, branded.

It's time for me—and you—to take a lesson from the big brands, a lesson that's true for anyone who's interested in what it takes to stand out and prosper in the new world of work.

Regardless of age, regardless of position, regardless of the business we happen to be in, all of us need to understand the importance of branding. We are CEOs of our own companies: Me Inc. To be in business today, our most important job is to be head marketer for the brand called You.

It's that simple—and that hard. And that inescapable.

Behemoth companies may take turns buying each other or acquiring every hot start-up that catches their eye—mergers in 1996 set records. Hollywood may be interested in only blockbusters and book publishers may want to put out only guaranteed best-sellers. But don't be fooled by all the frenzy at the humongous end of the size spectrum.

The real action is at the other end: the main chance is becoming a free agent in an economy of free agents, looking to have the best season you can imagine in your field, looking to do your best work and chalk up a remarkable track record, and looking to establish your own micro equivalent of the Nike swoosh. Because if you do, you'll not only reach out toward every opportunity within arm's (or laptop's) length, you'll not only make a noteworthy contribution to your team's success—you'll also put yourself in a great bargaining position for next season's free-agency market.

The good news—and it is largely good news—is that everyone has a chance to stand out. Everyone has a chance to learn, improve, and build up their skills. Everyone has a chance to be a brand worthy of remark.

Who understands this fundamental principle? The big companies do. They've come a long way in a short time: it was just over four years ago, April 2, 1993, to be precise, when Philip Morris cut the price of Marlboro cigarettes by 40 cents a pack. That was on a Friday. On Monday, the stock market value of packaged goods companies fell by $25 billion. Everybody agreed: brands were doomed.

Today brands are everything, and all kinds of products and services—from accounting firms to sneaker makers to restaurants—are figuring out how to transcend the narrow boundaries of their categories and become a brand surrounded by a Tommy Hilfiger–like buzz.

Who else understands it? Every single Web site sponsor. In fact, the Web makes the case for branding more directly than any packaged good or consumer product ever could. Here's what the Web says: Anyone can have a Web site. And today, because anyone can . . . anyone does! So how do you know which sites are worth visiting, which sites to bookmark, which sites are worth going to more than once? The answer: branding. The sites you go back to are the sites you trust. They're the sites where the brand name tells you that the visit will be worth your time—again and again. The brand is a promise of the value you'll receive.

The same holds true for that other killer app of the Net—e-mail. When everybody has e-mail and anybody can send you e-mail, how do you decide whose messages you're going to read and respond to first—and whose you're going to send to the trash unread? The answer: personal branding. The name of the e-mail sender is every bit as important a brand—is a brand—as the name of the Web site you visit. It's a promise of the value you'll receive for the time you spend reading the message.

Nobody understands branding better than professional services firms. Look at McKinsey or Arthur Andersen for a model of the new rules of branding at the company and personal level. Almost every professional services firm works with the same business model. They have almost no hard assets—my guess is that most probably go so far as to rent or lease every tangible item they possibly can to keep from having to own anything. They have lots of soft assets—more conventionally known as people, preferably smart, motivated, talented people. And they have huge revenues—and astounding profits.

They also have a very clear culture of work and life. You're hired, you report to work, you join a team—and you immediately start figuring out how to deliver value to the customer. Along the way, you learn stuff, develop your skills, hone your abilities, move from project to project. And if you're really smart, you figure out how to distinguish yourself from all the other very smart people walking around with $1,500 suits, high-powered laptops, and well-polished resumes. Along the way, if you're really smart, you figure out what it takes to create a distinctive role for yourself—you create a message and a strategy to promote the brand called You.

What Makes You Different?

Start right now: as of this moment you're going to think of yourself differently! You're not an "employee" of General Motors, you're not a "staffer" at General Mills, you're not a "worker" at General Electric or a "human resource" at General Dynamics (ooops, it's gone!). Forget the Generals! You don't "belong to" any company for life, and your chief affiliation isn't to any particular "function." You're not defined by your job title and you're not confined by your job description.

Starting today you are a brand.

You're every bit as much a brand as Nike, Coke, Pepsi, or The Body Shop. To start thinking like your own favorite brand manager, ask yourself the same question the brand managers at Nike, Coke, Pepsi, or The Body Shop ask themselves: What is it that my product or service does that makes it different? Give yourself the traditional 15-words-or-less contest challenge. Take the time to write down your answer. And then take the time to read it. Several times.

If your answer wouldn't light up the eyes of a prospective client or command a vote of confidence from a satisfied past client, or—worst of all—if it doesn't grab you, then you've got a big problem. It's time to give some serious thought and even more serious effort to imagining and developing yourself as a brand.

Start by identifying the qualities or characteristics that make you distinctive from your competitors—or your colleagues. What have you done lately—this week—to make yourself stand out? What would your colleagues or your customers say is your greatest and clearest strength? Your most noteworthy (as in, worthy of note) personal trait?

Go back to the comparison between brand You and brand X—the approach the corporate biggies take to creating a brand. The standard model they use is feature-benefit: every feature they offer in their product or service yields an identifiable and distinguishable benefit for their customer or client. A dominant feature of Nordstrom department stores is the personalized service it lavishes on each and every customer. The customer benefit: a feeling of being accorded individualized attention—along with all of the choice of a large department store.

So what is the "feature-benefit model" that the brand called You offers? Do you deliver your work on time, every time? Your internal or external customer gets dependable, reliable service that meets its strategic needs. Do you anticipate and solve problems before they become crises? Your client saves money and headaches just by having you on the team. Do you always complete your projects within the allotted budget? I can't name a single client of a professional services firm who doesn't go ballistic at cost overruns.

Your next step is to cast aside all the usual descriptors that employees and workers depend on to locate themselves in the company structure. Forget your job title. Ask yourself: What do I do that adds remarkable, measurable, distinguished, distinctive value? Forget your job description. Ask yourself: What do I do that I am most proud of? Most of all, forget about the standard rungs of progression you've climbed in your career up to now. Burn that damnable "ladder" and ask yourself: What have I accomplished that I can unabashedly brag about? If you're going to be a brand, you've got to become relentlessly focused on what you do that adds value, that you're proud of, and most important, that you can shamelessly take credit for.

When you've done that, sit down and ask yourself one more question to define your brand: What do I want to be famous for? That's right—famous for!

What's the Pitch for You?

So it's a cliché: don't sell the steak, sell the sizzle. it's also a principle that every corporate brand understands implicitly, from Omaha Steaks's through-the-mail sales program to Wendy's "we're just regular folks" ad campaign. No matter how beefy your set of skills, no matter how tasty you've made that feature-benefit proposition, you still have to market the bejesus out of your brand—to customers, colleagues, and your virtual network of associates.

For most branding campaigns, the first step is visibility. If you're General Motors, Ford, or Chrysler, that usually means a full flight of TV and print ads designed to get billions of "impressions" of your brand in front of the consuming public. If you're brand You, you've got the same need for visibility—but no budget to buy it.

So how do you market brand You?

There's literally no limit to the ways you can go about enhancing your profile. Try moonlighting! Sign up for an extra project inside your organization, just to introduce yourself to new colleagues and showcase your skills—or work on new ones. Or, if you can carve out the time, take on a freelance project that gets you in touch with a totally novel group of people. If you can get them singing your praises, they'll help spread the word about what a remarkable contributor you are.

If those ideas don't appeal, try teaching a class at a community college, in an adult education program, or in your own company. You get credit for being an expert, you increase your standing as a professional, and you increase the likelihood that people will come back to you with more requests and more opportunities to stand out from the crowd.

If you're a better writer than you are a teacher, try contributing a column or an opinion piece to your local newspaper. And when I say local, I mean local. You don't have to make the op-ed page of *The New York Times* to make the grade. Community newspapers, professional newsletters, even inhouse company publications have white space they need to fill. Once you get started, you've got a track record—and clips that you can use to snatch more chances.

And if you're a better talker than you are teacher or writer, try to get yourself on a panel discussion at a conference or sign up to make a presentation at a workshop. Visibility has a funny way of multiplying; the hardest part is getting started. But a couple of good panel presentations can earn you a chance to give a "little" solo speech—and from there it's just a few jumps to a major address at your industry's annual convention.

The second important thing to remember about your personal visibility campaign is: it all matters. When you're promoting brand You, everything you do—and everything you choose not to do—communicates the value and character of the brand. Everything from the way you handle phone conversations to the e-mail messages you send to the way you conduct business in a meeting is part of the larger message you're sending about your brand.

Partly it's a matter of substance: what you have to say and how well you get it said. But it's also a matter of style. On the Net, do your communications demonstrate a command of the technology? In meetings, do you keep your contributions short and to the point? It even gets down to the level of your brand You business card: Have you designed a cool-looking logo for your own card? Are you demonstrating an appreciation for design that shows you understand that packaging counts—a lot—in a crowded world?

The key to any personal branding campaign is "word-of-mouth marketing." Your network of friends, colleagues, clients, and customers is the most important marketing vehicle you've got; what they say about you and your contributions is what the market will ultimately gauge as the value of your brand. So the big trick to building your brand is to find ways to nurture your network of colleagues—consciously.

What's the Real Power of You?

If you want to grow your brand, you've got to come to terms with power— your own. The key lesson: power is not a dirty word!

In fact, power for the most part is a badly misunderstood term and a badly misused capability. I'm talking about a different kind of power than we usually refer to. It's not ladder power, as in who's best at climbing over the adjacent bods. It's not who's-got-the-biggest-office-by-six-square-inches power or who's-got-the-fanciest-title power.

It's *influence* power.

It's being known for making the most significant contribution in your particular area. It's reputational power. If you were a scholar, you'd measure it by the number of times your publications get cited by other people. If you were a consultant, you'd measure it by the number of CEOs who've got your business card in their Rolodexes. (And better yet, the number who know your beeper number by heart.)

Getting and using power—intelligently, responsibly, and yes, powerfully—are essential skills for growing your brand. One of the things that attracts us to certain brands is the power they project. As a consumer, you want to associate with brands whose powerful presence creates a halo effect that rubs off on you.

It's the same in the workplace. There are power trips that are worth taking—and that you can take without appearing to be a self-absorbed, self-aggrandizing megalomaniacal jerk. You can do it in small, slow, and subtle ways. Is your team having a hard time organizing productive meetings? Volunteer to write the agenda for the next meeting. You're contributing to the team, and you get to decide what's on and off the agenda. When it's time to write a post-project report, does everyone on your team head for the door? Beg for the chance to write the report—because the hand that holds the pen (or taps the keyboard) gets to write or at least shape the organization's history.

Most important, remember that power is largely a matter of perception.

If you want people to see you as a powerful brand, act like a credible leader. When you're thinking like brand You, you don't need org-chart authority to be a leader. The fact is you are a leader. You're leading You!

One key to growing your power is to recognize the simple fact that we now live in a project world. Almost all work today is organized into bite-sized packets called projects. A project-based world is ideal for growing your brand: projects exist around deliverables, they create measurables, and they leave you with braggables. If you're not spending at least 70% of your time working on projects, creating projects, or organizing your (apparently mundane) tasks into projects, you are sadly living in the past. Today you have to think, breathe, act, and work in projects.

Project World makes it easier for you to assess—and advertise—the strength of brand You. Once again, think like the giants do. Imagine yourself a brand manager at Procter & Gamble: When you look at your brand's assets, what can you add to boost your power and felt presence? Would you be better off with a simple line extension—taking on a project that adds incrementally to your existing base of skills and accomplishments? Or would you be better off with a whole new product line? Is it time to move overseas for a couple of years, venturing outside your comfort zone (even taking a lateral move—damn the ladders), tackling something new and completely different?

Whatever you decide, you should look at your brand's power as an exercise in new-look résumé management—an exercise that you start by doing away once and for all with the word "résumé." You don't have an old-fashioned résumé anymore! You've got a marketing brochure for brand You. Instead of a static list of titles held and positions occupied, your marketing brochure brings to life the skills you've mastered, the projects you've delivered, the braggables you can take credit for. And like any good marketing brochure, yours needs constant updating to reflect the growth—breadth and depth—of brand You.

What's Loyalty to You?

Everyone is saying that loyalty is gone; loyalty is dead; loyalty is over. I think that's a bunch of crap.

I think loyalty is much more important than it ever was in the past. A 40-year career with the same company once may have been called loyalty; from here it looks a lot like a work life with very few options, very few opportunities, and very little individual power. That's what we used to call indentured servitude.

Today loyalty is the only thing that matters. But it isn't blind loyalty to the company. It's loyalty to your colleagues, loyalty to your team, loyalty to your project, loyalty to your customers, and loyalty to yourself. I see it as a much deeper sense of loyalty than mindless loyalty to the Company Z logo.

I know this may sound like selfishness. But being CEO of Me Inc. requires you to act selfishly—to grow yourself, to promote yourself, to get the market to reward yourself. Of course, the other side of the selfish coin is that any company you work for ought to applaud every single one of the efforts you make to develop yourself. After all, everything you do to grow Me Inc. is gravy for them: the projects you lead, the networks you develop, the customers you delight, the braggables you create generate credit for the firm. As long as you're learning, growing, building relationships, and delivering great results, it's good for you and it's great for the company.

That win-win logic holds for as long as you happen to be at that particular company. Which is precisely where the age of free agency comes into play. If you're treating your resume as if it's a marketing brochure, you've learned the first lesson of free agency. The second lesson is one that today's professional athletes have all learned: you've got to check with the market on a regular basis to have a reliable read on your brand's value. You don't have to be looking for a job to go on a job interview. For that matter, you don't even have to go on an actual job interview to get useful, important feedback.

The real question is: How is brand You doing? Put together your own "user's group"—the personal brand You equivalent of a software review group. Ask for—insist on—honest, helpful feedback on your performance, your growth, your value. It's the only way to know what you would be worth on the open market. It's the only way to make sure that, when you declare your free agency, you'll be in a strong bargaining position. It's not disloyalty to "them"; it's responsible brand management for brand You—which also generates credit for them.

What's the Future of You?

It's over. No more vertical. No more ladder. That's not the way careers work anymore. Linearity is out. A career is now a checkerboard. Or even a maze. It's full of moves that go sideways, forward, slide on the diagonal, even go backward when that makes sense. (It often does.) A career is a portfolio of projects that teach you new skills, gain you new expertise, develop new capabilities, grow your colleague set, and constantly reinvent you as a brand.

As you scope out the path your "career" will take, remember: the last thing you want to do is become a manager. Like "résumé," "manager" is an obsolete term. It's practically synonymous with "dead end job." What you want is a steady diet of more interesting, more challenging, more provocative projects. When you look at the progression of a career constructed out of projects, directionality is not only hard to track—Which way is up?—but it's also totally irrelevant.

Instead of making yourself a slave to the concept of a career ladder, reinvent yourself on a semiregular basis. Start by writing your own mission statement, to guide you as CEO of Me Inc. What turns you on? Learning something new? Gaining recognition for your skills as a technical wizard? Shepherding new ideas from concept to market? What's your personal definition of success? Money? Power? Fame? Or doing what you love? However you answer these questions, search relentlessly for job or project opportunities that fit your mission statement. And review that mission statement every six months to make sure you still believe what you wrote.

No matter what you're doing today, there are four things you've got to measure yourself against. First, you've got to be a great teammate and a supportive colleague. Second, you've got to be an exceptional expert at something that has real value. Third, you've got to be a broad-gauged visionary—a leader, a teacher, a farsighted "imagineer." Fourth, you've got to be a businessperson—you've got to be obsessed with pragmatic outcomes.

It's this simple: You are a brand. You are in charge of your brand. There is no single path to success. And there is no one right way to create the brand called You. Except this: Start today. Or else.

THE LAST WORD

I liked the idea of Brand You, but do you really have to spend more time promoting yourself to become a successful brand?

Most of us have trouble finishing all the work that's already on our plates. Does succeeding as a brand really mean teaching night school or writing newspaper articles? I don't buy it.

I'm researching a book on successful number-two brands. One of the book's core themes is "sensed momentum." It's the perception among current and potential customers that a brand is dynamic, something to watch for—even if it's small. If you create positive word of mouth through sensed momentum, other people will build your brand for you—in their words and on their time.

Now that's appealing! You get to spend the evening having a beer with a friend—not teaching night school.

Adam Morgan
Director of account planning
TBWA
London, England

Free Agent Nation

From: Issue 12 | December 1997/January 1998 | By: Daniel H. Pink

---

In the hit movie *Jerry Maguire*, the title character gets fed up with the way things are done at his company, tries to change it, and fails. And so, in the parlance of the sports world in which he works, he becomes a free agent so he can do his work in accord with his values. Here's the thing: it isn't fiction. Writer Daniel H. Pink gave a name and a voice to a new breed of self-employed individuals hiding in plain sight. Empowered by mobile technology, so-called "third spaces" such as Kinko's and Starbucks, and a fierce spirit of independence, these free agents mix work and life on their terms. "Free Agent Nation" did more than just chronicle a subculture; it ignited a movement. To be sure, the world has changed significantly since the publication of this article, and the dark side of free agency has come to light. Most notably, affordable health insurance for the self-employed is an issue that has yet to be resolved. But cavils aside, the exuberance Pink captures among people who've broken free of one-size-fits-all careers remains as thrilling as ever.

Welcome to Free Agent, USA.

Federal census takers can't tell you how many people actually live here. Government mapmakers have yet to give it an official location.

But if you go look for it, as I did, you can't miss it. It's out there, from coast to coast, and it's growing every day. The residents of Free Agent, USA, are legion: Start with the 14 million self-employed Americans. Consider the 8.3 million Americans who are independent contractors. Factor in the 2.3 million people who find work each day through temporary agencies. Note that in January the IRS expects to mail out more than 74 million copies of Form 1099-MISC—the pay stub of free agents.

So let's hazard a guess. If we add up the self-employed, the independent contractors, the temps—a working definition of the population of Free Agent Nation—we end up with more than 16% of the American workforce: roughly 25 million free agents in the United States, people who move from project to project and who work on their own, sometimes for months, sometimes for days.

And if you're looking for a place to start making the map, you can mark Deborah Risi's home in Menlo Park, California. A 40-year-old marketing whiz, Risi worked for many years at companies like Apple Computer and Pacific Bell, climbing her way gracefully through their marketing divisions, securing ever-better positions at ever-higher salaries. Then, about two and a half years ago, she walked out of a company she'd rather not name and re-examined her life. "I looked back on my work history and realized I had never felt really, really good about it," she says. "I had maybe one boss I could both respect and learn from. I was tired of working incredibly hard for companies that lacked leadership and didn't share my values."

So she declared herself a free agent, landed her first client four days later, and hasn't looked back. Today Risi operates out of a room in her house that overflows with computer gear, file cabinets, and a Magic 8-Ball ("my managerial decision-making tool"). She consults on marketing strategy for high-tech giants like Sun Microsystems, Oracle, and Cisco Systems, usually juggling four to six clients at a time and bringing in a lot more money than she earned during her years in corporate America.

She feels more invigorated than she ever did in a traditional job. No surprise there. But—and this is one of the many counterintuitive truths of Free Agent Nation—she also feels more secure. She pilots her work life using an instrument panel similar to the one she uses for her investments: plenty of research, solid fundamentals, and, most of all, diversification. Just as sensible investors would never sink all their financial capital into one stock, free agents like Risi are questioning the wisdom of investing all their human capital in a single employer. Not only is it more interesting to have six clients instead of one boss, it also may be safer.

The concept eludes some. About a year ago Risi applied for a mortgage. The bank demanded to see every scrap of paper about her life and her finances, because a woman without a "job" was, in its old-economy view, an obvious credit risk.

"I showed them my resume and said, 'You're kidding me! I've been at Apple, Pacific Bell, Cullinet Software—all these high-tech companies. You're telling me that I would be a safer bet at one of those than I am with six active clients? If one of my clients goes away, I'm still going to make my payments. But if I'm employed by Apple and they let me go, I'm out on the street.' "

She got her loan.

"Unless you're into self-abuse, or you're incredibly lucky and avoid re-structuring," says Risi, "being a lifer is no longer an option."

As you take to the highways found on the new map of work, you'll soon learn the foremost rule of the road: freedom is the pathway to security, not a detour from it.

Like many free agents, I'm looking for Eldorado. Eldorado, New Mexico, that is. That's where you'll find June Walker, 53, a free agent who lives in an adobe house in this tiny, unincorporated area eight miles outside of Santa Fe. A tax and finance consultant, she advises other free agents on the intri-cacies and frustrations of the tax code. She says that if free agency changes the old equation between security and freedom—the either-or proposition of what Walker acidly calls the "W-2 world"—then the next challenging is-sue it raises goes straight to the heart of the matter: Why work?

"Free agency forces you to think about who you are and what you want to do with your life," she says. "Previously, it was only those wonderful, flaky artists who had to deal with this."

The old social contract didn't have a clause for introspection. It was much simpler than that. *You gave loyalty. You got security.* But now that the old contract has been repealed, people are examining both its basic terms and its implicit conditions.

Free agents quickly realized that in the traditional world, they were silently accepting an architecture of work customs and social mores that should have crumbled long ago under the weight of its own absurdity. From infighting and office politics to bosses pitting employees against one an-other to colleagues who don't pull their weight, most workplaces are a study in dysfunction. Most people *do* want to work; they *don't* want to put up with brain-dead distractions. Much of what happens inside companies turns out to be about . . . nothing. The American workplace has become a coast-to-coast *Seinfeld* episode. *It's about nothing.*

But work, free agents say, has to be about something. And so, instead of accepting the old terms, they're demanding new ones. Thus the second rule of the road for navigating Free Agent, USA: work is personal. You *can* achieve a beautiful synchronicity between who you are and what you do.

"A large organization is about submerging your own identity for the good of the company," says David Garfinkel, 44, from his apartment in San Francisco. "People have their game faces on." A few years ago, when he was a bureau chief for business publisher McGraw-Hill, Garfinkel decided he couldn't play that game any longer. "The appearance and title of the job were exciting, but the job wasn't using the best part of me. I felt like I was out of touch with who I really was." He's now a free-agent marketing strategist and copywriter.

Across the Bay, Sue Burish—a beefy, boisterous Oakland-based free agent who goes by the unlikely nickname of "Birdi"—concurs. "In traditional companies," she says, "people don't believe in themselves. How they act is so frequently not who they are. They put on masks for eight hours and then take them off when they're done."

Free agents gladly swap the false promise of security for the personal pledge of authenticity. "In free agency," says Burish, who now designs training programs, "people assume their own shape rather than fit the shape of some corporate box."

Burish, 45, knows about corporate boxes. She began her career in the mid-1970s, selling Parker pens. Since then she's worked at Southern Pacific Railroad, at Crocker Bank, and, for more than seven years, at Raychem Corp., the large electronics manufacturer.

"I have been riffed, merged, and bankrupted into unemployment," she says of her corporate life. But as a free agent for the last two years, she's been something altogether new: she's been *whole.* "I used to think that what I needed to do was balance my life, keep my personal and professional lives separate," she says. "But I discovered that the real secret is integration. I integrate my work into my life. I don't see my work as separate from my identity." The mask is gone. For this free agent, work is who she is.

And just as the first rule of the road leads to the second, the second yields the third: Work is fun.

For example, Burish came up with one of her best business ideas while taking the afternoon "off" to attend a day game of her beloved Oakland A's. "I don't know if going to a baseball game is business or fun," she says. "I've stopped worrying about it."

Because in Free Agent Nation, work is *supposed* to be fun.

It was the fun of her job that Theresa Fitzgerald missed when she rose from low-level designer to creative director at United Media, a New York company that syndicates columns and comic strips. She earned more and more money, got more and more responsibility, and moved further and further away from what she loved. Instead of doing art, she was managing people who did art. "I'd come into the studio and say, 'You guys are having all the fun,'" Fitzgerald explains. So, at the top of her career, she left to become a free agent.

It's yet another way that free agents have reversed the organizing premises of work in America. Remember the Peter Principle? That old chestnut held that people rise through the ranks until they reach the level of their incompetence. Fitzgerald embodies the Paul Principle: people rise though an organization until they stop having fun. Then they leave to become free agents.

Today Fitzgerald, 35, operates out of a 10×12 room in an apartment on Manhattan's Upper West Side. The ceiling is low, and the ceiling fan makes it seem even lower. A plastic Gumby dangles from the cord, dancing to the sound of the jackhammers devouring West 83rd Street. The Paul Principle propelled her here, where she designs children's clothing, toys, and promotions for clients including Playskool, Scholastic Publishing, and Major League Baseball. As much as she treasures her years as a corporate honcho, she knew she was losing touch with who she really was.

"I'm a doer," Fitzgerald says. "I would have very busy days at United Media, but I wouldn't have *done* anything."

She does not consider this boxy room the East Coast version of a Cupertino garage—the incubator for a large design operation of her own. "If I become a studio," she says, "I begin to lose me."

Tacked above her drafting table is a newspaper photo of Norman Rockwell with a small knot of people. "Why do you have a picture of Norman

Rockwell?" I ask. She points to a young man at the edge of the frame, almost cropped out of the photo: "That's my dad. He took drawing classes from Norman Rockwell."

"Was he a professional artist?" I ask.

"No," she answers. "He worked at General Electric for 35 years, but he was a very talented artist." Back then, freedom and security *were* a trade-off, and with five kids to feed, he understandably chose security. Work wasn't personal, and it damn well wasn't supposed to be fun.

"It was," Fitzgerald says, "a different world."

"I'm wiped," says Joanna Baker from her cell phone as she drives to a meeting somewhere near Chicago. "I've been working every night until 10."

Baker, 36, is the founder of an executive search firm. She's off to see another client. Like many in her field, Baker has sterling academic credentials—an undergraduate degree from Barnard College, an advanced degree in management from Northwestern University's Kellogg School. But unlike the legions of squeaky-clean MBAs who make their way lemminglike from on-campus interviews to socially acceptable "jobs," Baker has been a free agent from day one of her career. Smart, talented, driven, she is a first-round draft pick who's opted to play in a league of her own.

She recalls her B-school days as she pilots her Toyota Corolla wagon to her next stop: "Everybody was looking for that big plum job. Everybody wanted to be a brand manager." She too was tending that way—until she attended a few recruiting receptions. "They were fake, they were plastic." She was looking for authenticity.

She had entered Kellogg's Class of '93 after working in social services in New York City: "I worked at a nonprofit. I didn't know what the hell a balance sheet was." But gradually Baker grew to love the world of business, in particular the talent side of business—hiring and recruiting people to join companies.

By her second year of B-school, she figured she could do that sort of work on her own, but she covered her bets by talking to the megacompanies that were interviewing on campus. A pharmaceuticals company offered her a job as a recruiter at a juicy starting salary. But she decided she'd rather go it alone. Then, in the spring of her second year, the dean of Kellogg took Baker to lunch and told her not to do anything rash. Take the job at the drug company, he advised. You won't regret it.

For a time, she considered it. Here was the dean of one of the nation's top business schools giving her private career counseling.

But in the end, she turned down the offer: "I did a gut check. And my gut said that I'm going to be a little sick to my stomach when I wake up in the morning. I didn't want to give up Joanna Baker to be a cog in their machine."

So, haltingly, she struck out on her own. She joined a professional association, The Research Roundtable, and visited other recruiters. She didn't always like what she saw. These recruiters, she says, "put a high value on having mahogany and brass. There's no mahogany in my house."

In her Evanston, Illinois, home office, there are two phone lines and a black Labrador retriever—elements that Baker considers essential to her free-agent success. The dean has become a friend and even introduces her to prospective clients. And when she attends alumni meetings and sees her old classmates, she realizes that she makes about as much money as they do but has fringe benefits they probably can't even imagine.

"I get to do yoga every day in my house," Baker says. "Other people are commuting while I'm doing yoga."

Deep in the Hudson Valley, across the abandoned railroad tracks, past the rural cemetery, beyond the stone lions, in a cedar-paneled house at the foot of the Shawangunk Mountains, Terri Lonier is working solo. Literally.

Lonier, 45, is the founder of Working Solo, a consulting and publishing operation that advises free agents on how to navigate this new world; it also helps larger businesses understand and reach this growing new market. She is both evangelist and ambassador. She spreads the word, urging the growing flock of free agents to have faith—in themselves. And she journeys to the more established land of business to decode what's taking place in the strange new realm that she represents.

At her home here in New Paltz, New York, one of the most compelling subplots in the Free Agent Nation story is unfolding in Lonier's basement and across her telephone lines. Throughout the country, small groups of free agents are helping one another succeed professionally and survive emotionally. These groups belie another of the central myths about free agency: that without that office watercooler, free agents become isolated and lonely. As Lonier puts it, "Working solo is not working alone."

These groups—at once hard-headed and soft-hearted—are creating new communities. One part board of directors, another part group therapy, these small, self-organized clusters are part of the emerging free-agent infrastructure. Along with Kinko's, Office Depot, Staples, and Web sites too numerous to count, they are forming the new foundation of our economic and social lives.

Every other week, usually on a Friday morning, Lonier and three colleagues—including Elaine Floyd, 36, a newsletter impresario based in St. Louis, and Pam Davis, 47, a television producer based in San Diego—hold a conference call to discuss their microbusinesses. They solicit and receive advice, set goals for the coming weeks, and give one another an emotional boost.

David Garfinkel, the free-agent copywriter from San Francisco, is the fourth participant in the biweekly call. He says that being accountable to peers has forced him to get things done that he might have let slide. "I have a lot of great friends," Garfinkel says, "but they haven't chosen this path. No matter how kindhearted they are, they just can't cheer you on. They're on a different emotional frequency."

Adds Davis: "A lot of people don't understand what I'm going through. I see this look on their faces, and I say, 'I'm going to go talk to my group about it.' "

A different Friday morning, a different group. This time I'm in Miriam Krasno's living room in Skokie, Illinois, with a plate of bagels to my left and her parrot BooBoo to my right. This is the Strategy Group, which includes Joanna Baker, the executive recruiter, and three other women: Krasno, 41, a career coach; Cheryl Rodgers, 41, an educational technology consultant; and Beth Sirull, 34, a free-agent marketing guru.

The Strategy Group has fun, but it's structured fun. At their meetings, each participant has a maximum of 20 minutes to speak, with the time divided into four periods. The first period is called Accomplishments and Insights; here, a participant must talk for at least two but no more than five minutes about what she has achieved in the past month—personally, professionally, and, yes, spiritually. Next comes Struggles and Dilemmas, a two-to-five-minute chance to discuss problems while avoiding self-flagellation. That sets the stage for the nine-minute interactive session, during which the group offers advice (like a corporate board) and encouragement (like a support group). Then comes the one-minute finale, in which each woman makes commitments to herself that the group will enforce.

For this session, Rodgers—sitting cross-legged on Krasno's couch—begins. She reports on her month, which has been a bit up-and-down. She likes some of the work she's doing, dislikes some of the rest. Midway through a sentence, Baker's black pocket timer screeches to signal the end of this period. "Struggles and Dilemmas," Baker says. "Let's go."

Rodgers's main difficulty is that a contract she's working on looks as if it will take significantly longer than she expected. She feels she's not getting paid a fair amount. "I have no idea whether it's appropriate to go back to my client and say that I'm uncomfortable with this," she says.

"Did you give the client a written proposal?" Krasno asks, peering from behind her birdlike glasses.

Rodgers, head turned down, says, "No."

"That's the problem," says Sirull. "You've got nothing to fall back on, nothing to point to."

Rodgers also thinks she might want to work full time for an operation for which she's now a contractor. Her group debates the merits of such a move. "If you can get health insurance, it might be worth it," Sirull offers.

The rapid-fire squeal of Baker's timer sounds again: now it's Krasno's turn. Then comes Sirull.

Baker goes last, and she has a lot going on. She's secured office space because new business has flooded in. And she's landed even more work. But her report quickly turns personal: "I'm going to start teaching yoga soon." Later she adds, "I haven't had an actual date since last time we met."

Her first struggle: for one large project, she's had to spend a lot of time in a cubicle inside a large company. "I remembered all those things I'd forgotten—pantyhose being stupid, commuting being stupid, not seeing light during the day. I want not to work there so badly I can taste it."

Another struggle: her schedule is so packed that she's having a tough time doing things like shopping for groceries and sustaining a social life.

The group helps her decide which time commitments to honor and which to discard. They also validate her decision to secure new office space, and they help her navigate an ethical dilemma that she faces with one client. All in all, they provide useful and compassionate advice.

Baker's commitments for next time run the gamut—from having lunch with a new business contact to cleaning her house.

Unprovoked, Sirull offers a prediction: "I think you'll have a date in the next month too."

In a spartan eighth-floor office of a mangy building in the Union Square section of Manhattan, Sara Horowitz is busy writing the new rules of labor. Horowitz, 34, is executive director of Working Today, a two-year-old organization made up of nine professional groups and comprising 35,000 people—including 2,500 individuals who have signed up on their own. By joining Working Today, free agents can secure some of the economies of scale enjoyed by traditional workers. Working Today's $10 membership fee buys access to health insurance, office supplies, computer software, and airline tickets, all at group discounts.

What makes this idea so innovative is that it leads to the exact opposite of a labor union. Traditionally, labor unions have derived their strength from seeking to establish a monopoly on the sale of labor in a certain industry or region. In this radically new economy, Horowitz is establishing more or less a monopoly of *buyers*—in short, a consumer union. It's practically impossible for free agents to bargain for wages as a group. But it's relatively easy for them to bargain together for better prices on the things they all must buy. Free agents represented by Working Today can say, "Sell us health insurance and office supplies at a reasonable price, or we'll take our business—and there's a lot of it—elsewhere."

Her work unsettles many in the labor establishment, because it abandons many of the movement's core strategies, revises its central vocabulary, and calls for a new architecture of laws and regulations. Horowitz thinks she has the standing to reinvent the game. Her grandfather was vice president of the International Ladies' Garment Workers' Union. Her father was a labor lawyer. So is her husband. And so is she. When she graduated from Cornell University, she went to work as a union organizer at a nursing home.

At a Manhattan coffee shop, Horowitz reaches across our table, grabs my notebook, and begins scribbling. "This is the structure of work," she says, drawing an enormous box. "The big building, the office." She then draws a stick figure. "This is an employee. An employee goes and works on a job. From that base, because they're called employees, they can unionize. They have labor rights, administrative benefits. This notion that you are working on your job—all these things flow from that. You get your health insurance, your pension, your unemployment insurance."

She draws another diagram—a bunch of tiny, disconnected circles. "This is the 1990s. This is the new structure of work. Any rights you have come from being an individual. This *job* notion, which used to undergird everything, doesn't exist here."

Horowitz pauses. "We need to look at the new ways people are working and say, 'These legal distinctions don't make sense. You don't tie these rights to the job. You tie them to the individual.' "

She has a point. There's no economic or moral reason why Americans get health insurance and pensions from their jobs. It's an accident of history. During World War II President Franklin Roosevelt imposed a wage freeze throughout the economy. Companies faced a labor shortage, and since they were prohibited from raising wages, they enticed workers with fringe benefits. They offered health insurance, and the custom stuck. In the United States most people who have health insurance receive it from an employer. Horowitz is willing to upset the status quo with what amounts to a moral argument: we should get health insurance not because we have some artificial Industrial Age construct called a job, but because of our dignity as individuals.

She cites Alexis de Tocqueville, who believed that what made the young American republic strong was its citizens' penchant for forming associations. Unions are declining, Horowitz says, but free agents "have been forming associations like crazy. This is going to be a new kind of democracy," she says.

"But Working Today isn't building a big, gargantuan bureaucracy," she says. Instead, she's drawing lessons on building her organization from Dee Hock, who used complexity theory and the principle of distributed power to create Visa International.

Yet Horowitz remains animated by the union ideals that seem imprinted on her genes: "If we're going to say that people are going to work on their own, then we have to put mechanisms in place so that more people can do that—and not just the well-to-do, the extraordinarily talented, or the extremely lucky."

There's no way to know at first, no way even to suspect. The building is stylish—two sleek stories and lots of wood—but not much different from many here in downtown Los Altos, California. The office I enter is pleasant but hardly on the cutting edge.

But the instant I meet him, the moment he begins talking, I know. *I've met Jerry Maguire*—the pop culture icon of the free-agent economy.

Actually, he's what you'd get if you genetically combined Jerry Maguire with Frank Zappa. His name is Bo Rinaldi. As executive vice president of the Trattner Network, which dubs itself the "Digital Talent Source," Rinaldi, 49, is the agent for some 1,000 software developers. In this land where lords and ladies of the digital renaissance construct their kingdoms, Rinaldi represents the traveling minstrels of software, the developers whose code can make or break a company. He finds them work, negotiates their contracts, and soothes their easily inflamed egos. Forget all the talk about Siliwood— the convergence of Silicon Valley and Hollywood. Rinaldi is Siliwood. He's brought the techniques of the Hollywood agent to the closed culture of Silicon Valley. And he's become a powerful force.

But visiting Bo is not like visiting a power broker. It's more like having an audience with a Zen master.

"We're in the center of the hourglass," Rinaldi explains in a voice that reveals his Southern California origins. "The sands are right in the center of the hourglass, speeding through it."

Corporations have foundered, he says, because they have neglected individuals and their psychic needs. "But it's an error to think that you can be a different person depending on where you are," Rinaldi says from behind the red-tinted sunglasses that he's wearing indoors. "I'm going to go to sleep Bo, and I'm going to wake up Bo. And that is the ghost in the machine."

This afternoon, the ghost is garbed in Silicon chic—a white *guayabera* shirt, a pair of jeans, and funky gray sandals pulled over rag-wool socks.

"We are at our very best—whether we're spiritual beings or mechanized beings—when we are purely on our path. Work is part of our path just as home is part of our path."

"Who you are and what you do should be in sync," I offer.

"Amen," Rinaldi says. "I'm in church."

Rinaldi saw the free-agent light about 10 years ago—after a stint as an executive at ComputerLand, an early PC retailer, and while working as a headhunter at the Trattner Network. His revelation was at once economic and emotional. He discovered that companies needed top-notch coders more than the coders needed them. And he knew that for these workers, the emotional value of work came from creating a product and making a difference—rather than from affiliating with a particular company.

So he started exploring. He talked to sports agents and Hollywood types, and he figured out the rules—and then changed them. His first rewrite: software writers weren't geeks; they were artists. The software developers whom he represents work for companies like Sun Microsystems and Netscape Communications; they've designed products like Adobe Acrobat. To Rinaldi, they are "product architects" and "applied visionaries."

"I believe in a talent-driven model," he says. He has in mind something like the film industry. "In a temp agency, you test 'em and roll 'em out. In my model, everyone is a star." The new realities of computers and networking make several of the old structures obsolete. "In the new metaphor of work, the loyalty factor is still very high. In the new metaphor of work, you have a smaller-team model and a greater sense of loyalty to the team than to this artifact known as a company. Companies do not exist. Countries do not exist. Boundaries are an illusion. But the team exists," Rinaldi says. "The loyalty is also to you. This is the summer of love revisited, man!"

Our conversation is almost over, but Rinaldi is still grasping for a way to describe what he does. Then he almost bounces out of the seat he's been swiveling in for the last two hours.

"I create code farms—places where people can sow the seeds of great code, work with these great geniuses, and grow these tremendous products."

I consider the implications: "If you bring enough talent onto this farm, you'll be able to build any piece of software that anybody needs."

Rinaldi flashes an inscrutable grin. "That's the idea."

The office is really an attic—an upside-down flower box of a room with wood floors and a sloping ceiling. Out one window is a neighbor's green roof; out the other is another neighbor's green tree. There's a nifty laptop on a desk and a fax-copier-printer combo on a crate, but not much else of economic value. The only things saving the walls from complete bareness are a Roy Lichtenstein poster and three snapshots of a stunningly cute little girl with her very attractive mom. This is where I work. I'm a free agent.

A few months ago I was working in the White House. Now I tell people I'm working in the Pink House, since my office is on the third floor of our compact home in Washington, D.C. For many years, I'd held down a job—often one that people considered a "good job." But I'd grown tired—tired of politics in general and of office politics in particular, tired of doing assignments I didn't enjoy on a schedule I couldn't control, tired of wingtips that felt like vises and neckties that seemed like nooses, and most of all, tired of seeing my stunningly cute daughter only when she was asleep and her very attractive mom only when I was complaining.

So I left. On Independence Day.

I became a free agent. That makes me a bit like the guy in those commercials who boasts that he's not simply president of Hair Club for Men: he's also a client. I'm not just a chronicler of Free Agent Nation: I'm also a citizen. And what has surprised me most—both during my rookie season of free agency and throughout my dozen-city, 7,000-mile jaunt through Free Agent, USA—is the extraordinary distance between this new world and the one I left behind.

For example, a new economic infrastructure is being built, and few people seem to notice. Since there's no well-stocked supply room here in the Pink House, I buy my wipeboards and Sharpies at Staples. If I've got major copies to crank out or a big presentation to prepare, I head for one of the three Kinko's within a four-mile radius of our house. Add e-mail and the Web—plus a nearby Mail Boxes Etc.—and I've got as good a foundation to do my work as I'd have in a regular office. But still, people seem surprised that I'm able to function at all.

Or take public policy. While the private sector eagerly fashions this new free-agent infrastructure (in 1996, for example, Staples opened two new superstores every week), the public sector barely recognizes the forces driving all this construction. In conventional political dialogue, most of the talk continues to be about saving "jobs" or rewarding "entrepreneurs," with little understanding that lots of us—and pretty soon, most of us—live somewhere between those poles. The tax code is still geared to employees, and it imposes extra costs and annoying accounting demands on free agents. For free agents, keeping health insurance is a pain; getting it is even worse. Labor laws don't apply to us—even though we make up more than one-sixth of the labor force.

But majority public attitudes still can't see it. For example, during my first month as a free agent, I described my switch to a friend, and he responded, "I really admire you for doing that. Most people wouldn't be able to handle the change in status."

On his map, the direction from the White House to the Pink House is straight down. Free Agent Nation is a land of exiles, an economic Elba. Many people like him ask me whether—sometimes when—I'll return to the other, more traditional world. It's a question that I posed to the 100 or so free agents whom I've spoken to in recent months. As it turns out, Deb Risi's answer is also mine—and soon, I think, it will be the answer of millions more.

Would you go back?

"I can't imagine why."

THE LAST WORD

As a resident of free agent nation, I applaud Daniel H. Pink's story about the millions of people leaving the corporate world to strike out on their own. I urge Fast Company's readers to take Pink's advice: Go for it! That's what I did.

I slaved away in a high-tech company for 10 years. Then, at age 40, I turned down a promotion and had a baby. Some might say that I checked out. In fact, with child in arms, I started on my own free-agent journey—and haven't looked back.

The leap is not that scary, if you make the right preparations. That means planning your finances, assessing your talents, and seeking out free-agent associations that will support you along the way. It's not as lonely or as hard as you might imagine. For instance, I often refer pieces of projects—the pieces I'm not qualified to do—to people who can do them. These associates are always grateful for the business, and my "networking" gets returned tenfold.

In the end, you're not going to be remembered for loyalty to "the company" or for how much money you make. You're going to be remembered for your contributions to your friends, your family, your society—and yourself. Free agents can make these kinds of contributions.

Dotti Lackey
President, The Parsons Group
Atlanta, Georgia

Genius at Work

From: Issue 17 | September 1998 | By: Sara Terry

The genius here is Bill Strickland, a potter turned social entrepreneur who defines the best of what we mean when we discuss applying business acumen to social causes. When he was in high school in early-1960s Pittsburgh, the city was changing, and not for the better. He easily could have gone the wrong way, too. But one man changed all that, and Strickland devoted his life to emulating the compassion of the man who saved him with a guiding hand at the right moment. As problems in the world mount, Strickland's methods are an inspiring lesson in the very best way to save the world, one person at a time.

Bill Strickland can tell you when his life began: It was a Wednesday afternoon in September 1963.

And he can tell you how it began: It started with a lump of clay.

Strickland, then a 16-year-old black kid, was bored by school and hemmed in by life in a decaying Pittsburgh neighborhood. He wanted a way out, but he didn't have a clue about how to find it—until that Wednesday afternoon, when he went wandering through the hallways of his high school. It's a moment etched so clearly in his memory that, 35 years later, he can still recall the quality of the sunlight streaming in through the school windows. That's the day he came face to face with hope.

Looking through an open classroom door, Strickland saw something he'd never seen before: a rotating mound of clay being shaped into a vessel by a man absorbed in his work.

"If ever in life there is a clairvoyant experience, I had one that day," says Strickland, now 51. "I saw a radiant and hopeful image of how the world ought to be. It opened up a portal for me that suggested that there might be a whole range of possibilities and experiences that I had not explored. It was night and day—literally. I saw a line and I thought: This is dark, and this is light. And I need to go where the light is."

So Strickland walked into the sunlit classroom, introduced himself to ceramics teacher Frank Ross, the man at the potter's wheel, and said, "I'd like to learn whatever that is." With Ross as his mentor for nearly 20 years, Strickland not only found the way out—one that led to college—he also found the way in: the path that lets one person make all the difference in the world.

He mastered the art of social entrepreneurship, applying his potter's hands to reshape the business of social change. As a result, the people who now work with him and come to his programs at the Manchester Craftsmen's Guild (MCG) and at the Bidwell Training Center Inc. (BTC)—his Pittsburgh-based organizations for urban change—will tell you that the day Bill Strickland walked into that ceramics classroom was the day that he began reinventing this country's approach to social entrepreneurship.

For nearly three decades, Strickland has worked at his craft back in the same Pittsburgh neighborhood he grew up in—creating a model for turning people with dead-end lives into productive workers. And it's working.

In the Manchester neighborhood of Pittsburgh's North Side, Strickland has forged a series of programs to bring new life to the community. At one end of the lifeline is the MCG, which aims to rescue at-risk school kids by using the arts to teach them life skills. At the other end is the BTC, an innovative partnership with local companies to train displaced adults for real work in real jobs. Since their inception, the two programs have each grown into more than $3-million-a-year operations, with a combined staff of 110 people. Strickland serves as president and CEO, the linchpin that holds all of the parts together.

And there's more. Like any true entrepreneur, Strickland has filled the space between the two programs with other ventures: a jazz concert hall and an innovative Grammy Award–winning record label. Next year, he plans to roll out the Denali Initiative—a national three-year effort funded by the Kaufmann Foundation to teach nonprofit leaders how to think like entrepreneurs.

The source of it all is Strickland's single flash of insight on that long-ago Wednesday afternoon. "You start with the perception that the world is an unlimited opportunity," Strickland says. "Then the question becomes, 'How are we going to rebuild the planet?' "

The question may seem presumptuous, but plenty of people think that Strickland not only has the right to ask it, but that he has also discovered some of the answers. Although he isn't dealing in big numbers—his combined programs reach about 400 kids and 475 adults each year—Strickland is dealing in success: For the past five years, 75% to 80% of the high-risk high-school kids who've come to his after-school arts program have gone on to college. At the same time, 78% of the adults who graduate from his vocational program find jobs.

Just as impressive as the numbers are Strickland's supporters and believers. There's George Bush, who named Strickland to a six-year term on the board of the National Endowment for the Arts. And there's Hillary Rodham Clinton, who visited Strickland's center—and then invited Strickland to visit the White House.

There's the Harvard Business School—which hailed Strickland as a "social entrepreneur." And there's the Harvard Graduate School of Education—which invited him to share with its students his lessons on teaching.

There's San Francisco Mayor Willie Brown and jazz musician Herbie Hancock, who teamed up with Strickland to replicate his Pittsburgh program in San Francisco—an undertaking that Strickland hopes will be the first of 100 "franchises" that he plans to set up nationwide over the next 30 years. And there's the MacArthur Foundation, which awarded Strickland a $295,000 "genius" grant in 1996.

Not bad for a man who, 30 years ago, set out to learn how to throw a pot.

"This Is My Clay"

Bill Strickland's story starts in the 1950s, when the Manchester community he grew up in was filled with neat row houses and green trees. People in the neighborhood could find good jobs nearby in thriving small businesses and at prosperous industrial firms such as Allis-Chalmers, Steel City Electric, and Midland-Ross Corp.

The neighborhood was culturally rich, a melting pot of roughly 40,000 people. But in the early 1960s, hard times caused many local businesses to shrink or shut down. The character of the community began to change. And Strickland, a teenager, felt his world narrowing.

"I'd watched my neighborhood go from a healthy community to a ghetto. I needed to find a way out," he says. "But there weren't many examples of successful people in my community who could serve as role models." And then came that day in high school when Strickland discovered Frank Ross, ceramics, and the possibility that the world might have something more to offer.

"Mr. Ross brought a kind of gutsy quality to public education that said, 'Look, there's nothing wrong with you. There's a lot wrong with the circumstances that you find yourself in,'" Strickland says. "He said, 'You have the talent and the resources to take control of your life and to do something more than you've done up to this point.' And I believed him."

After that first encounter, Strickland devoted his remaining two years in high school to learning everything that Ross could teach him. When he graduated in 1965, Strickland went on to the University of Pittsburgh, entering on probation because he'd neglected his high school academics in favor of ceramics. But he quickly proved himself, landing on the dean's list by the end of his first year—and winding up on the university's board of trustees 32 years later.

Even as his world expanded during college, Strickland remained bound to the old neighborhood. Then, in 1968, when the social upheaval and rioting that were rocking the nation reached Manchester, Strickland decided it was time for him to do something to bring hope back to the streets. While still in college, he opened the Manchester Craftsmen's Guild, an after-school program to teach neighborhood children the same pottery skills that had originally motivated him. A local Episcopalian church donated space for the program in the basement of a row house.

After college, Strickland continued his work with MCG, building a staff of volunteers, and earning a name for himself as a local activist. He ran the program on an annual budget of less than $50,000, cobbling together funds from small grants, and from contributions by community leaders who had begun to support his work.

Three years later, a second piece of Strickland's program fell into place: He was asked to take over the Bidwell Training Center, a three-year-old neighborhood vocational-training program. Like MCG, BTC had been started in response to the 1968 riots. But the Presbyterian church that had administered the program had run afoul of the Internal Revenue Service for failing to pay withholding taxes. The options: Shut down the program—or find somebody to take it over and rebuild it.

Strickland was the ideal candidate—and he accepted the challenge. The way he saw it, BTC offered him an opportunity to play out his ideas on a larger stage. On the surface, however, it was an unlikely marriage of programs: arts and kids on the one hand, vocational training and adults on the other. But to Strickland, combining the programs meant he could approach community rebuilding from two directions: by saving troubled kids and getting them on to college; and by reclaiming adults who'd been discarded and giving them the opportunity to make a second start in life.

For the next decade, Strickland worked at both programs, quietly forming his own vision of social change, and attracting people to his cause. By 1983, Strickland was ready to take a new leap, ratcheting up both programs to have more impact and more presence. The move was equal parts vision and audacity: With $112 in the bank, he launched a fund-raising drive to construct an $8 million building on the site of an abandoned industrial park.

What might have been a futile gesture turned into a natural expansion. For years, Strickland had nurtured relationships with business and community leaders; now that work paid off. In three years, he raised enough money from foundations, corporations, and government sources to build a showplace, a center for social innovation that would allow him to demonstrate exactly how his ideas worked—and what they could do.

Designed by a pupil of Frank Lloyd Wright, the 62,000-square-foot, honey-colored brick building houses Strickland's vision of a thriving community-learning center. Each day, struggling high schoolers and adult vocational students enter a stunning building of arches and circles designed to allow the sun to pour through—the way Strickland remembers the light in Ross's ceramics studio. "The worst thing about being poor is what it does to your spirit," says Strickland, "not just your wallet. I wanted to build something that would give the people who come here a vision of what life could be, to create an environment that says that life is good."

Strickland's done that—and more. He's brought all of his talents as an artist to bear to create a template for social change. "The planet's changing," says Strickland. "The whole culture, the language, the relationships—it's all new. The millennium is defining a different kind of artist, a different kind of entrepreneur, a different kind of leader than we've known before. This is my clay."

"Entrepreneurs and Artists Are Interchangeable"

It's a typical classroom: Computers are lined along one wall, a few dozen institutional chairs with attached desktops are gathered in the center of the room. A bunch of ninth-grade students crack jokes or ask questions as they consider a fable about a cat and a fox.

But there is something just a bit, well, odd in this learning situation. First, there are the questions: One teenage boy asks, "Are we allowed to sew today?" And there are the materials: strips of papier-mache, bits of fabric, and pieces of string scattered everywhere.

The subject is a fable. But the teaching method is pure Manchester Craftsmen's Guild. These students—most of them considered "at risk" by the public school that has sent them here—are making puppets of the two lead characters in the fable. They've made papier-mache heads and bodies, and now they're sewing small costumes by hand.

Their work is the hands-on, creative phase of a lesson that began one month earlier. The Puppet Project, as it's called, started with a discussion of folktales, focusing on the way that stories can teach morals. The students watched a video of *Pinocchio* and discussed the story's lessons. Next they wrote a folktale of their own, with a clearly defined moral. Then they studied the fable of the cat and the fox. And now they're learning to approach the fable as an artistic endeavor—a hands-on, problem-solving exercise of constructing puppets that they will then use to stage the fable as a play.

This is Bill Strickland's take on the art of learning. It's got little to do with tradition, plenty to do with education, and everything to do with art. For three hours a day, these students come from nearby David B. Oliver High School—Strickland's alma mater—to study at MCG. The medium is art—the teaching staff uses photography, ceramics, painting, and drawing to convey academic subjects. The message is life.

This part of Strickland's program, called the Arts Collaborative, costs

$500,000 a year, an operating budget that is funded by local foundations. Like MCG's after-school arts program, it builds on mentoring relationships that create educational learning and individual self-knowledge. Unlike that project, which runs as a voluntary arts-education drop-in center, attendance at the Arts Collaborative initiative counts for part of an accredited school day for participating kids from Oliver High School.

So far, it's working—and working more effectively than Oliver High School. The numbers tell the story: According to an independent consultant's analysis of the program's first two years, students in the Arts Collaborative missed far fewer days of class than did their peers at Oliver High School. And their grade-point averages were better—by a half-point for ninth graders and three-quarters of a point for tenth graders.

The use of art to change students' attitudes is at the heart of Strickland's vision of education. The goal is not to produce artists. It's to find an individually tailored approach to learning that will redirect troubled young people, and get them into college and on to productive lives. But Strickland does see a connection between the creativity instilled by a love of the arts, and the skills needed for business success in the new economy.

"Artists are by nature entrepreneurs, they're just not called that," Strickland says. "They have the ability to visualize something that doesn't exist, to look at a canvas and see a painting. Entrepreneurs do that. That's what makes them different from businesspeople. Businesspeople are essentially administrators. Entrepreneurs are by definition visionaries. Entrepreneurs and artists are interchangeable in many ways. The hip companies know that."

"There Has Got to Be a Deal Here"

It's 4:15 on a foggy, drizzly April afternoon, and inside one of the amphitheater-style classrooms at the Harvard Business School, the subject is Bill Strickland.

There are 145 students in the room—leaders of nonprofit organizations from across America and Europe. They're here as part of an Executive Education seminar hosted by the school's Initiative for Social Enterprise. Most of the people in this room have just had their first exposure to Strickland:

They have finished reading a 22-page case study; set in 1993, the case lays out the situation that Strickland and his twin programs faced at that time.

Under the gentle prodding of visiting professor John Vogel, the nonprofit leaders voice their opinions of Strickland and his work: "It's one of the most moving case studies I've ever read," offers one. "He consistently challenged the community to help itself," says another. "It's a customer-focused organization," comments a third.

But they remain divided on the big question raised in the case study: Where should Strickland focus his next efforts? Should he concentrate on fund-raising for BTC, which at the time had a dicey record of getting money from the state government? Should he expand his operation into a real-estate development project? Should his for-profit food-services company— a spin-off of BTC's culinary training program—make a bid to manage the employee cafeteria at the newly expanded Pittsburgh International Airport? Or should he try to franchise his programs in other cities?

The choices that Strickland faced back in 1993 prompt a heated debate among the students. Everyone has an opinion about which strategic move Strickland should make, but no clear consensus emerges in the room. One thing is clear: Nobody—absolutely nobody—thinks that it makes sense for Strickland to pursue all four options simultaneously.

When the debate ends, Strickland stands up. In his usual, understated way, he announces, "I've got some pictures to show you of what I do for a living." And then he proceeds to blow everyone in the room away: As Strickland runs through his slide show, it becomes clear that what he did back in 1993 was, in fact, to pursue all four of the case-study options. Simultaneously.

Yes, he concentrated on fund-raising: Through relationships built with Pennsylvania statehouse politicians, Strickland secured a permanent place for BTC as a line item in the state budget, guaranteeing funds of $3.5 million a year.

Yes, he pursued the real-estate development option: He just broke ground on a new project—a 60,000-square-foot office building that will sit across from the existing facility. Part of the space will be used to accommodate expanded training programs for BTC. But the new building will also turn Strickland into a commercial landlord: UPMC Health Systems at the

University of Pittsburgh has committed to leasing 30,000 square feet of office space.

As for the bid on the employee cafeteria at the airport, yes, his food-services company made a bid and got the contract. No, it didn't work out. But he's continued to build the food services company—which has revenues of about $1.5 million—and this year expects it to show its first profit. What's more, Strickland is now aiming for a food-services contract with Pennsylvania's turnpike authority, a deal worth roughly $250 million a year.

And franchising? Yes, that's going forward as well. In fact, Strickland reports, he has just teamed up with San Francisco Mayor Willie Brown and musician Herbie Hancock to build a project in a poor neighborhood on the shores of the San Francisco Bay. If all goes according to plan, the San Francisco program will be up and running in three years.

Strickland winds up his comments by turning the spotlight back onto his peers in the room. "If this country has a future," he says, "it's because of you guys. Because of your ability to form visions and to form partnerships. I believe that we can change the United States of America in my lifetime, and I'm not out of my mind. We've got to change the way this country sees itself."

The crowd goes wild. Strickland gets a standing ovation and is soon surrounded by people who want to exchange business cards, learn more, come to visit, change the world. They are believers.

Later, Strickland turns the tables, and offers his views on the challenges facing nonprofits. "Nonprofits have to recognize that they're businesses, not just causes," he says. "There's a way to combine the very best of the not-for-profit, philanthropic world with the very best of the for-profit, enterprising world. This hybrid is the wave of the future for both profit and nonprofit companies."

It's a message that Strickland repeats over and over again on his travels, which keep him on the road as many as 12 days a month. It's a message that is winning over the toughest, most bottom-line-oriented businesspeople, people who are interested in concrete results, not wishful thinking.

Strickland won over Peter Benzing, 69, a decade ago. Benzing had retired as a vice president at Bayer Corp.—the U.S. subsidiary, headquartered in Pittsburgh, of the giant German chemical-pharmaceutical conglomerate—but he had stayed active with the company. When he met Strickland,

Benzing's biggest concern was the need for an educated local workforce that could meet Bayer's needs.

Benzing recalls his meeting with Strickland. Thirty minutes into the session, Benzing asked whether Strickland could train chemical technicians. "Bill said, 'I don't have the slightest idea about how to train somebody for that, but if you'd be willing to help, maybe we could do that at Bidwell too,'" Benzing says. It was a classic Strickland response, going straight to the core of his market-oriented operating philosophy: I've got poor people who want to learn how to work. You can't find people who've been trained to do the jobs you've got. Let's do it together.

Benzing was so impressed that he immediately went back to Bayer, got the company to contact other chemical companies nearby, and wound up with a business consortium that partnered with Strickland to create a one-year-long curriculum to train chemical lab technicians. It's a tough program—many students drop out because of the demanding work. But in 12 months, it turns out trained workers who can compete with college graduates for jobs. More than 100 students have finished BTC's program; of those, 81% have found jobs in a field where the annual minimum starting salary is between $20,000 and $25,000.

Companies have found there's another reason why it's good business to do business with Strickland: It makes them look good. Case in point: the creation of a Grammy Award–winning jazz record label, another Strickland innovation that happened almost by accident. When Strickland brought MCG and BTC under one roof in 1986, he made sure that the blueprint included a 350-seat jazz concert hall. His rationale? He loves jazz.

But Strickland knew nothing about booking concerts, so he hired someone who did: jazz musician and promoter Marty Ashby, 37. Under Ashby's direction, MCG quickly gained a reputation as a great venue for live music. Although the musicians were just coming to play another gig, they inevitably left impressed by Strickland's community. "He's like a Dr. King," says singer Joe Williams, 79, whose award-winning career has spanned more than 50 years, and who has performed at MCG three times. "I've watched Bill's project grow to become an integral part of the community. And when I say community, I mean the community of the United States."

Strickland's team made sure that each live concert was recorded on state-of-the-art equipment, videotaped, and archived. But it wasn't until 1994, when Strickland and Ashby were at Bayer for discussions about BTC's training program, that the idea of a record label began to take shape. While touring the company, Strickland asked about one machine in the plant, and was told that it was for making compact discs. Bayer, it turned out, is a leading producer of polycarbonate, the plastic from which CDs are made.

"Bill said, 'You've got the CDs. We've got the music. There has got to be a deal here,' " recalls Ashby. Bayer liked the idea so much that it helped broker an extraordinary relationship. Using Bayer's contacts with Sony, Benzing helped put together a classic Strickland-style hybrid, combining the for-profit and nonprofit worlds.

What ultimately emerged was a five-record deal, with taped live perfor-mances provided by MCG; plastic provided by Bayer; pressing done by Sony Disc Manufacturing; and jewel boxes, liner-note production, and printing donated by three other companies. Under the deal, proceeds from the sale of the first 25,000 units of each record go directly to MCG.

It was an inspired move. In 1997, the first record of the deal—the Count Basie Orchestra with the New York Voices—won a Grammy for best perfor-mance by a large jazz ensemble. A second release, by Paquito D'Rivera and the United Nations Orchestra, is in the stores and selling briskly, and a third, by Brazilian artist Ivan Lins, has just been released.

As for Bayer and Sony, explains Benzing, the corporations benefit by having their names attached to a socially responsible project. "It's a big deal when a large company works with an inner-city organization," he says. "It's good news, and it fits into Bayer's philosophy of working with the commu-nities in which we're located."

"Welcome to the Conversation"

There's one other thing about the break-the-mold way that Bill Strickland does business: It's about the payoff. No, Strickland isn't in this for the money. But he's also not into being a starving artist. Strickland is looking for something in-between, like his hybrid model of social entrepreneurship. In fact, he's striving for the one thing that he thinks is missing in the world today: balance. A balance of resources, equity, and opportunity—a socially responsible mind-set that asks the haves in this country, How much is enough?

For Strickland, $125,000 a year is enough—that's his combined salary for running MCG and BTC. A house in the neighborhood he grew up in, a 1998 Volvo station wagon, a savings account to pay for his daughter's college education, and a closet full of impeccable suits and pressed shirts—for Strickland, these things are enough.

"I don't need the money," he says. "It's not my thing. Don't get me wrong—I do like money. But I don't know that it's ecologically appropriate to hoard millions and millions of dollars. We don't need to have so much wealth concentrated in so few hands. Our culture needs to recognize that having $20 million in the bank is not an absolute requirement for being happy. We have got to be more attuned to the idea that the life experience has its own value."

Strickland speaks with a moral authority that rings true with one particularly unlikely group: young business-school students. After having spent tens of thousands of dollars on a postgraduate education that presumably has them primed for a high-paying job in a high-flying company, business-school grads are probably the least likely group of people to find the nonprofit world attractive.

But they are, in fact, drawn to it—or at least to Strickland's version of it. And that fact alone may be one of the most important indicators that Strickland's hybrid approach to business and philanthropy has a future beyond Pittsburgh. At business schools across the country, Strickland finds that each time he lectures, more students are ready to enlist in the cause.

"At the end of the lecture, students are lined up wanting to work for me," Strickland says. "It's startling. I have students coming up with tears in their eyes, saying, 'You are doing what I want to do with my life.' I say, 'I thought you were in business school because you wanted to run Xerox.' And they say, 'We're here because we wanted to find an opportunity where life could make some sense. You make sense.' Then I tell them, 'We're going to take all this genius, all your enthusiasm, and see the world as a set of possibilities. This is a new game, and I'm one of the guys who's right in the middle of it. Welcome to the conversation.' "

THE LAST WORD

What a great article on Bill Strickland! I am forwarding it to my high-school art instructor, a man named Dick Ressel. Dick has long been a successful teacher—and for many of the same reasons that Strickland is successful in his line of work. Dick had a profound effect on me, and he had an even bigger effect on my brother, who has gone on to become an accomplished potter.

People like Bill Strickland and Dick Ressel make salaries that are modest by today's lofty standards. But they are constantly seeking ways to make a difference in the lives of others. That attitude is a pleasant change from today's get-it-as-fast-as-you-can corporate environment.

Scott Rempe
Coleman Resources
Greensboro, North Carolina

The Agenda—Grassroots Leadership

From: Issue 23 | April 1999 | By: Polly LaBarre

On the surface, the United States Navy might not appear to be a place where you'd find a paragon of forward-thinking leadership. Aren't the armed forces an exemplar of top-down command and control, the very style readers were rebelling against in their corporate iterations? Think again. D. Michael Abrashoff, the commander of the USS *Benfold*, a $1 billion Naval warship, will not only upend any preconceived notions you have about military leaders, but will offer a model of leadership that can work anywhere. Perhaps the military—and corporate America, too—could use more people like him.

You expect to be *awed* by the view from the deck of the USS *Benfold*. The $1 billion warship is one of the U.S. Navy's most modern, most lethal fighting machines: 8,300 tons of steel armed with the world's most advanced computer-controlled combat system; revolutionary radar technology; a stock of missiles capable of taking out precise targets on land, sea, or air; and a crack crew of 300 highly skilled, totally committed sailors. In 1997, a year and a half after its commission in the Pacific fleet, the guided-missile destroyer spearheaded some of the most critical missions in a confrontation with Iraq. Now tethered to a dock on San Diego's sprawling naval base, the *Benfold* gleams with power. When eating up the sea at full throttle, she generates a plume of froth that's two stories high.

What you don't expect to find on board the *Benfold* is a model of leadership as progressive as any celebrated within the business world. The man behind that model is Commander D. Michael Abrashoff. His career includes a sterling service record, combat experience, and prestigious posts in Washington, D.C. He has won dozens of medals. He is also credited with building the *Benfold*'s reputation as the best ship in the Pacific fleet. Last year, in fact, the ship won the prestigious Spokane Trophy for having the best combat readiness in the fleet—the first time in at least 10 years that a ship of its class had received that honor. Yet Abrashoff doesn't quite look the part: Think of a military leader, and you may envision George C. Scott's depiction of General George S. Patton. Abrashoff, however, has an easy smile and electric-blue eyes.

Behind Abrashoff's relaxed confidence is his own brand of organizational zeal. Settling into his stateroom, Abrashoff, 38, props his feet on a coffee table, sips a soda, and says, "I divide the world into believers and infidels. What the infidels don't understand—and they far outnumber the believers—is that innovative practices combined with true empowerment produce phenomenal results."

That the ranks of the nonbelievers include most of his superiors and fellow commanding officers doesn't deter Abrashoff one bit. "I'm lucky," he says. "All I ever wanted to do in the navy was to command a ship. I don't care if I ever get promoted again. And that attitude has enabled me to do the right things for my people instead of doing the right things for my career. In the process, I ended up with the best ship in the navy—and I got the best evaluation of my career. The unintended benefit? My promotion is guaranteed!" After completing his 20-month tour of duty as commander of the *Benfold* this past January, Abrashoff reported to a top post at the Space and Naval Warfare Systems Command.

Abrashoff continues to see his mission as nothing less than the reorientation of a famously rigid 200-year-old hierarchy. His aim: to focus on purpose rather than on chain of command. When you shift your organizing principle from obedience to performance, says Abrashoff, the highest boss is no longer the guy with the most stripes—it's the sailor who does the work. "There's nothing magical about it," he says from his stateroom on the *Benfold*. "In most organizations today, ideas still come from the top. Soon after arriving at this command, I realized that the young folks on this ship are smart and talented. And I realized that my job was to listen aggressively—to pick up all of the ideas that they had for improving how we operate. The most important thing that a captain can do is to see the ship from the eyes of the crew."

That perspective provided Abrashoff with two insights about change:

First, there's always a better way to do things. In the first few months of his command, Abrashoff took apart every process on board and examined how each one helped the crew to maintain operational readiness. "I pulled the string on everything we did, and I asked the people responsible for—or affected by—each department or program, 'Is there a better way to do things?'" Most of the time, he discovered that there was.

Abrashoff's second insight about change: The more people enjoy the process, the better the results. Spending 35 days under way in the Persian Gulf is anything but enjoyable—but Abrashoff managed to lead his sailors through their missions and to have fun in the process. An ingenious supply officer procured pumpkins—not an easy task in the Middle East—thereby allowing the *Benfold* to sponsor a pumpkin-carving contest for the fleet in October 1997. During replenishments alongside supply tankers, the *Benfold*'s crew became known throughout the Gulf for projecting music videos onto the side of the ship. The crew took its entertainment detail a step further during Christmastime, when K.C. Marshall, the ship's highly skilled Elvis impersonator (and chief navigator), serenaded the admiral's ship with a rendition of "Blue Christmas."

Abrashoff first developed his inclination to skirt standard operating procedure during his post as military assistant to then–Secretary of Defense William Perry, in 1994. He sat beside Perry during the arduous implementation and assessment of the Defense Acquisition Reform Initiative, and he took every opportunity to apply lessons from that initiative on the *Benfold*. For example, in purchasing food for the ship, Abrashoff switched from high-cost naval provisions to cheaper, better-quality name-brand food. With the money he saved, Abrashoff sent 5 of the *Benfold*'s 13 cooks to culinary school—and as a result made the ship a favorite lunchtime destination for crews across the San Diego waterfront.

Abrashoff's leadership formula produces benefits that are both financial and operational. In fiscal year 1998, the *Benfold* returned $600,000 of its $2.4 million maintenance budget and $800,000 of its $3 million repair budget. Abrashoff notes that because any surplus goes back to the navy's top line, "there's no rational reason for saving that money—except that we've created an environment in which people want to do well." The navy's bean counters slashed the ship's maintenance budget this year by exactly

$600,000—yet Abrashoff expects the ship to return 10% of its reduced allotment.

At the same time, the *Benfold*'s performance has set new standards. For the past two years, the ship's "readiness indicators" have featured the lowest count of "mission degrading" equipment failures and the highest gunnery score in the Pacific fleet. The crew also completed the navy's predeployment training cycle in record time. That process normally requires 22 days in port and 30 days under way. The *Benfold*'s crew required 5 days in port and 14 days under way to complete the cycle—and to earn coveted shore leave.

Another critical performance measure is a ship's retention rate. The *Benfold*'s rate is off the charts. On average, only 54% of sailors remain in the navy after their second tour of duty. Under Abrashoff's command, 100% of the *Benfold*'s career sailors signed on for an additional tour. Given that recruiting and training costs come to a minimum of $100,000 per sailor, Abrashoff estimates that the *Benfold*'s retention rate saved the navy $1.6 million in personnel-related costs in 1998.

Yet the most compelling sign of Abrashoff's success may be the smooth interaction that now exists among the ship's company. The *Benfold*'s experienced department heads, its divisional officers (most of them fresh out of the naval academy or ROTC), and its enlisted sailors all show a deep appreciation of the ship's relaxed discipline, its creativity, and its pride in performance. Commander Abrashoff walked *Fast Company* through six principles that have made the USS *Benfold* a working example of grassroots leadership.

Don't Just Take Command—Communicate Purpose

The *Benfold* is a warship. Our bottom line is combat readiness—not just in terms of equipment but also in every facet of training and organization. But the military is an organization of young people. Many of them go into the military to get away from bad situations at home. Many have been involved with drugs or gangs. Although they know what they don't want, they don't quite know what they do want. Getting them to contribute in a meaningful way to each life-or-death mission isn't just a matter of training and discipline. It's a matter of knowing who they are and where they're coming from—and linking that knowledge to our purpose.

Within two days of when new crew members arrive, I sit down with them face-to-face. I try to learn something about each of them: Why did they join the navy? What's their family situation like? What are their goals while they're in the navy—and beyond? How can I help them chart a course through life? Ultimately, I consider it my job to improve my little 300-person piece of society. And that's as much a part of the bottom line as operational readiness is.

Leaders Listen Without Prejudice

Most people in this organization are in "transmit mode"—meaning that they don't "receive" very well. But it's amazing what you discover when you listen to them. When I first took charge of the *Benfold*, I was having trouble learning the names of everyone in the crew, so I decided to interview five people a day. Along with Master Chief Bob Scheeler, the senior enlisted guy on the ship, I met with each person individually and asked three simple questions: What do you like most about the *Benfold*? What do you like least? What would you change if you could? Most of these sailors had never been in a CO's cabin before. But once they saw that the invitation was sincere, they gave me suggestions for change that made life easier for the whole crew and also increased our combat-readiness ratings.

From those conversations, I drew up a list of every practice on the ship and divided those practices into non-value-added chores and mission-critical tasks. I tackled the most demoralizing things first—like chipping-and-painting. Because ships sit in salt water and rust, chipping-and-painting has always been a standard task for sailors. So every couple of months, my youngest sailors—the ones I most want to connect with—were spending entire days sanding down rust and repainting the ship. It was a huge waste of physical effort. A quick investigation revealed that everything—from the stanchions and metal plates to the nuts and bolts used topside—were made of ferrous material, which rusts. I had every nut and bolt replaced with stainless steel hardware. Then I found a commercial firm in town that uses a new process that involves baking metal, flame-spraying it with a rust inhibitor and with paint, and then powder-coating it with more paint. The entire process cost just $25,000, and that paint job is good for 30 years. The kids haven't picked up a paintbrush since. And they've had a lot more time to learn their jobs. As a result, we've seen a huge increase in every readiness indicator that I can think of.

I not only know the names of my crew members—I also know where they're from, as well as a little bit about their families; I know what they aim to do in life. I learned from the interviews that a lot of them wanted to go to college. But most of them had never gotten a chance to take the SAT. So I posted a sign-up sheet to see how many would take the test if I could arrange it. Forty-five sailors signed up. I then found an SAT administrator through our base in Bahrain and flew him out to the ship to give the test. That was a simple step for me to take, but it was a big deal for morale.

Practice Discipline Without Formalism

In many units—and in many businesses—a lot of time and effort are spent on supporting the guy on top. Anyone on my ship will tell you that I'm a low-maintenance CO. It's not about me; it's about my crew. Those initial interviews set the tone: In my chain of command, high performance is the boss. That means that people don't tell me what I want to hear; they tell me the truth about what's going on in the ship. It also means that they don't wait for an official inspection or run every action up and down the chain of command before they do things—they just *do* them.

Lieutenant Jason Michal, my engineering-department head, recently had to prepare for engineering certification. That's one of the most critical and stressful inspections on the ship, but I kept away until he asked me to come down to review his work. What I saw blew my mind. He had been tweaking procedures for months and had implemented about 40 changes in the operating system. Of course, he aced the inspection. When the people who do the work know that *they*—not the manual or policy—have the last word, you get real innovation in every area.

One of our duties during the 1997 Gulf crisis was to board every ship going to or coming from Iraq and to inspect it for contraband. This inspection was a laborious process that involved filling out a time-consuming four-page report each time a ship made a crossing. One of my petty officers created a database to store information about each ship and to generate reports automatically. I gave a copy of the database to another CO, who showed it to the admiral. Now that database method is policy throughout our battle group.

None of this means that we've sacrificed discipline or cohesion on the ship. When I walk down the passageway, people call attention on deck and hit the bulkhead. They respect the office but understand that I don't care about the fluff—I want the substance. And the substance is combat readiness. The substance is having people feel good about what they do. The substance is treating people with respect and dignity. We gain a lot of ground and save a lot of money by keeping our focus on substance rather than on extraneous stuff.

The Best Captains Hand Out Responsibility—Not Orders

Companies complain about turnover, but a ship's company isn't a static population. Not counting dropouts and other separations, about 35% of a ship's crew transfers out every year. That means that I must be constantly vigilant about cultivating new experts. After improving the food on this ship, my next priorities were to advance my people and to train my junior officers, who are called on repeatedly to make life-and-death decisions.

I not only have to train new folks, I also have to prepare higher-level people to step into leadership roles. If all you do is give orders, then all you'll get are order takers. We need real decision makers—people who don't just sleepwalk through the manual. That means that we have to allow space for learning. Removing many of the nonreadiness aspects of the job—from chipping-and-painting to cleaning—lets us spend more time on learning how to use all of the sophisticated technology in our combat-information center and on running through war scenarios on our computer system.

And because we're more interested in improving performance than we are in pomp, we can create learning experiences at every turn. When something goes wrong on a ship, the traditional attitude is "Hurry up and fix it, or we'll look bad." Well, if you don't care about getting promoted, you'll give a sailor time to learn how to do the job right—even if you run the risk of having the admiral stop by before the problem is fixed.

As a result, we have the most proficient training teams on the waterfront and a promotion rate that's over the top. In the last advancement cycle (that's the process that determines base pay, housing allowance, and sea pay), *Benfold* sailors got promoted at a rate that was twice as high as the navy average. I advanced 86 sailors in 1998. That amounts to a huge chunk of change and a lot of esteem for roughly one-third of my crew.

Successful Crews Perform with Devotion

At a conference for commanding officers that I attended recently, more than half of the officers there argued that paying attention to quality of life (QOL, as we call it) interferes with mission accomplishment. That's ridiculous. It doesn't make sense to treat these young folks as expendable. The navy came up 7,000 people short of its 52,000-person recruitment goal in 1998, and it expects to be 12,000 people short of its goal in 1999. In every branch of the military, one-third of all recruits never complete their first term of enlistment. We've got to provide reasons for people to join, to stay—and to perform. The leader's job is to provide an environment in which people are not only able to do well but *want* to do well.

I looked at what usually happens when new 18- or 19-year-old recruits check in: They fly in from boot camp on a Friday night. They feel intimidated and friendless. They stow their gear in their berths and immediately get lost in San Diego. To change all of that, we've created a welcoming plan: Now, when new recruits come on board, their bunks are assigned, their linen and blankets are there, and we match them with a hand-picked sponsor who shows them the ropes. They can even call home—on my nickel—to tell Mom and Dad that they've made it.

The biggest complaint when we're out to sea for weeks on end is military-issue entertainment. When we pulled into Dubai—one of the better liberty ports in the Persian Gulf—a sailor took me aside to tell me that the crew members were frustrated because their tour-bus drivers didn't speak English and wouldn't deviate from assigned routes. On the spot, I rented 15 10-passenger minivans. I told the crew to divide into groups, and I assigned a senior petty officer to serve as a monitor on each bus.

Now, that wasn't strictly legal, but it helped morale so much that it has become a popular procedure for ships throughout the Gulf. A more serious issue for crew members at sea involves time away from their families. Most ships report several family problems during every deployment, and most of those problems result from lack of communication. I created an AOL account for the ship and set up a system for sending messages daily through a commercial satellite. That way, sailors can check in with their families, take part in important decisions, and get a little peace of mind.

Back in port, the top frustration for the crew involves 24-hour shipboard duty between deployments. The standard practice is to divide the crew into four sections that stand duty in rotation—with each section serving a 24-hour shift every 4 days and getting only 1 weekend off each month. That's criminal! So I suggested an eight-section duty rotation, which would require a 24-hour shift every 8 days while providing 2 weekends off each month. In order to maximize flexibility, I cross-trained all of the sailors to perform every function of their duty section. The system has worked so well that many ships on the waterfront are now copying it.

Maintaining "quality of life" is simply a matter of paying attention to what causes dissatisfaction among the crew. You do what you can to remove those "dissatisfiers" while increasing the "satisfiers." Increasing satisfaction may be as simple as recognizing that everybody loves music and then setting up a great sound system or buying a karaoke machine. "Quality of life" is also a matter of creating an environment in which everyone is treated with respect and dignity. The *Benfold* is one of the first ships in the navy that was built from the keel up to accommodate women. It's no secret that the military has had problems with sexual harassment and with prejudice in general. Yet when we do equal-opportunity surveys for the *Benfold*, we get stunning results: Only 3% of minorities on board reported any type of racial prejudice, and only 3% of women reported any form of sexual harassment.

That's not because I give long lectures on prejudice or sexual harassment—it's because I talk about the effects of community and about the need to cultivate unity and teamwork with as much care as we give to maintaining our equipment.

True Change Is Permanent

Ships in the navy tend to take on the personality of their commanding officers. But neither my crew nor I worry about what will happen now that I've moved on. We've set up a virtuous circle that lets people know that their contribution counts. This crew has produced phenomenal results, and now it's motivated to do even better. My attitude is, once you start perestroika, you can't really stop it. The people on this ship know that they are part owners of this organization. They know what results they get when they play an active role. And they now have the courage to raise their hands and to get heard. That's almost irreversible.

THE LAST WORD

I want to congratulate Fast Company *for writing about Commander Abrashoff. I spent the first five years after college as a junior officer on the West Coast. Abrashoff's views and philosophies about leadership totally inspired me. A leader who considers his troops' best interests and who helps them to achieve great feats is a refreshing and reinvigorating notion. I plan to take that lesson on leadership with me wherever I go.*

During my short naval career, I experienced both good and not-so-good examples of leadership. I realize that these experiences can have an impact on careers beyond the duty station and can mark a young person's life for years. I certainly hope that Abrashoff recognizes the lifelong impact that he's had on the men and women under his command. All great leaders should!

> *Sam Kamel*
> *Director, Business Development*
> *E-Loan Inc.*
> *Dublin, California*

Why We Buy

From: Issue 29 | November 1999 | By: Charles Fishman

Apple's history is inextricably linked to the power of design. In the company's 30 years, its greatest successes have come when it has focused on designing elegance and simplicity into what it sells—the Macintosh, iMac, and iPod. When Apple loses sight of those principles, the company struggles. The behind-the-scenes person responsible for Apple's unlikely second act in American business is Jonathan Ive, chief designer. *Fast Company* caught up with him in 1999, when Ive's iMac woke up the computer industry—and the rest of corporate America—to the impact smart design can have. In this piece, you'll hear Ive's design philosophy from the man himself, a telling enumeration of ideas that not only produced the iMac but later led to the iPod and arguably still guide Apple as it continues to innovate. Every company envies Apple's design, but just how many are living what Ive espouses?

About the tamest description offered of Apple's saucy iMac computer is that it is "postbeige"—a neat phrase that is simultaneously descriptive and hopeful.

More typically, the 15-month-old iMac has inspired a blossoming of puns, metaphors, colorful language, and just plain silliness:

The iMac is egg-shaped, gumdrop-shaped, pear-shaped, hood-shaped, and beach-ball-like.

It is cute 'n' jazzy, retro-curvy, funky and snazzy, and extremely friendly.

It is a glowing, fruit-hued, Lifesaver-colored, trendoid status symbol.

It is an accessory, not just a tool.

You want to touch it, to hug it, to tickle it under its chin.

The iMac has put the crunch back into Apple. It is electrifying the entire computer industry. It is a design breakthrough.

Buying an iMac makes you feel hopeful again. It is a revolution in a box.

The iMac's design evokes such an emotional response that it even fires the imaginations of its critics. Tom Wolfe, who might have been prefiguring the iMac when he wrote *The Kandy-Kolored Tangerine-Flake Streamline Baby*, recently grumped that the iMac symbolized the death of 20th-century American design. The iMac, he said, is a "blobjet." On its own Web site, Apple calls it a "rocket computer."

Call it what you will, the iMac is indisputably successful. In its first year on the market, 2 million iMacs were sold. During most of that time, the iMac was the number one–selling computer model in the country.

And, not surprisingly, the computer has had a direct impact on Apple's bottom line: The iMac has helped pull Apple back to profitability for two years in a row and has helped boost the company's stock price from 15 to 70.

As no computer has done since the early days of Apple computers, the iMac has captivated consumers. Apple claims that one-third of individuals who bought iMacs never owned a computer before; independent surveys cut that figure in half. Either way, it's an amazing statistic. People have been moved to purchase a first computer because of the image that the iMac conveys—because of its colors, its approachability, its simplicity. The iMac has even managed to silence the decadelong crossfire—PC or Mac? Apple seems to be winking broadly at that question and asking one of its own: Which color? It may be difficult to believe, but until the iMac came along, no manufacturer had produced a computer in a rainbow of colors. Colors pose inventory problems. Who needs the extra hassle? Khaki computers work just fine.

The iMac won a spot in popular culture almost instantly—it has come to represent all turn-of-the-century computers. On shows like *Ally McBeal*, office workers use iMacs simply because their appearance says, "I am a cool computer in a cool office."

The iMac's role as icon is no accident. Orchestrated by Steve Jobs,

Apple's cofounder and interim CEO (iCEO), the iMac is the labor of Jonathan Ive and the industrial-design group that he heads. Ive, 32, a Brit, started his career in London, designing everything from washbasins and bathtubs to TVs and VCRs for Japanese companies. As a contractor, Ive also helped design Apple's early PowerBooks, and he headed from London to Cupertino, California, to join Apple full time in 1992.

Almost everything that's striking about the iMac—its unassuming shape, its candy-shop colors, its inviting cable cover—had been carefully calculated. A case in point: Ive himself talked to companies that produce translucent candy to make sure that the iMac's translucence worked just right.

Ive's development group—which also produced the iMac's new sibling, the iBook—is intensely secretive. Reporters aren't allowed to interview Ive in his office because there's too much cool, futuristic stuff lying around. Ive won't say how many people work in industrial design, and he won't hint at what will come after the iBook, except to say, "We feel that we're just getting going."

Fast Company talked with Ive about the design principles that infuse the iMac, the iBook, and the ongoing work of his design group. From bathtubs to computers, here are some of Ive's fundamental rules for creating a design that sells.

Good Design Starts a Good Conversation

The right conversation is one that's meaningful to customers. Part of that is about design. And a lot of that is about making the design understandable. Because the technology is powerful, and because we're very confident about that, we don't have to obsess about trying to communicate just how powerful the iMac is. We can be more overtly concerned about, and put a lot of energy into, other attributes.

When people shop for an iMac, I love that the discussion is now much more egalitarian, more accessible, and more open, instead of being about technologies that many people don't understand. I like that you can go into a store and have a discussion about which color you want. That's something that the whole family can do. That's exciting. We've made the whole process of buying and using computers more accessible.

A Computer Is Not a Teacup . . .

The iMac is a holistic product. The price is right, the performance is right, and the combination of those two attributes, along with the design, has made it a well-balanced, relevant product.

But design alone would not have been sufficient to make it successful. It's important to understand the contribution that design can make. It's significant. But if factors like performance and price are not right, then design would be fairly irrelevant.

One thing that is in the genes of Apple Computer, the company, is connecting people with technology in a friendly and accessible way. If you've got technology on the one hand and you've got people on the other, then an object's design—no matter what that object is—defines the nature of that connection.

That's particularly true of high-technology products, because the internal workings of the machine are enigmatic. The majority of people simply do not understand how those things work. And there is no physical expression of the object's function. Unlike, for example, a teacup or a comb, which are what they do.

A washbasin is a good example; that's something I've actually designed in the past. A washbasin's form and function are exactly the same. The object's appearance and meaning are completely accessible: It looks like a washbasin, because that's what it is. You look at it, and you think, "Okay, I understand that." People make an immediate connection with it.

With technology, the function is much more abstract to users, and so the product's meaning is almost entirely defined by the designer. I think that's an incredible opportunity, but with that opportunity comes an enormous responsibility. If you are designing an object, you are defining what it means to people: You are conveying what the object is, what it does, how it does it, where it does it, and how much it's going to cost. So especially if you're dealing with incredibly compelling technology like computers, the responsibility is to make the relationship between people and the technology as effective, as natural, as accessible, and as enjoyable as possible.

. . . But a Computer Might Be an Entire Tea Set

When we started designing the iMac, we were wrestling with the question, What is the function of a computer? One thing that really struck us was that a computer's function can change radically: It can be a digital video-editing station, a content browser, or a typewriter. That's a unique ability—for something to change its function so dramatically. So we were wrestling with the fluid nature of the object. At the same time, we were trying to make the technology as accessible, as friendly, and as nonthreatening as possible. That involves focusing on a couple of levels.

The first level we focused on was the overall form of the product. It absolutely needed to be about tomorrow, and we really wanted to define something new. But something dramatically new can actually alienate people. That design challenge represented an interesting paradox for us: how to create something for tomorrow that people are comfortable with today.

A lot of energy went into defining an overall form that was in some senses "strangely familiar" but that was also about tomorrow.

Design Is All About Understanding

We didn't come up with an architectural solution. That's one of the things that struck us about how a computer's function changes. The design should be something that feels fluid and dynamic. I think the iMac looks like it's just arrived or is just about to leave. It's not something that's grounded permanently to the surface that you put it on.

A number of details reflect that sense as well. The handle, for instance, clearly makes the iMac something that's not permanent. It makes it approachable, accessible. Obviously, the primary function of a handle is to be able to carry a product around. Another thing about the handle is that when people see it, they immediately understand its purpose. It unambiguously references your hand. So when you first meet the product, you understand something about it, and it understands something about you.

People don't necessarily understand the internal components and the essential function of the machine. But they can look at its exterior and actually understand elements of it immediately.

Beyond understanding the iMac, people want to touch it. When you see a handle, you want to use it: That reaction is instinctive, immediate, and universal. When you look at an object like a handle, you instantly form sub-conscious opinions about it.

Another attractor is the nature of the surfaces. The surfaces look like they'd be good to touch. There's a real unity to the iMac. There's no tradi-tional front, top, back, and sides. I think that makes it inviting. Most design tends to focus on an object's front—as the one surface that people will address themselves to. But inherently, when you present the front, people assume that the front is better than the back. The back is merely a conse-quence; it's just hanging on for the ride. One of the things that we've ac-complished with the iMac is to create a design that gives integrity to the shape of the whole: The computer's back and sides are as interesting, arrest-ing, and important as its front.

Also, there's the nature of the translucent material. Most computers are made of materials that keep everything on the surface. But with the iMac, you get this fluid effect, the way the light transforms the material and the color. It's not just about surface, it's about depth.

Sometimes a Designer Has to Think Inside the Box

The primary purpose of the handle, of course, is to make the product easy to move, which is what we knew people would want. But it also suggests something else: When you can move something, you dominate it. Making it easy to move helps people feel less intimidated by the object or by the tech-nology, which many, many people are.

In fact, one of our goals for designing the packaging was to have the handle be one of the first things you see when you open the box. The idea is that the first piece of packing foam you pull out becomes a little table for the manual, the keyboard, and the accessories. After you remove that piece of foam, you see the handle. You know what to do next. That's the great thing about handles: You know what they're there for.

Once you take the iMac out of its packaging, you can put the accessory box on the little table. You open that, and it's clear what to do next. One ca-ble is for power, one is for Internet access, and one connects the keyboard.

It sounds simple and obvious. But often, getting to that level of simplic-ity requires enormous iteration in design. You have to spend considerable energy understanding the problems that exist and the issues people have—even when they find it difficult to articulate those issues and problems themselves.

So when you ask why the iMac has been such a success, the answer is, the design combined with the Macintosh interface. It's just how easy the product is to take out of the box, set up, and use. That simplicity is about removing the obstacles that have made so many people intimidated by the technology in the past.

Before It Persuades Customers, a New Product Has to Persuade Its Own Company

What drove the design of the iMac was a vision and a commitment to create the best consumer computer that we could. In other words, we made the needs of the customer our highest priority. And when you do that, it places significant demands on different parts of the company.

For example, we found that the right place for a lot of the cable connectors was on the side of the iMac, which is where they are more accessible. You don't have to get up and go around to the back or move the entire machine to get to them. That was an example of trying to address issues of utility and function.

But from an engineering perspective, the easiest place to put connectors is on the back. Putting them on the side was actually very difficult and would mean elevating the concerns of the user way above those of the engineers. That drove having an easy-to-adjust keyboard and also the flip-out foot. It's sort of intuitive.

Another example: We knew people wanted a choice of colors. But if we offered people one color, we knew the next question would be, When can we have other colors? That poses a number of significant challenges for manufacturing, distribution, and managing inventory—especially if you have demands for a certain color. Color options have never been offered in our industry.

In that sense, I think the iMac reflects the original mission: to create a great consumer product. More broadly than that, it stands as a testament to a company that not only shared the same vision but could also implement that vision. Somebody asked me how we'd convinced the people at Apple that what we were proposing with the iMac and the iBook was the right thing.

The more I thought about it, the more I realized that we'd spent zero energy trying to cajole the people at Apple into believing that what we were proposing was right. We'd put all of our energy into coming up with the content and into creating just the right design. We'd been incredibly self-critical. And as a result, it took us many iterations to get to the right solution—the one that we ultimately wanted to develop and to market.

But, by genuinely trying to design a product for people in a very natural way, people were intrigued by the product—whether they were our managers or our customers.

What You Can't Measure Is Often What Matters Most

The computer industry is immature; it has been preoccupied with technology and driven by technologists. In some senses, the value proposition for consumers has degenerated into an argument that "Five is a greater number than two." Go back a year, and the value proposition was, "Our machine has a larger hard drive than yours," or "Our machine is cheaper than yours."

There was an obsession with product attributes that you could measure with numbers. And that's an easy value proposition to articulate: Five is a bigger number than two. It's much more difficult to articulate the value of product attributes that are less tangible. I think it's at the heart of Apple, in the genes of the company, that these other attributes do matter.

A lot of that is knowing how an object elicits an emotional reaction from people. The response can range from a perception to a physical reaction. That is, people touch it and pat it. One of the things we've seen repeatedly with the iMac is that people in stores want to touch it.

There are a number of simple ways that you can physically connect with the iMac. You can pick it up by the handle. Or you can open the door on the side to get to the connectors. When you open that door, you discover that it's a really simple circle—a hole. It's obvious. You put your finger inside the hole to pull the door open.

Now there were lots of solutions we could have used to open that door, including discreet, technical latches. But there was something so simple and so human about the solution we eventually pursued.

These are the less-tangible product attributes, but they're still important. We made some major life decisions based on stuff that's difficult to assign a number to.

With the iBook, we're trying to engage people even more. If you think about people touching an object, the iBook takes that experience to another level. We're combining materials with different attributes and properties. We're combining rubber with polycarbonate to get strength and warmth.

We're doing those things because when we started working on the iBook, we defined a list of all the attributes that we wanted the product materials to have. That list ranged from robust, strong, structural, and hard, to attributes like soft, yielding, and warm. We included those attributes because the iBook is something you'll be taking with you. That makes it a highly personal product; you're going to spend a lot of time carrying it.

That list of attributes contained polar opposites. Although we couldn't find one material with all those properties, we found that by developing some processes to combine materials, we could design a case that really did have all those properties.

Another example of less-tangible attributes is the sleep light on the iBook. When traditional products go into sleep mode, the light blinks on and off. That solves the functional problem, which is to describe a state the object is in. But we felt that a blinking light did it in a machinelike way.

For the iBook, we developed a sleep light that glows on and off. When people describe it, they say that it looks like the computer is breathing or beating. Rather than just having it switch on and off in a very mechanical way, the iBook *breathes* on and off. It's actually been remarkable how many people have commented on that. The design of that one feature has made the iBook seem more fluid, more organic.

That light illustrates the difference we're seeking to make in the industry. The traditional blinking light works; it addresses the functional imperative. But I knew that we could find a more organic, human solution. When you see the iBook, when you pick it up, when you turn it on, or even when you put it to sleep, you get a sense that it was designed and manufactured by a group of people who care—maybe fanatically—about the details.

Do we acknowledge that it's not functionally critical to care about all those details? Absolutely. We know that. But we also know that we've got overarching design principles that we're seeking to express: simplicity, accessibility, honesty—and enjoyment. We're really seeking to design products that people will enjoy.

Why does it matter whether you enjoy using something?

Because it makes you happy. And it's good to be happy.

THE LAST WORD

I loved your piece on Jonathan Ive, designer of the iMac. You conveyed perfectly why the design of that computer matters. Now my wife understands why I just sit and stare at my iMac—without using it!

> *Andy Halper*
> *President*
> *Social Imaginations Inc.*
> *Minneapolis, Minnesota*

Are You on Craig's List?

From: Net Company 02 | Winter 2000 | By: Katharine Mieszkowski

---

The Internet era has given us any number of unlikely heroes, and Craig Newmark may be the most surprising of all. A humble computer programmer, Newmark inadvertently stumbled into creating the paragon of Internet community with his Web site. He also turned a hobby into a valuable piece of Internet real estate, the envy of both venture-backed dot-coms that devalue the word "community" with all their chatter about it and of the old-school newspapers that are watching craigslist devour their lucrative classifieds business. When *Fast Company* interviewed Newmark in early 2000, he happily shared his blueprint for success. His ideas on community have since proven essential for the generation of leaders building Web 2.0.

Community. It is one of those charged-with-meaning words that is meant to distinguish what happens on the Web with what happens in less virtual (and less virtuous) segments of the economy. One promise of the Web is that it blends the value of commerce with the values of personal interaction. Why be content to sell one-size-fits-all products to a disparate collection of individuals when you can meet the shared needs of a single community? Why be content to create a marketplace when you can create a "market space" that lets people swap ideas, trade experiences, learn from one another—and then buy products that reflect their shared interests?

Community. It is one of those devoid-of-meaning words that inspires bemused grins from Internet insiders. Is a stock-market chat room a "community"—or a rumor mill? Is a collection of customer reviews (of books, software, or cars) a community forum—or just a bunch of ill-informed opinions from never-satisfied consumers?

Craig Newmark knows a community when he sees one—because he's built one of the Web's most influential communities. If you ask around, you'll soon find someone who's participated in "craigslist" (www.craigs list.org), which acts as a virtual community bulletin board for the San Francisco Bay Area—the unofficial capital of the Internet economy. It's the plugged-in place to find a job, a roommate, a neighborhood dog walker, or the latest Internet-industry schmooze. And hardly a week goes by without at least one plaintive posting: Is there a list like this in New York? Portland? Boston? Seattle?

Craig Newmark, 47, is a Java programmer who describes himself as a "recovering nerd." This self-proclaimed "Forrest Gump of the Internet" became the Bay Area's best-known online community organizer by "happy accident." Five years ago, while he was working as a computer-security architect at Charles Schwab, he took on the role of Internet evangelist. "I'd give talks about the Internet, saying that this is how we should do business someday," he says.

A year later, he started a small, informal "cc list" to keep his friends updated on local techie-art events. As more people joined, the number of posts snowballed, and the subject matter sprawled: from "Sublet my room!" to "We need a Web designer!" Today, the craigslist site receives 5 million page views a month from thousands of visitors and has more than 7,700 e-mail subscribers, who receive the postings in their in-boxes every day. There are now so many postings that the list is divided into 27 categories, ranging from tech events to writing/editing jobs. "What we do," says Newmark, "is give people a voice, and that's pretty powerful."

And extremely valuable. What was once a Java programmer's part-time avocation is now a fast-growing nonprofit that receives full-time devotion from Newmark and five other staffers; it's run like a scrappy startup out of Newmark's Cole Valley flat. The business model is simple: Charge companies $45 to list job openings. All other listings are free. The community does the rest.

"Our intent is inclusive—to humanize and democratize the Internet," Newmark explains. "Too much of life is whom you know. We're trying to open that up a little more." Part of that vision is to bring the community-building experience of craigslist to other cities—the grassroots way. "We're not carpetbaggers," says Newmark. "We're interested in working with people in other places who want to do similar things. And we're creating technology that will allow people anywhere to build community sites, including neighborhood ones. We're trying to find the right ways to give this technology away."

In the Bay Area, craigslist has fast become a local institution, and Craig Newmark himself, much to his bashful chagrin, has become at once an urban legend and a local celebrity. Some people don't believe that there is a real guy named Craig, and they express incredulity when meeting him in person. Others seek him out to tell him how craigslist has changed their lives—how a roommate became a spouse, or how a gig jump-started a career. "That feels pretty good," he says with characteristic understatement.

Newmark does concede that he knows a little something about organizing a community on the Web: "I've been trying to pay attention and to learn something about it along the way." He's even taught a course called "How to Create a Successful Online Community Web Site." In a series of interviews with *Fast Company*, Newmark explained what it takes to build a community on the Web.

How Do You Know a Community When You See One?

Defining what constitutes a community—as opposed to a crowd—involves lots of subjective judgments. But I'd say that a community involves people who have the potential to interact with one another while having a shared experience. In a community, there's more than just communication—there's a sense of connection, a sense of intimacy, a feeling that we're in this together.

Of course, if all we're talking about is connection, then 50,000 people cheering the home team in a football stadium would be a community. But being an observer is qualitatively different from taking part in a community. You're sharing a little bit when everyone cheers or gasps at the game, but you're still just part of an audience. That's why you also need the opportunity for interaction. That's what differentiates a community from a crowd.

What Are the Prerequisites for Building a Community?

Community starts with people having something in common, whether that is a subject that interests them or the city where they live. There's a reason why people in a geographic community feel—or want to feel—connected.

We've lost contact with our neighbors. We don't know who they are, but we crave contact with them. So creating a new place for people to interact with others in their own town is one way of establishing community. Geography is something that we all already have in common with our neighbors.

That doesn't mean that members of a community must have the same values or beliefs. Shared values are useful to a community, but a common set of values is not mandatory. Neighbors have lots of important things in common, but they don't necessarily have the same religious beliefs or vote for the same political candidates come election time.

What's the Right Kind of Technology to Support Communities?

People need a convenient arena or forum where they can interact. It can be at a café, around the company watercooler, or at the fax machine. On the Net, that arena is created electronically; it might be a mailing list, a bulletin board, a chat room, or a Web site that publishes information that helps bring people together in person.

But let's be clear: The Net is not about technology, it's about people—a fact that is obvious to everyone except to us programmers. The most important things we, as humans, need to do—commercially or socially—is to connect with others. An online community is no substitute for real-world interactions. In fact, the most successful online communities are the ones that throw parties, sponsor events, host get-togethers—help members meet one another face-to-face in the real world.

We live our lives, for the most part, in the physical world (although in San Francisco, that's optional). Virtual life is a great complement to real life, but it's only a complement. Usually people find it more meaningful to make an online connection with someone local whom they might have the opportunity to meet, or might already know, than with someone who is half a world away.

You may not care so much about the personal home page of a guy with his dog if he happens to live in another country. You just see a guy and his dog. Big deal. But if this person lives a couple of blocks away from you, then you may be very interested to learn about him. The exception to this, of course, is communities of interest, where people come together by virtue of their passion for a common subject—say, basset hounds. If you think about it, we're all in a bunch of sub-subcultures.

But I still think that if you're interested in basset hounds, then you're more likely to feel a connection to a community at a basset-hound site that draws people who live in your own neighborhood than you would at a site about basset hounds in general.

What Else Does It Take to Build and Sustain a Community?

The best communities aren't just interesting, they're useful. On craigslist, there's not a lot of abstract discussion. We address everyday, real-world, down-to-earth stuff—finding a place to live, a roommate, a job, a technology event to attend. The community has grown out of these practical concerns. At its most mundane, what we're doing is basically creating a different version of classified ads. The difference is that they're free. Because we're not charging by the word, people can say as much as they want. And in their postings, people reveal something of themselves—and others feel a sense of connection. One woman told me that she reads our lists just for the personal stories. It's a window into what's going on around her, and it provides a sense of connection and intimacy with others. That's the common theme: What's going on around us?

Think about when you move to a new city or town. How long does it take to feel connected, to feel as though you know what's going on? Six months? Two years? This approach makes that process happen much faster. So if you want to build community, the most important question to ask yourself is, What needs are you serving? When you go to the Web to feel connected, you don't need another site to provide stock quotes. And you don't need to see pictures of somebody's nieces and nephews. What you need is to hear someone's opinion about a local bar or restaurant, or what that person thinks about a nearby store or another part of the city. It's real-world, everyday stuff. It's so ordinary that it may sound obvious. Keeping it simple works.

So the Way to Build a Community Is to Give People Information.

Actually, the most poignant use of Web community is when you give people a voice. And if you provide the right kind of forum, anyone can have a voice. In any large organization, whether it's a company or a part of the government, the people on the front lines know how to do things well. But the nature of large organizations is that they stifle those people. Over time, these people give up trying to be heard because they have the sense that no one is listening.

In that sense, community is about connecting people who need a break with people who might be able to give them one. It's all about people helping one another. This idea is not new. For a long time, people in technology have been helping others online. You ask a question, you get an answer. It's a pretty good deal. When you go to a technical conference and read someone's name tag, you may realize that you're meeting someone who may have helped you a year ago, or someone whom you've helped.

What Are Some Pitfalls as You Try to Create a Community?

Scale is one. Web sites that attempt to build community quickly on a grand scale will not succeed. People in different areas and in different cultures know what's right for their areas and cultures. It is possible to create a big community site, but it has to be a network of affinity groups—a community of communities.

Some big "communities" are basically collections of free home pages. But these sites aren't communities if people aren't interacting with one another. I don't hear about anyone who is passionate about these big sites. It may be because people perceive big sites as merely a way to sell ads. I have nothing against commercialism; everyone should get rich on the Web. But people will accept commercialism in a community only if they think they're getting a fair exchange of value in return.

What Are Some Other Challenges?

One is the "tragedy of the commons." It's a term that describes what happens when you have a limited resource, but there's no controlled access to that resource—like a field that has a common grazing area for sheep. If too many ranchers use that field, then it becomes overgrazed and doesn't work for anyone. To some extent, that's what has happened to Usenet, the early newsgroups on the Internet. Take one of the 50,000 groups, like "Bay Area Jobs Offered." Recruiters just dump in listings to collect résumés. It's impossible to distinguish real jobs from headhunters' come-ons.

This is one of the hazards of not having moderation—there's no quality control. Also, most communities need to be moderators to keep the momentum going. The discussion needs to be encouraged and directed in some way. At craigslist, we avoid the tragedy of the commons through very light moderation. Between light moderation and self-policing, the quality of what's on the list remains very high, and it doesn't get overrun. And when a category does become overrun, such as engineering, we'll split it off into different categories—for example, Web-building jobs and system-administration jobs.

What Other Advice Can You Give Aspiring Web Organizers?

You've got to keep it real. That means being down-to-earth and open. And it means no hidden agendas. In our case, that means not using the community stuff as a way of selling ads, or selling anything else.

I spend lots of time maintaining the trusted relationship we have with everyone who uses craigslist. We don't even know how many visitors come to our site, because we don't use "cookies." We never sell any of our mailing lists or anything personal about visitors to our site. That's because the foundation of the community is that trust.

Another way we keep it real is with the name. I was embarrassed to call it craigslist, and I still am, but people want something personal. They want something that feels real.

What Can Traditional Companies Learn from the Community That You Have Created?

They can learn how to improve their customer service. At craigslist, we do customer service, which, to the best of my knowledge, far exceeds the vast majority of for-profit businesses. We tell the community about the changes that we're going to make on the site before we make them. And we solicit feedback from all our customers—subscribers and people who just visit our site. Once a month, we ask them how we're doing. We actually change our site in response to what members of the community request. We ask people all the time if we're doing our job right, and if we're not, we change.

For example, we'd thought about adding chat, but our community told us that there are already lots of places to chat on the Net, so we didn't do it. That's not what they wanted. Sponsorships are another great example. People are telling us that the very lightest of sponsorships or underwriting is cool, but it has to be very light. So we may do our first real example of that soon.

Why don't more companies interact with their customers this way, using public forums as a source of consumer feedback? Certainly, using any kind of public forum for support means that a company will be faced with disgruntled customers. But much of the time, disgruntled customers are right—and they're giving you valuable feedback. Make disgruntled customers happy, and the process will probably improve the quality of your product. Of course, some disgruntled customers are just never happy, but other customers reading their posts can see that. The community will recognize the never-happy customers for what they are.

THE LAST WORD

I've been told that there are persons signed up on craigslist who are surfing the ads only to send harassing comments to sellers. If there is to be a healthy business experience on craigslist, sellers should be as protected as the sellers who are doing business on eBay. EBay has a spoof department and SquareTrade to monitor, and in some cases, investigate and prosecute, the unlawful behaviors of their buying members. Even in the simplest case, harassments by these individuals should not be tolerated.

Tommy Budd
Via the Internet

Built to Flip

From: Issue 32 | March 2000 | By: Jim Collins

Things had clearly gotten out of hand. The NASDAQ seemingly knew only one direction: up. High-tech startups sprouted like weeds, with one goal: to cash in. Dot-commers had forgotten the true meaning of the new economy: You were supposed to love your work, and because of your devotion and excellence, you'd create and share in wealth. As Silicon Valley became the land of milk and money, you no longer needed to create anything of long-standing value to earn riches. Who better than the author of *Built to Last*, Jim Collins, to deliver a stinging rebuke to this ugly culture? Collins's passionately argued essay fortuitously appeared at the absolute peak of the Internet bubble; it serves as an excellent autopsy of what went wrong in the late 1990s. But "Built to Flip" is more than a depiction of a single moment in time; it endures as a well-reasoned argument against any culture of entitlement that emerges in our society. It's a bracing response to any mania.

"I developed our business model on the idea of creating an enduring, great company—just as you taught us to do at Stanford—and the VCs looked at me as if I were crazy. Then one of them pointed his finger at me and said, 'We're not interested in enduring, great companies. Come back with an idea that you can do quickly and that you can take public or get acquired within 12 to 18 months.'"

A former student was reporting to me on her recent experiences with the Silicon Valley investment community. As an MBA student at Stanford, she had taken my course on building enduring, great companies. She had come up with a superb concept that involved doing just that. But when she took the idea to Silicon Valley, she quickly got the message: Built to Last is out. Built to Flip is in.

Built to Flip. An intriguing idea: No need to build a company, much less one with enduring value. Today, it's enough to pull together a good story, to implement the rough draft of an idea, and—presto!—instant wealth. No need to bother with the time-honored method of most self-made million-aires: to create substantial value by working diligently over an extended period. In the built-to-flip world, the notion of investing persistent effort in order to build a great company seems, well, quaint, unnecessary—even stupid.

The built-to-flip mind-set views entrepreneurs like Bill Hewlett and Dave Packard, cofounders of Hewlett-Packard, and Sam Walton, founder of Wal-Mart, as if they were ancient history, artifacts of a bygone era: They were well-meaning and right for their times, but today they look like total anachronisms. Imagine Hewlett and Packard sitting in their garage, sipping lattes, and saying to each other, "If we do this right, we can sell this thing off and cash out in 12 months." Now that's an altogether different version of the HP Way! Or picture Walton collecting a wheelbarrow full of cash from flipping his first store after 18 months, rather than building a company whose annual revenues now exceed $130 billion. These entrepreneurs and others like them—Walt Disney, Henry Ford, George Merck, William Boeing, Paul Galvin of Motorola, Gordon Moore of Intel—were pedestrian plodders by today's built-to-flip standards. They worked hard to create a superb management team, to develop a sustainable economic engine, to cultivate a culture that could withstand adversity and change, and to be the best in the world at what they did. But not to worry! In the built-to-flip economy, you can get rich without any of those mundane fundamentals.

We have arrived at a unique moment in history: the intersection of an unprecedented abundance of capital and an explosion of Internet-related business ideas. But, for all of the incredible opportunities unleashed by this combination, there is one monumental problem: The entrepreneurial mind-set has degenerated from one of risk, contribution, and reward to one of wealth entitlement. We all have friends and colleagues—often mediocre friends and colleagues at that—who have struck gold after 18 or 12 or 6 months of work in a built-to-flip company. And we have all entertained the thought "I deserve that too." Here's another thought: When I and a lot of other people began talking and writing about the new economy in the early 1980s, little did we know that it would engender what we most despised about the old economy—an entitlement culture in which the mediocre flourish.

Worse, the creative drive behind the new economy at its best has been superseded by a way of thinking that recalls the 1980s at its worst: a Wall Street–like culture that celebrates the twin propositions that "greed is good" and that "more is better." The hard truth is that we're dangerously close to killing the soul of the new economy. Even worse, we're in danger of becoming the very thing that we defined ourselves in opposition to. Those who kindled the spirit of the new economy rejected the notion of working just for money; today, we seem to think that it's fine to work just for money—as long as it's a lot of money.

Have we labored to build something better than what members of previous generations built—only to find their faces staring back at us in the mirror? Is the biggest flip of all the flip that transforms the once-promising spirit of the new economy back into the tired skin of the old economy?

Invasion of the Mind Snatchers

Built to Last appeared in 1994, and I was more surprised than anyone when the book took off and became both widely read and highly influential. After all, what my coauthor, Jerry I. Porras, and I had produced was a huge analytic study of the underlying principles that could yield enduring, great companies. In the book, we drew examples from such 20th-century icons as Disney, General Electric, HP, IBM, and Wal-Mart. These were not hot companies—nor was this a sexy topic.

And yet the book hit a chord, generating more than 70 printings, translations into 17 languages, and best-seller status (including 55 months on the *Business Week* best-seller list). That wasn't planned; we were lucky. The book appeared just as the whole reengineering, everything-is-change-and-chaos wave crashed down—just as people were beginning to ask themselves, "Is nothing sacred? Is nothing timeless? Is nothing sustainable?"

In retrospect, I think that *Built to Last* gave people three perspectives that they desperately craved. First, it said, "Yes, there are some timeless fundamentals. They apply today, and we need them now more than ever." Second, the book affirmed that the essence of greatness does not lie in cost cutting, restructuring, or the pure profit motive. It lies in people's dedication to building companies around a sense of purpose—around core values that infuse work with the kind of meaning that goes beyond just making money. Third, the book tapped into powerful, albeit latent, human emotions: Readers were inspired by the notion of building something bigger and more lasting than themselves. In quiet moments, we all wonder what our lives will amount to, what we're going to leave behind when we die. *Built to Last* pointed people toward a path that they could follow if they wanted to leave behind a legacy. The book also rooted its answers in rigorous research, lending hard-nosed credibility to principles that people knew in their gut were true but that they could neither prove nor precisely articulate. It gave voice to their inner sense of what must be right, and it backed up that intuition with empirical evidence and clear, logical thinking.

Finally, there is one other reason why *Built to Last* struck a chord, and it is the most important reason of all: The book spoke not only of success but also of greatness. Despite its title, *Built to Last* was not about building something that would simply last. It was about building something worthy of lasting—about building a company of such intrinsic excellence that the world would lose something important if that organization ceased to exist.

Implicit on every page of *Built to Last* was a simple question: Why on Earth would you settle for creating something mediocre that does little more than make money, when you could create something outstanding that makes a lasting contribution as well? And the clincher, of course, lay in evidence showing that those who opt to make a lasting contribution also make more money in the end.

That was the state of play in 1994, when the book hit the market and captured the public's imagination. Then, on August 9, 1995, Netscape Communications went public and captured the market's imagination. Netscape stock more than doubled in price within less than 24 hours. This was the first of a wave of Internet-related IPOs that saw the value of shares double, triple, quadruple—or increase by an even greater margin—during the first days of trading.

The gold rush had begun. The Netscape IPO was followed by IPOs for such high-profile enterprises as eBay, E*Trade, and priceline.com. Companies with no significant products, profits, or prospects scrambled to position themselves in the "Internet space." The point of this new game was impermanence: Start-ups flip their stock to underwriters, who flip the stock to individual buyers, who flip the stock to other individual buyers—with everyone looking for a quick, huge financial gain.

In some cases, the results were mind-boggling. When the financial Web site MarketWatch.com went public, on January 15, 1999 (with a quarterly net profit margin of −168%), its basket of public shares flipped over not once, not twice, but three times within the first 24 hours, driving the opening-day price up nearly 475%. The flipping continued to escalate, creating a slew of stunning debuts: From November 1998 to November 1999, 10 companies had first-day price increases that exceeded 300%, despite minimal or no profitability. As Anthony B. Perkins and Michael C. Perkins calculate in their superb book, *The Internet Bubble* (HarperBusiness, 1999), less than 20% of the top 133 "flip" IPOs showed any profits as of mid-1999. In fact, their current market valuations would be justified only if revenues for the entire portfolio of companies grew by 80% per year for the next five years—a rate considerably faster than that achieved by either Microsoft or Dell within the first five years of their IPOs.

Fueling the built-to-flip model has been a nearly unprecedented rise in venture-capital investment: From a steady state of about $6 billion per year for the 10-year period from the mid-1980s to the mid-1990s, venture-capital investment exploded, reaching more than $17 billion in 1998. Simultaneously, a flight of angel investors began looking for a piece of the next big flip. As my former student found out, if you have a flippable idea, you won't have much trouble finding capital. It doesn't matter whether the idea is a good one—whether the idea can be built into a profitable business, or a sustainable organization, or indeed a great company. All that matters is that the idea be flippable: Get in, get out, and get on to the next idea before the bubble bursts.

All of this happened overnight, at the blinding pace of change known as "Net speed." One day, I was teaching eager students, entrepreneurs, and businesspeople how to build enduring, great companies. The next day, that goal had become passé—an amusing anachronism. Not long ago, I gave a seminar to a group of 20 entrepreneurial CEOs who had gathered at my Boulder, Colorado, management lab to learn about my most recent research. I tried to begin with a quick review of *Built to Last* findings, but almost immediately a chorus of objections rang out from the group: "What does 'building to last' have to do with what we face today?"

Scenes from the science-fiction classic *Invasion of the Body Snatchers* ran through my head. I went to bed one night in my familiar world and woke up the next morning to discover that my students had been taken over by aliens.

Built Not to Last

I believe as strongly as ever in the fundamental concepts that came from the *Built to Last* research. I also know that building to last is not for everyone or for every company—nor should it be. In fact, there are at least two categories of companies that should not be built to last.

The first category is "the company as disposable injection device." In this model, the company is simply a throwaway vessel, a means of developing and injecting a new product or an innovative technology into the world. Most biotechnology and medical-device ventures fall into this category. They function as a highly decentralized form of large company R&D—in effect, serving as external labs for one or another of the large, powerful pharmaceutical companies that dominate the world market. With most such ventures, the only question is which large company will end up owning a given technology. One example: Cardiometrics Inc., a Mountain View, California, company that set itself up in 1985 for the purpose of developing a device that could gather data on the actual extent of coronary disease in a patient. (The goal was to reduce the number of people who undergo unnecessary bypass surgery.) Cardiometrics was not built to last, and in 1997 it was acquired by EndoSonics Corp., a heart-catheter company in Rancho Cordova, California, that has a distribution network capable of reaching millions of patients. In this case, acquisition by another company made perfect sense—economically, organizationally, strategically, entrepreneurially. And the acquisition in no way demeaned the contribution that the founders and employees of Cardiometrics had made in developing a vital new technology. For companies like this one, it is eminently reasonable to do the hard work of creating a product that can make a distinctive contribution—and then to sell the product to a company that can leverage it faster, cheaper, and better.

In retrospect, we can all point to companies that *should* have viewed themselves as "built not to last." Confronting that reality would have helped them understand that they were never more than a project, a product, or a technology. Lotus, VisiCorp, Netscape, Syntex, Coleco—all of these companies would have served themselves and the world better if they had accepted their limited purpose from the outset. Ultimately, they squandered time and resources that might have been applied more efficiently elsewhere.

The second category is "the company as platform for a genius." In this model, the company is a tool for magnifying and extending the creative drive of one remarkable individual—a visionary who has immense talent but lacks the temperament required to build an enduring, great company. Once that person is gone, so is the company's reason for being. The best historical example is Thomas Edison's R&D laboratory. The purpose of that enterprise was to leverage Edison's creative genius: Edison would spin his ideas and then flip them out to people who could build companies around them. That's what he did with the lightbulb, and that's how General Electric came into being. When Edison died, his R&D laboratory died with him—as indeed it should have.

Recent adaptations of the genius model include Polaroid (Edwin Land) and DEC (Ken Olsen). And the jury is still out on what may prove to be the most successful and powerful genius platform of all time—Microsoft. Despite the company's profitability and stature, there is no moral or business-logic reason why Microsoft must outlast the guiding presence of Bill Gates.

Not New, Not Even Improved

Like many aspects of the new economy that we celebrate as revolutionary, Built to Flip has been around for a long time. For three decades, entrepreneurs have followed a Silicon Valley paradigm—a set of assumptions about how to handle a start-up. The model isn't all that complicated: Develop a good idea, raise venture capital, grow rapidly, and then go public or sell out—but, above all, do it fast. Even 20 years ago, there was an ethic of impatience: A company that hadn't made it big within 7 to 10 years was deemed a failure. There was also an ethic of impermanence: The expectation that a company would be built to last was largely absent from Silicon Valley business culture. Remember Ashton-Tate? Osborne Computers? Businessland? Rolm? Today, none of those outfits exist as stand-alone great companies—but each was a successful example of the Silicon Valley paradigm.

My first encounter with the Silicon Valley built-to-flip mentality came in 1982. While completing my graduate studies, I did a research project on entrepreneurship in the Valley. My target of study was a workstation startup called Fortune Systems. As I explored the internal workings of the company, what struck me wasn't its technology, its business model, or its culture. No, what struck me was what I perceived to be its founders' utter lack of interest in building a great company. Fortune Systems was built to flip from the get-go. Workstations were hot, capital was plentiful, and the stock market was starting to look good for IPOs. I remember asking a member of the management team about plans for building the company after the IPO, and he just looked at me: Clearly, I didn't get it. The point of it all, I concluded, was simply to go public as fast as possible. Even the company's name—Fortune Systems—was a none-too-subtle tip-off to its underlying purpose.

That was almost 20 years ago. Today, we've arrived at a whole new level of flippability. In the old Silicon Valley paradigm, "fast" meant flipping a company within 7 to 10 years. By today's standards, that time frame seems preposterously glacial. Fortune Systems aside, most people operating within the old Silicon Valley paradigm at least gave lip service to the idea of creating a great company—of inventing products that make a significant contribution and then building a sustainable economic engine around those products. People are now proselytizing the bizarre notion that it's better not to have profits: Today's upside-down logic says that a company will get a better valuation if it has nothing but upside potential—because the casino players care about nothing else. In a recent column in the *New York Times*, technology writer Denise Caruso described the phenomenon: "The desire to cash out big is not a new motivating force in the technology industry. But what is striking about today's Internet economy is how much of that money lust is focused on selling business plans for their own sake, rather than planning viable businesses."

The High Cost of the Pursuit of Money

The great irony of all this is that we now enjoy the best opportunity in 100 years to build great companies that fundamentally change the world in which we live. Somewhere out there, a small group of people are laying the foundation for the great, enduring companies of the 21st century. They will be for us what Henry Ford, George Merck, and Gordon Moore were for our predecessors. They will fashion organizations that will dominate the economic landscape and the business conversation for the next 50 years. And 50 years from now, most of today's built-to-flip companies and their founders will be as relevant to the world as the gold diggers who flocked to California 150 years ago. That doesn't mean that those who build to flip won't get rich. Many will—perhaps more people than at any time in modern history. In fact, amassing unlimited personal wealth may well be the defining goal of our era. At no time in history has it been easier to reallocate capital without creating lasting value. Of course, in doing so, we run the risk of missing the best opportunity in decades to create something great.

But so what? What's wrong with Built to Flip run rampant?

If Built to Flip were to become the dominant entrepreneurial model of the new economy, one almost-inevitable outgrowth would be a rise in social instability. At the heart of the American commitment to democratic capitalism is a shared ideal: From the Industrial Revolution to the Information Revolution, Americans at all levels of society, in all walks of life, and in all occupations have bought into the proposition that the United States offers economic opportunity for all. What we've already seen, even in this relatively early phase of Built to Flip, is a growing socioeconomic disparity—and, perhaps most troubling, a perceived decoupling of wealth from contribution. Not only is there an increasing sense that the social fabric is fraying, as the nation's wealth engine operates for a favored few; there is also a gnawing concern that those who are reaping more and more of today's newly created wealth are doing less and less to "earn" it.

But here's the good news: Built to Flip can't last. Ultimately, it cannot become the dominant model. Markets are remarkably efficient: In the long run, they reward actual contribution, even though short-run market bubbles can divert excess capital to noncontributors. Over time, the marketplace will crush any model that does not produce real results. Its self-correcting mechanisms will ensure the brutal fairness on which our social stability rests.

The most significant consequence of the Built to Flip model isn't socioeconomic, however. It is personal. When it emerged in the early 1980s, the new-economy culture rested on three primary tenets: freedom and self-direction in your work; purpose and contribution through your work; and wealth creation by your work. Central to that culture was the belief that work is our primary activity and that through work we can achieve the sense of meaning that we are looking for in life. Driving the new economy were immensely talented, highly energetic people who sought a practical answer to a fundamental question: How can I create work that I'm passionate about, that makes a contribution, and that makes money? By fostering a culture of entitlement, Built to Flip debases the very concept of meaningful work. And, as is always the case with any form of entitlement, it ultimately debases the person who feels entitled.

Even for those with exceptional talent and drive, money seems to have become the central point of it all. The poster children of the new new economy are people like Jim Clark, the founding genius of Netscape, who is vividly portrayed in Michael Lewis's riveting book *The New New Thing* (W. W. Norton, 1999). Despite his impressive resume, Clark comes across as a man who is stuck on a monetary treadmill: He seems addicted to running after more and more, and then more still, without ever stopping to ask why. Late in the book, Lewis describes a scene in which he presses Clark on this very issue. Earlier, Clark had said that he would retire after he became "a real after-tax billionaire." Now he was worth $3 billion. What about his plans for retiring? "I just want to have more money than Larry Ellison," he says. "I don't know why. But once I have more money than Larry Ellison, I'll be satisfied."

But Lewis pressed further. In about six months, Clark would surpass Ellison in terms of net worth. Then what? Did Clark want more money than, say, Bill Gates? Lewis writes, " 'Oh, no,' Clark said, waving my question to the side of the room where the ridiculous ideas gather to commiserate with each other. 'That'll never happen.' A few minutes later, after the conversation had turned to other matters, he came clean. 'You know,' he said, 'just for one moment, I would kind of like to have the most. Just for one tiny moment.' " In the biggest flip of all, by running aimlessly on the new-wealth treadmill, we have come to resemble previous generations. In the old economy, our parents got jobs not because of the work itself but because of the pay. In the new economy, we got jobs not just for the pay but also for the chance to do meaningful work. In the new new economy, we've come full circle. This time, though, the drive for money is not about putting bread on the table (in other words, achieving comfort and security); it's about getting a bigger table. It's about keeping up with the Ellisons.

Comparison, a great teacher once told me, is the cardinal sin of modern life. It traps us in a game that we can't win. Once we define ourselves in terms of others, we lose the freedom to shape our own lives. The great irony of the Built to Flip culture is that its proponents see themselves as freethinking people in search of the Holy Grail. And yet, when they do one successful flip, they invariably discover that it isn't enough. So they go off in pursuit of bigger numbers—not one set of options but a whole portfolio of options—in an escalating, never-ending game. If the Holy Grail isn't $10 million, then maybe it's $50 million. And if it's not $50 million, then surely it's $100 million. . . . Meanwhile, those who don't play Built to Flip view their "no better than me, but luckier" colleagues with seething envy—a form of self-imprisonment that's even uglier than greed. The Holy Grail will forever elude those who imprison themselves, no matter how gilded the prison. As Joseph Campbell pointed out, the Holy Grail can be found only by those who lead their own lives.

Built to Work

So which are you striving for: Built to Last or Built to Flip? In fact, that's the wrong question. Some companies will be built to last; some won't. Some should be; others shouldn't. Ultimately, that's an artificial distinction.

The real question, the essential question is this: Is your company *built to work*? The answer rests on three criteria: excellence, contribution, and meaning. Again, consider Cardiometrics. The company may not have been built to last, but in all of its activities, it adhered to the highest possible standards: Instead of relying on expedient studies and marketing hype, it conducted rigorous, costly clinical trials in order to demonstrate the value of its technology. And the company clearly made a significant contribution—to the market, to its investors, and to the lives of patients all over the world.

Finally, the people of Cardiometrics found their work to be intrinsically meaningful: They worked with colleagues whom they respected and even loved, and they pursued a worthy aim to the best of their ability. Built to Flip? Built to Last? Cardiometrics embodies neither of these models: It was built to work.

If the new economy is to regain its soul, we need to ask ourselves some tough questions: Are we committed to doing our work with unadulterated excellence, no matter how arduous the task or how long the road? Is our work likely to make a contribution that we can be proud of? Does our work provide us with a sense of purpose and meaning that goes beyond just making money?

If we cannot answer yes to those questions, then we're failing, no matter how much money we make. But if we can answer yes, then we're likely not only to attain financial success but also to gain that rarest of all achievements: a life that works.

THE LAST WORD

Thank you for Jim Collins's article on the get-rich-quick phenomenon that seems to be taking over the new economy. People who build companies that exist merely to make a quick buck are participating in the greatest non-indictable crime in business history. Those who are out just to create companies and then "flip" them right away are responsible for the biggest scam of all. And, unfortunately, it's the small investors who usually end up getting burned.

I've begun shopping around my own idea for a long-lasting company. It may be quaint to do something because it provides value, or to do something that I plan to commit a good portion of my career to, but I want to create something that lasts longer than the next year. I hope to be around longer than the just-add-smoke-and-mirrors business-plan approach that is so prominent today. Built to Last *is good business sense—and an honorable way to conduct one's life.*

Frank John Giovinazzi
CEO
Globalepic.com
Alexandria, Virginia

"What Are We After?
We Are Literally Trying to Stop Time"

From: Issue 34 | May 2000 | By: Bill Breen

Hunter S. Thompson's line "Faster, faster, until the thrill of speed overcomes the fear of death" was once *Fast Company*'s guiding mantra. The thrill of this story by Bill Breen is the surprising advice he brought back from his time with the world's best track coach. When the difference between success and also-ran status is measured in hundredths of a second, the techniques that elite sprinters use to win contain enlightening insights into how to compete in today's cutthroat global marketplace. On your mark. Get set.

"Runners, take your mark," intones the Madison Square Garden announcer, quieting a crowd of 16,000 that has turned out for New York City's Millrose Games, the most illustrious stop on the U.S. indoor-track-and-field circuit. Six Olympic-quality sprinters step up to the starting line and prepare to run the men's 60-meter race.

Built like streamlined NFL running backs, the athletes each begin a meticulous, 30-second choreography of twitches and flexes. Maurice Greene—the reigning world champion in the 100-meters and the world-record holder in both the 60 and the 100—crouches and, in one quick, catlike motion, springs backward on both legs, briefly testing his ankles, calves, quads, and hams. Jon Drummond, a 1996 Olympic silver medalist in the 400-meter relay, presses his fingertips into the Mondo track, aligning his hands on the starting line like a pool player lining up a break. Ato Boldon, the 200-meter gold medalist in the 1997 World Championships, locks his eyes on the finish line, then bows his head and waits for the next word.

"Set," commands the announcer. A moment later, the starter pistol cracks. In a microsecond, the sprinters vault forward.

As they burst out of the blocks, they collectively unleash enough force to make a Ferrari go from 0 MPH to 60 MPH—in 4 seconds flat. They hurtle down the straightaway with a fury that is simultaneously beautiful and terrifying. Hands slash through the air like switchblades. Runners reach maximum velocity in 3.5 seconds. At top speed, they cover 8 feet per stride. They are so swift, it is almost impossible for the unschooled observer to take it all in.

But not for John Smith, a six-foot, one-inch combination of track smarts and street charm who stands near the track's edge. Smith, 49, was once a renowned world-class runner. In 1971, as a member of the UCLA track team, he clocked 44.5 seconds in the 440-yard dash, setting a world record. More recently, in 1996, he cofounded HSI, an Irvine, California–based sports agency.

Smith is also the track world's foremost teacher of speed. Greene, Drummond, and Boldon are three of his pupils. But they are not alone. His circle of speed demons also includes Inger Miller, the women's 200-meter world champion; Marie-Jose Perec, the women's 200- and 400-meter gold-medal winner in the 1996 Olympics; and Quincy Watts, the men's 400-meter champ in the 1992 Olympics.

The lessons that Smith passes on to the world's fastest runners have obvious implications for businesspeople who want to win a competitive race that's measured in Internet time. To learn how fast companies—and the people who work for them—can move even faster, we caught up with Smith, who has embarked on a title fight with time itself. At stake is nothing less than his ambition to reinvent the way that the race is run, to shatter the physical and psychological barriers that prevent the world's fastest sprinters from doing what they were born wanting to do—that is, to fly.

"What are we after? We are literally trying to stop time," says Smith. "Running 100 meters in 10 seconds won't bring you fame. But running it in 9.79 will. He who finishes closest to zero wins. Freeze the clock—that's what we're all about."

Here, then, are five of Smith's clock-stopping rules for competing in a race where there is no speed limit.

To Go Fast, Take Your Time

Half a step. That was the margin of victory in the Millrose 60-meters, as Greene barely nipped Drummond at the tape. Drummond has one of the best starts in the business, and he challenged Greene for the entire race. But Greene's searing finish managed to hold Drummond off in the final few meters.

So how did Greene win? "He took his time," Smith replies. Huh? Greene edged out Drummond by 0.05 seconds—roughly the length of time that it takes a hummingbird to flap its wings once. When did Greene have the time to "take his time"?

The answer, it turns out, is that he ran a smart race. Smith has used 400-meter tactics to help him radically rethink the way that shorter distances are run. "The 400 sucks up everything you've got, so you have to be very careful about how you distribute your energy throughout the race," he says. "You need to structure the race, and you need a plan. I took everything that I knew about the 400 and used it to teach the 100."

Smith analyzed the shorter race, trying to clip off a few thousandths of a second here, another few thousandths there. He saw an opportunity in the final 20 meters, when a runner is assumed to have lost the capacity to maintain his top speed. If Smith could stretch out a sprinter's speed for the entire distance, the sprinter would have some fuel left for the finish.

Smith divided the 100-meter race into five stages. First comes "reaction time," a bloodless phrase for the violent moment when sprinters explode out of the blocks. Next, there's the "drive phase," when the runners leverage their forward momentum to propel themselves down the track. Then they make the "transition"—often visualizing gear changes as they shift into overdrive and fly into the fourth stage, "maximum velocity." The goal at this stage is to maintain top speed for as long as possible—for 30 or even 40 meters.

As they approach the final stage, the runners try to "hold on." They have pushed their bodies to the limit, and now their exhausted muscles stop obeying. Their limbs start to seize up. But if an athlete has run the first four stages correctly, he's in a position to control the inevitable deceleration. And that is Smith's great secret: The runner who slows the least over the final 20 meters usually gets the gold.

Smith's point about Greene's "taking his time" is that Greene didn't rush through those stages. He maxed them out, refusing to shift into the next gear until his RPM was just right. That allowed him to relax as he surged to the finish. He won because he stayed fast.

"Sprinters are most vulnerable in the middle of a race, because they want to punch that accelerator," says Smith. "But if you hit it too soon, you'll run out of gas. You've got to give your body enough time to unfold, so that you'll be in the best position to apply great force.

"People think that all a sprinter needs to do is to run all out, but that's so Hollywood. I want my sprinters to do just the opposite. I want them to show how *easy* it is to run fast."

The point, concludes Smith, is that there's a world of difference between "haste" and "speed." Haste doesn't win races. Taking your time just might.

Make Your Competitor Your Partner

In the world of track and field, says Smith, long-distance runners often get along because they share a common obstacle: the race's distance. Marathoners, for example, must channel all of their competitive aggression into conquering a 26-mile, 385-yard course.

But sprinters are stripped of any such distraction. Their only obstacle is the competitor who lines up next to them, separated solely by the thin white line that demarcates the track's eight lanes. Metaphorically, that line is often crossed, as the rivals engage in race-day hazing: the territorial staredown during warm-ups; the trash talk before the start; the winner's chest-thumping, fist-pumping strut after the finish; the loser's determination to ignore it all.

"You couldn't write the stuff that sprinters say to get one another off their game," says Smith. "They'll talk about you. They'll talk about your parents. [Olympic sprinter] John Carlos used to line up and announce, 'You guys figure out how you're going to place, because first is gone—I got that. I'll be waiting for you at the finish.' "

It's all the more remarkable, then, that Smith has made teammates out of natural-born rivals. Greene, Boldon, and Drummond are among the world's top men in the 100- and the 200-meter races. Each of them is gunning for the other, as they vie for their sport's ultimate grail: the hard gold of the 2000 Summer Olympics, in Sydney, Australia. Most elite runners avoid one another, going head-to-head only when big money and a big title are at stake. Yet these three train together nearly every day, with Smith and his stopwatch at their side.

Smith's workplace is the rust-colored track inside Drake Stadium, on the campus of the University of California, Los Angeles. On a damp, late-winter day, he leads two of his charges—sprinter Gentry Bradley and 400-meter runner Danny McCray—through an advanced tutorial on speed.

After 45 minutes of stretching and warm-ups, the work begins. Smith tells his runners to do three "350s"—sprinters' shorthand for 350-meter laps run at near-race speed, with 8-minute rest intervals. "This is going to be a little grueling," understates Smith. "At 300 meters, you're at the limit of a human being's ability to go all out. That's when all shit stops, and real men start running."

McCray toes the starting line. Bradley lines up directly behind him. "Set," barks Smith. "Go!" They take off from a standing start and quickly leg into maximum velocity. As the runners fly into the backstretch, Smith parses out split times and advice over a megaphone: "Don't lose him, G. Elbows in. Keep your rhythm up. Stay focused. Don't float on me. Now you're running. Take it in."

Watching Bradley and McCray push each other, the coach's game plan becomes searingly clear: By working together instead of alone, his athletes work harder. The more intense the workouts, the faster the two men run. Ultimately, the day-to-day grind of competing one-on-one will make them get fast—faster.

Smith doesn't try to control his athletes' rivalry or ensure that it stays healthy off the track. "They can be friends after practice. But when they're out here, I throw gasoline onto the fire. I want them to challenge each other. When someone raises the bar and achieves a higher level of performance, everyone else must rise to meet that person. When that happens, I've done my job."

Work on Your Weakness

Two minutes, 15 seconds. Take away the warm-up time, and that was the total length of Bradley and McCray's speed workout. Sprinters are fast—but not all the time. They pick their moments.

To the inexperienced observer, sprinters are experts at wasting time. Their workout seems to consist almost entirely of stretching and resting, punctuated by brief moments of maximum exertion. More accurately, explains Smith, they are using their downtime to recover, so that they can focus on the few seconds that really matter.

A sprinter's season consists of perhaps 10 major races—less than 100 seconds of performance. To prepare for those do-or-die moments, sprinters submit to a continuous round of bearing down and snapping back. They lay themselves out one day, ease up the next. Weight work is followed by speed work. The goal is to stress the muscles, rest, and allow the body to build itself back up—to become more powerful than before. In a variation of the old adage, their suffering will only make them stronger—if it doesn't kill them.

"I don't need to get maximum effort every day," says Smith. "But whenever they can give it, I want it. Last year, Maurice [Greene] told me that he wanted to work with the quarter-milers. It was awesome. They dragged him around the track, but he stayed with them. After every workout, he was doubled over, fertilizing the grass." Smith flashes a smile and scuffs his foot across a swath of browned grass where Greene and the other sprinters had vomited.

"And that's a big deal, because it's no longer a matter of me wanting them to work harder. I have to be smarter in the work that I give them. In Maurice's case, we were already working smarter. He had a problem handling a short recovery, so he put himself in a position where he *had* to endure a short recovery again and again and again, until he was able to deal with it. Most people work on their strengths. I admire a man who's smart enough to work on his weaknesses."

Move Fast, and Time Will Slow

It happened nearly 29 years ago, but Smith clearly recalls the moment when he reached the "Edge"—that magic zone where it feels as if gravity is pulling the body along, rather than impeding it. That was the day when he felt the effortless, flowing sensation of moving fast, faster than he'd ever run before. It was the day he nailed the world record in the 440.

To get to the Edge, sprinters must be at their peak physically—maximum power emanating from the lightest possible body. And their mechanics must approach perfection. For the 100-meter race, that means a total of 45 steps from start to finish, each step striking and lifting from the track in 0.083 seconds—just enough time to plant the ball of the foot and explode forward with maximum efficiency. Every stride is a balancing act, with the body making countless microadjustments so that it can continue moving in a precise line down the straightaway.

That's not all. When a sprinter has reached the Edge, he has absorbed race tactics and proper mechanics to the point where they have become instinctive. Now, at the crack of the starter's gun, all thought reverts to feeling. There's a vibration, a hypersensitivity to the feel of the track itself. As the runner reaches maximum velocity, breathing and movement are one. He is moving exceedingly fast. But he feels relaxed, in total control.

Smith describes the Edge in near mystical terms. "Everything you've trained for, everything you've learned, is focused on this single, concentrated moment," he says. "And that's the moment when you have your breakthrough. That's the moment when you steal the light."

Smith's moment came in Eugene, Oregon, during the 83rd running of the National Amateur Athletic Union championships. "I couldn't sleep the night before, but I wasn't tired," he remembers. "I felt a kind of lightness about me. The race started, and it felt like my feet weren't even touching the ground. Between 200 and 300 meters, all I saw was blur. I was passing people so fast. I put my foot to the pedal in the backstretch, and suddenly everything was moving in slow motion. That's what happens when you're in that zone: Time itself seems to slow."

A clip from the archives of *The New York Times* shows Smith breaking the tape. His mouth is curled upward in the slightest of smiles. Otherwise, his face is expressionless. There's no painful grimace—none of the intensity that you'd expect from someone who'd just pushed the limits of human endurance.

"When you look at someone who's moving fast, the thing that's being expressed is movement, which is effortless," says Smith. "The guys who are tense, the guys who are straining, have lost the race. The race goes to the athlete who's in control—of his body, of his breathing, of his rhythm. Guys who have just run incredibly fast always say the same thing: 'That was so easy.' "

Lose Like a Winner

It's inevitable. At some point, even the world's fastest man will lose. Maurice Greene had a dream season in 1999. He set a world record. He took four world titles. But he was blistered in two races. And defeat hammers at the most vulnerable spot in a dynamo's armor: his psyche.

Each race inflicts on sprinters a taffy pull of conflicting emotions. They won't win unless they are convinced that they will win, even though they know in their heart that they can be defeated on any given day. In victory, they must hold on to at least a scintilla of humility, lest they get too cocky—and ripe for a takedown. In defeat, they must be arrogant, or they risk losing the confidence that fuels a winning performance.

"It's kind of a paradox. Just when you start winning a lot and really begin to master the sport, you've got to become more humble and realize how much more you still need to learn," says Smith. "And when you lose, you've got to stick your chest out and take on the persona of a winner. Other runners can beat you, but you can never, never let them defeat you. If you do, they'll take over your market."

According to Smith, no one was better at losing like a winner than Carl Lewis, arguably the greatest track-and-field athlete in history. Case in point: the 1994 Grand Prix meet in Lausanne, Switzerland. In the 100, Leroy Burrell didn't just blow by Lewis; he shattered Lewis's world record. "Carl lost," recalls Smith. "But Carl did the interview. I've never seen anything like it.

"Leroy was very emotional. He was crying and celebrating because he'd broken Carl's record. And Carl was genuinely happy for him. He hugged him. Then, during the TV interview, he talked about how well Leroy had run. It was Leroy's moment, but Carl was determined to share it. *He wasn't going to let it get him down.* As far as Carl was concerned, he didn't lose; he just didn't win. How did Leroy feel after that? He was probably pissed. You'll have to ask him.

"Mind games," says Smith with a hearty chuckle. "Man, they're just beautiful."

THE LAST WORD

Your issue dedicated to "Speed" surely fueled the fire of internal chaos that many of your readers feel today—myself included. As the boundaries between work life and home life continue to blur, we need to be fast but to eat slow; to be fast but to smell the roses; to be fast but to make sure that we have time to go to our daughter's soccer game. At the rate we're all going, the battle between speed and sanity will lead to a mass diagnosis of bipolar disorder. How can we fix this?

The challenge today is to edit out all of the noise that comes disguised as information. Am I the only person in business who has grown weary (and wary) of talk about "paradigm shifts," a "new breed of entrepreneurs," and "value-adds"? I would much rather read about successful companies that espouse grace, humility, gratitude, and honesty. Will I become someone else's lunch because I hold this view? No. In working to start companies that can stand the test of time, I've learned a very important lesson: The key thing to remember is not that we need to be fast but that we are running a race that has no finish line. So the fuel that drives us needs to be made of something substantial— something for the heart that the head can also follow.

Vincent Kralyevich
President
Videoschoolhouse
New York, New York

The Permatemps Contratemps

From: Issue 37 | August 2000 | By: Ron Lieber

What if a free agent wasn't really free? A permatemp is a person who does full-time work for one employer but who isn't a full-time employee—so he's not eligible for full benefits, stock options, or even playing on the company softball team. It's the worst of both worlds: Independent contractors lose the flexibility they became independent for, and those who want full-time jobs can't get them. That's what was going on at Microsoft during the 1990s, leading to an ugly class-action lawsuit that asked the courts to hash out the meaning of a full-time employee. Writer Ron Lieber took a unique approach to covering the issue, profiling some of the various players on all sides of the controversy. He didn't find any easy answers, and his dispatch signaled the first indication that people who choose the life of the free agent would pay a high cost for their desired freedom. In December 2000, not long after our story appeared, Microsoft settled the case for $97 million. But the permatemps, in a final indignity, had to wait until October 2005 before they started receiving their checks. The average payout? $8,425. The dark side of free agent nation, indeed.

The e-mail message from Microsoft's then-president seemed innocuous. Dated Wednesday, January 17, 1990, and addressed to Bill Gates and Steve Ballmer, among others, it explained the consequences of a recent altercation that pitted Microsoft against the Internal Revenue Service. The IRS had noticed that the company was employing lots of independent contractors for long periods of time and was not withholding taxes from their paychecks. Having determined that there were few differences in substance between what kind of work those contractors did and what kind of work Microsoft's full-timers did, the IRS had forced the contractors to pay back taxes—some of which were covered by Microsoft—and had asked the company to change its policies so that all employees would be giving the government its fair share of their paychecks every two weeks.

The IRS had left it to Microsoft to decide how it would do that; by early January 1990, one option had emerged that seemed sensible: Ask the independent contractors to sign up with Seattle-area temp agencies and to have those agencies withhold taxes. The e-mail message began by explaining the nuances of this practice to company managers: "First do not have your people just make all the freelancers temps. That should only happen in the cases where there is a clearly defined end date to a project and a firm commitment to let the person go when that project is completed." Certain contractors who had been working on existing products that had longer timelines would be offered full-time jobs. "This is really the elimination of a longtime cheat to hold down headcount," the e-mail continued. "Don't try to go around it, we could have severe legal problems if this is not done according to the law."

That was in 1990. Today, that e-mail seems prescient, since it resurfaced as a result of "severe legal problems": a class-action lawsuit that a group of temp workers filed against Microsoft in 1992. But even that lawsuit didn't stop Microsoft from employing long-term temps. Throughout the 1990s, Microsoft took on thousands of workers through local personnel agencies, certain that it had a right to employ contract workers—as long as those workers knew that an assignment at Microsoft did not include company benefits or guarantee full-time employment in the future.

Those temps who did sign on to work at Microsoft often stayed for so long that they eventually developed a collective nickname: "permatemps." Whoever coined the term must have had a sharp sense of irony. Legitimate free agents—the "temps" in "permatemps"—are deliberately impermanent. In a perfect world, they work whenever and wherever they want to work, and they pick up stakes and move on whenever the learning curve levels off or whenever a better deal comes along. But employees who are "permanently temporary"—the "permas" in "permatemps"—are looking for the opportunities that are afforded by a full-time job, including all of the fringe benefits that come with full-time status.

To be a permatemp is to sit in the oxymoronic crosshairs of the new economy. You enjoy—or you suffer—the worst of both worlds. Free agents choose to work as independent contractors because they want to, because it gives them more leverage in the job market and more control over their lives. Permatemps work as not-so-independent contractors often because they feel as though they must. They're stuck—or at least that's how they feel. The ones who worked at Microsoft are case studies of the dark side of free agency, examples of how an experimental human-resources policy that was intended to encourage flexibility can have unintended consequences.

Microsoft didn't plan to serve as the setting for the new economy's defining trial on the meaning and limits of free agency, but it has become just that. And the results of this experiment? None of the people involved in the temp controversy have gotten exactly what they wanted. Although Microsoft has grown and prospered, the lawsuit has generated lots of bad publicity and has lowered morale dramatically among the company's temps, who have at times made up as much as 25% of Microsoft's Seattle-area workforce. The temps may well end up as the beneficiaries of a lawsuit that awards them millions of dollars, but a judgment in their favor will have consequences too. Even if the workers do win the case, free agents may find themselves constrained in their ability to work on their own terms, and permatemps may still not land the full-time jobs that they want. Meanwhile, the courts have taken over the role of chief policy maker on matters that could not be settled by the talent market and by human-resources strategists.

The cast of characters who live out this drama of the new-economy workplace include an unwilling full-time employee, an unwilling perma-temp, two aspiring permatemp union organizers, a permatemp agency operator, and the head of the temp workers at Microsoft. Their stories—like the permatemp lawsuit, the advantages of free agency, and free agency's dark side—are still evolving.

Sylvia Moestl: The Unwilling Full-Timer

When Sylvia Moestl graduated from the University of North Carolina in 1989, she was an interdisciplinary-studies major with little background in technology. For several years after college, she traveled abroad and did volunteer work. She then returned home to Charlotte, where she found a temporary job at a Microsoft technical-support facility. After six months of hard work, a long evaluation process, and several interviews, she got an of-fer from Microsoft for a full-time position, making her one of 5 temps in her group of about 80 that the company hired. In 1994, Moestl pulled up stakes and moved to the Seattle area.

For most young people with technology smarts in the pre-Internet 1990s, landing a full-time job at Microsoft would have been a chance-of-a-lifetime coup. But for Moestl, the full-time job soon became a daily re-minder of the attraction of free agency. "I was always on the phone with people who had skills like mine, and who were making four times the money that I was making," she says. Her new job did come with some Microsoft stock options—but not enough to make her feel either destined for riches or trapped by golden handcuffs. "Talking to all of those people on the outside got me completely in tune with the idea of moving on to do my own thing."

Moestl, now 32, undoubtedly would have made more money in the long run had she stuck with her full-time job and garnered even more stock op-tions. But when she made her decision to quit her full-time job, she wasn't thinking only about her income. She was looking for work that fit her inter-ests, and she felt uncomfortably pigeonholed while she was working in the technical-support department at Microsoft.

In the fall of 1995, Moestl left Microsoft to become a free agent. Over the course of the next four years, she did contract work on five different Microsoft projects, playing a number of different roles and honing a variety of skills.

Even though Moestl hasn't done temp work for Microsoft recently, her job experience at the company and her exposure to the permatemps con-troversy left her with a strong opinion about the lawsuit. "Just because someone *wants* a full-time job doesn't mean that person is going to get one," she says. "The market has ways of regulating situations like this. There are job opportunities elsewhere, and if people are unhappy, they should take advantage of those opportunities."

As unsympathetic as Moestl is to the cause of the permatemps, the con-troversy has had a direct impact on her life. In February 2000, Microsoft an-nounced a new permatemp policy: No temp worker would be allowed to stay at the company for more than a year without a break in service. In the wake of that announcement, many other local companies—and companies elsewhere around the country that have been tracking this high-profile case—decided to follow the practice to avoid becoming the next target of a class-action lawsuit.

"Some large companies are trying to avoid hiring any contractors at all," says Moestl. "And there are others who don't want to risk giving a contractor longer projects to work on, because they're afraid that they might be sued if contractors think that they're doing full-time work for them. All of it directly affects my bottom line and my ability to choose the way that I want to work."

Barbara Judd: The Unwilling Permatemp

Two years ago, accepting a temporary assignment at Microsoft seemed like a pretty good bet to Barbara Judd. An MBA, Judd, who was in her late forties at the time, was one of what would eventually become 60 temps who signed on to help the company develop a piece of software that was designed to compete with Intuit's popular TurboTax program. What Judd really wanted was a full-time job at Microsoft; taking a temp position would at least get her foot in the door, she figured. "The company made it clear to us that there were no guarantees that the project would succeed," she says. "But my take on temp work has always been that it's a good way to prove yourself to an employer. Plus, it was a chance to work on a piece of software from the ground up. It's always more exciting to build than it is to fix. I saw that job as a chance for me to be a pioneer."

One year later, Judd was still a temp and was still working on the same project. That was when she attended an annual meeting of the Institute of Management Accountants in Seattle—and inadvertently found out how at least one high-ranking Microsoft executive really felt about permatemps. Greg Maffei, then the chief financial officer of Microsoft, was the speaker at the summer event. At the end of his remarks, an audience member asked him about the company's use of temps, and Maffei fired away. "We are very tough in hiring [full-time workers] in terms of standards, but we aren't as tough on temps," he said. "So you found that the quality of the temps is not as good as the quality of the full-time people."

Sitting in the audience, listening to Maffei's remarks, Judd felt "like I was being punched in the stomach. I must have looked like it too. People kept whispering to me, 'Are you okay? Are you okay?' He was telling my peers that I wasn't good."

The incident not only made Judd uneasy; it also reminded her that she had some serious, unanswered questions about her future and about the role of permatemps at Microsoft. On one hand, she knew that it would be foolish for her to feel entitled, or even attached, to her job at Microsoft. The company had guaranteed her nothing except a specific wage and had told her explicitly that it could let her go at any moment. She made $32 an hour plus overtime—more than she might have made on an hourly basis as a full-time employee—but she had no Microsoft stock options and a less-than-ample benefits package through the temp agency. On the other hand, temps like Judd were questioning what made permatemps different from regular employees. Why couldn't she join the club?

For all of the uncertainty and all of the unanswered questions, several signs cropped up that seemed encouraging to temps looking to land full-time positions. Within one year of the project's start, Microsoft converted four of Judd's colleagues to full-time status. Judd and many of her coworkers had worked together on tax software for a different company in the past, and four managers from that previous project got those four full-time slots at Microsoft. Once those four workers were promoted, Microsoft's project managers spent the next year trying to encourage Judd and the other temps to be patient, reminding them that Microsoft needed their tax product in order to have a full suite of financial software to bring to market.

While Judd waited, she had to live by a long list of rules that come with a temp worker's status at Microsoft. Temporary employees, whether they have worked at the company for a week or for two years, are not allowed to play on the Microsoft ball fields, get a free membership to a local gym, or join any of the employee-affinity groups. Badges that the company issues to temps are orange, rather than blue. And, on the Microsoft e-mail system, an "A" is printed before the name of temps who are assigned through local staffing agencies—a designation that temps say makes their e-mail opinions easier to dismiss. There's more: Temps can't buy discounted software at the company store. In fact, they can't buy it at all, for any price, even if they wrote the instructions inside the box.

With her day-to-day work constrained by demeaning employment rules and her future job status uncertain, why didn't Judd simply leave? "Getting another job isn't quite as easy as you might think," she says. "Microsoft doesn't want us to put their company name on our resume as our employer. They say that the temp agency is our employer, even if we worked at Microsoft for two years. When people see that you've been working through a temp agency, they think that you have an unstable work history, so they toss your resume into the trash can."

Besides, Judd argues, why *should* she have to leave? "The courts have ruled that Microsoft controls the terms of our work, that we're common-law full-time employees. So don't ask me why I didn't leave," she says. "Ask Microsoft why it didn't do what the courts say it should have done and given me the privileges that all full-time employees get when they work for the company."

But to Microsoft, the job never was permanent. After more than two years, Microsoft announced on March 22 that it was discontinuing work on its tax software that very day. The company gave Judd and her colleagues 48 hours to clean out their desks.

Marcus Courtney and Mike Blain: The Permatemps Organizers

To many outsiders, there is a simple solution to the permatemps problem at Microsoft: They should just quit and strike a better deal somewhere else. But to Marcus Courtney, that line of reasoning doesn't match his understanding of how most people work. "The 'love it or leave it' argument might make sense for some people," Courtney says. "But why should you have to love every single term that comes along with an employment contract? If you're at Microsoft, working with cutting-edge technology in areas that interest you, isn't it possible that you might want to stay and try to improve the things that bother you?"

Courtney, 29, knows firsthand how logical it is to try to make your work better, rather than bailing out—and how frustrating it can be to try to effect change as a temp. In 1998, having worked at Microsoft for almost two years, Courtney was still classified as a temp. His hourly wage had improved only slightly over those two years, the benefits were less than generous, and he was frustrated with his failed attempts to land a full-time job. He found a similarly disillusioned, long-term temp worker in Mike Blain. Besides their frustration, both men shared a passion for organizing. "High-tech temp workers had no effective representation at Microsoft, let alone at a state or a national level," says Blain, 33. "At the time, Microsoft was a member of an industry group that was trying to make overtime pay for hourly software workers optional, and staffing agencies were bending the ears of government officials in Washington's statehouse. But temps had no one speaking for them." While Microsoft did not lobby for the industry group's position, the group's effort still served as a wake-up call for what might happen if no one was representing the voice of the temps.

So the pair, along with 25 other high-tech workers, launched the Washington Alliance of Technology Workers (WashTech). Blain and Courtney quit their temp jobs eight months later, after they got the financial backing of the Communications Workers of America (CWA). Microsoft had never been a target of high-tech union activity before. Blain and Courtney planned to change that through their work at WashTech. They also saw themselves as part of something larger: the first attempt to organize and represent the interests of workers who don't want to be employees of any one company, or who are contract workers unable to secure a full-time position.

If permatemps is an oxymoronic job description, then Blain and Courtney sought to create an oxymoronic labor union—a union of people who, by definition, are temps. But who would want to join a group like that? Blain and Courtney didn't start out with all of the answers, but they did know that, given the level of dissatisfaction among Microsoft's temps, they had a fertile testing ground for their new union. Setting union dues at $11 per month, they went to work to demonstrate the value of membership and focused immediately on training, an opportunity that the two organizers recognized from their own experience as a missing element for most temps. The offer struck a nerve, and members began to sign up.

Still, like any union, WashTech needed specific grievances to rally around in order to gain visibility and to alert potential members that it was attempting to make Microsoft executives take it seriously. For years, temporary workers at Microsoft had not been able to request formal performance reviews directly from their managers at the company. Instead, Microsoft told temps to get their reviews from their employer of record: the temp agencies. "Your agency rep would send an evaluation form to your manager at Microsoft," Courtney says. "The manager would fill out the form and send it back to your agency, and then your rep would call you on the phone and read the manager's comments to you. Most agency reps were just regurgitating what the manager had written on the form."

But WashTech was aware of another review process that the temps were not privy to. "We'd known for several years that there was some sort of database that secretly tracked the performance of each temp worker," says Blain. "Someone stumbled onto it on the Microsoft corporate network and discovered that the company had been evaluating its temps and storing comments about them all along. So we quietly got the word out to people so that they could peek in and review their records. We knew that once Microsoft found out that we had discovered its database, the company would shut it down."

Microsoft did, in fact, cut off access to the database—around the same time that WashTech went public with the news on its own Web site. "Because WashTech is around, people who missed the chance to see their file felt like it was safe to demand that Microsoft give them access to it," Courtney says. "Microsoft tells people that only their agency can make that evaluation, but then it keeps secret files that blackball some of them from ever working at the company again. When people can't get a straight answer about their performance, it really devalues their contribution as a worker."

For its part, Microsoft claims that WashTech encouraged temps to break the law by trespassing on the Microsoft network in search of those personnel files. Earlier this year, WashTech asked the state Department of Labor and Industries to issue an opinion about whether the temps have a right to see the files, and the state issued an opinion in favor of the temps.

WashTech is now moving more formally on other fronts, starting with wages. Most temp agencies refuse to disclose to temps how much money they charge for a temp worker's labor. "Many of these agencies are just parasites," says Blain. "They hire whomever Microsoft tells them to put on their payroll. Then they process their paychecks, and that's it. They're just glorified money launderers." WashTech and its members believe that, like lawyers and accountants who work for a firm, temp workers should be told by their agencies the rates at which their services are billed out. The group was influential in drafting a bill in Washington's state legislature that would force agencies to disclose their markups.

But for all of its activity and public-relations successes, WashTech has found the actual organizing of new members slow going. By May 2000, the union had signed up only about 260 members—far short of the 1,500 that it needs to be self-sustaining at its current staffing levels. As of last December, Microsoft had 18,525 full-time employees working in the Puget Sound area near Seattle and had between 5,000 and 5,500 other employees working as temporary workers in that same region. WashTech's own surveys suggest that nearly 60% of those temps would prefer to have a full-time job with the company—an estimate that suggests that there are ample numbers of temps for the union to sign up.

Why, then, has it been so hard to get temps to join? Courtney points to a number of reasons. A lot of temps are scared to join, he says, and they're caught in a catch-22: Those who are most unhappy tend to be temps who want full-time jobs but can't get them, and those same temps are least likely to make waves and jeopardize their chances of getting those full-time jobs. Meanwhile, true temps are generally not joiners by nature. "They have a strong sense of individual spirit, and none of them has ever encountered an organization like ours," Courtney says. "The word 'union' comes with a certain amount of baggage for white-collar workers in general, and for individualist workers, in particular. So we try to get people interested in the issues that we're working on without using that term to describe what we do."

Perhaps the biggest challenge that WashTech's organizers face comes from the transient nature of many free agents. Over the past two years, 400 people have joined WashTech at one time or another but then have left town or have dropped out of touch. "For the past two generations, unions have appealed to people who would hold the same job for 30 years," Courtney says. "The power of a union contract has come from being able to go back to the bargaining table over and over again to improve it."

In fact, despite Courtney's arguments to the contrary, "love it or leave it" does describe the way that many temps approach their work. Courtney remains confident, however, and so far his CWA sponsors have shown no sign of withdrawing their support, even though they'll likely have to cover the shortfall in WashTech's budget for the foreseeable future. "For the CWA to remain viable in the 21st century, it needs to have a strong presence among information-technology workers, and it's looking for us to lead the way," Courtney says. "As long as we're making changes at companies like

Microsoft, building support for our organization, and translating that support into new members, they'll want to be a part of that. Their support is not based upon a membership quota."

Peg Cheirrett: The Permatemps Agent

For the owners of many Seattle-area temp agencies, Microsoft's decade-long permatemp experiment has been extremely good for business. For Peg Cheirrett, who has spent the past 15 years running WASSER Inc., an agency for technical writers, it has been just plain extreme. First she rode to the top of the business, filling Microsoft's demands for employees. Then she rode out of the business, accepting a lucrative offer from a company that wanted to buy her firm. "Microsoft made WASSER's growth feasible," Cheirrett says. "If we had been in Kansas, this would be a very different company."

According to Cheirrett, 51, the true free agents who worked through WASSER enjoyed their work at Microsoft but often felt conflicted. "I recall one conversation with someone who was particularly mistrustful of me," she says. "The whole reason that he had gone independent in the first place was because he felt that agencies were exploitative and that they didn't give anything back to workers. Working through an agency in order to do work for Microsoft, to him, was a loss of control, a loss of prestige."

The evolution of the permatemp, Cheirrett says, was largely a matter of inertia. "It just seemed to *happen* to some people," she says. "There was one person who worked for me at Microsoft for six years, and at some point during the beginning of year number three, he began to notice that the whole thing was just going by itself. Once we put workers like him into the Microsoft system, those workers would find more projects there on their own and would stay on."

Some permatemps kept working at Microsoft simply because staying was easier than leaving and trying to find a new job at a different company; others remained with hopes of landing a full-time job. Either way, Cheirrett thinks that her agency played a useful role. "These were not people who would have been good at marketing themselves or at negotiating their own rates," she says. "Our agency handled payroll and benefits for them, and gave them easy access to new assignments if they needed it."

And, says Cheirrett, the setup became more and more convenient for Microsoft as well. "In the old days, much of the demand for technical writers really was seasonal," she explains. "They would jam stuff through during the summer in order to get it out in time for Comdex in the fall, and then they would lay everybody off and go into hibernation for the winter." But as Microsoft expanded its offerings, demand grew for year-round help writing manuals and other technical documents. And individual projects became more complex. "It took three years to write the first version of Exchange, the e-mail program that eventually became Outlook," Cheirrett says. "We had contractors actually bailing out of that one because they didn't want to continue working on such a stressful, troubled product. They wanted to go somewhere else and have a better time."

In the early-to-mid-1990s, with all of this activity going on, Microsoft did hire more full-time technical writers, but the demand for Cheirrett to provide more contract writers also increased. Why didn't Microsoft simply hire more of those writers on a full-time basis? To Cheirrett, the answer lies in the company's DNA. "Microsoft is a hacker culture," she says. The company has always valued people with programming smarts above all else— followed by those with the marketing skills to find millions of customers to buy the company's software products. "For people who have talent, our doors [to full-time work] are open," Bill Gates told the *Los Angeles Times* in 1997, commenting on the permatemp controversy. To many temps, Gates's comments confirmed the company's internal division that put programmers at the top—and assigned to interchangeable temps the lowly tasks of writing manuals and creating content for the company's Web properties.

Cheirrett began to notice that her firm's role in the labor market was changing. It went from being a technical-communications company to being a human-resources services company, and those services were becoming a commodity. "Our profit margins were already around 5%, and we didn't want to see what might happen if competitive pressure pushed them lower," she says.

So, in 1997, Cheirrett and her husband, with whom she owned WASSER, sold the company and signed a three-year contract with the new owner that would allow her to run the agency during the transition. She did not renew her contract this year, and she plans to spend the next several months as a free agent herself.

Her first two self-appointed tasks: researching cutting-edge human-resources policies and studying the Hollywood model of deploying independent professionals. "I can't believe that I haven't looked into this until now," she says. "That model could serve as an example of what to do in the tech world."

Sharon Decker: The Permatemps Director

This is not a morality tale or a Hollywood movie with heroes and villains—which is why inside Microsoft's verdant corporate campus, you will not find a snarling executive who is responsible for keeping "those lowly temps" down. Instead, for the past three years, the director of contingent staffing has been Sharon Decker, herself a former Microsoft temp who did a three-month stint in customer service in 1985. Decker, 55, began her full-time Microsoft career in sales support, moved on to marketing, and then landed in human resources in the late 1990s.

Three years ago, she moved into her current job. "We are a company that's always been good at technology," she says. "And at that point, we had become a fully grown-up company, so I thought that the human-resources department might benefit from some fresh perspective. It seemed as if the next logical thing for me to do was to try to make change happen by working with people."

At the time, Microsoft's policies on the employment of temporary workers had not changed much since 1989, when the IRS first identified the issue of tax withholding and long-term contractors. To Decker, Microsoft's solution of sending its temps to staffing agencies was neither a grand strategy nor a nefarious plot. It was just a way of going about the company's business. "To my knowledge, there was no 'big decision' where people sat in a room and said, 'This is how we are going to staff the company, and this is why we're going to do it,'" she says. "We've just always wanted to maintain flexibility and to avoid big fluctuations in the number of full-time workers."

But as the move played out, it had both unforeseen and unfortunate consequences. By the time Decker started her job overseeing the temps in 1997, there was clear dissension in the ranks over Microsoft's personnel policies. At that point, the class-action suit that was filed by the temps had been wending its way through the legal system for five years, publicly pitting the company against a number of independent contractors who worked in its Seattle-area offices. The effect on morale was subtle but profound.

Decker knew that the time had come to make major changes in her company's culture. At the same time, she knew that there were certain things that she simply could not fix. Take, for instance, seemingly trivial—and presumably easy-to-change—rules that restrict temps from using the company's ball fields. Because the temps are not on the company payroll, Decker says, Microsoft's insurance company will not permit it to allow its contract workers to use its corporate ball fields or to get a free membership at a local gym through Microsoft's benefits program. As for policies that would exclude temps from bowling nights or forbid them from buying software at the company store, those were generally set by Microsoft's lawyers specifically to enable the courts to see a clear line between full-time employees and contract workers.

Decker eyes the party line carefully. "If agency employees want to participate in parties and outings, they need to ask their employers to contribute to the cost of their attending," she says. "Rarely have we been turned down when we've asked one of the agencies to do that." Decker has also approached the personnel firms about providing temps with discounts at the Microsoft store so that they wouldn't have to pay full price for the products that they had helped create. "We should have done it before now," she says.

In other areas, Decker has had more leeway to improve the standing of temporary workers at the company. In 1998, for example, she instituted a platform of changes that requires every temp agency that works with Microsoft to pay for at least half of a temporary worker's medical and dental insurance, to give workers at least 13 paid days off each year, to grant them at least $500 worth of training annually, and to establish a retirement-savings plan with at least some matching contribution from the agency. And, for the first time, all temps in every job category have a choice between at least two agencies that they can sign up with. "If you're going to use a contingent workforce, then you need to make sure that there's a safety net in place for those workers, and you need to underwrite the costs associated with that net," Decker says, noting that Microsoft now pays 20% more per worker to agencies than it did just a year ago.

This year, clearly tired of bad press and union pressure and wanting to put the lawsuit behind them, Decker and Microsoft declared that permatemps will no longer be fixtures on company grounds. Most recently, the company announced that it would not allow anyone to work as a temp at the company for more than a year. Once contractors hit the 365-day mark, they must take 100 days off before working for the company again. Decker insists that she'll strictly enforce this policy—a departure from past performance—and the announcement has compelled Microsoft managers to make tough decisions about which positions are truly temporary.

"They're going to have to map out each assignment and determine whether it has the characteristics of a regular, long-term position that fits into their long-term strategy," Decker says. "Are they part of an emerging group in a growth area, or a mature area that's downsizing? What sort of unique skills might they need year-round?"

As Microsoft creates more full-time jobs as a result of this analysis, many of those positions are open to contract workers. At any given time, Microsoft has about 3,000 openings for full-time jobs, and Decker figures that at least 40% of those jobs will go to former temps *this year*. Another result, however, could be that contractors who never wanted full-time jobs will be unable to string together one temp position after another. "It's unfortunate," Decker says. "But we have no other way to really make sure that people are filling positions in a manner that makes them true temporary employees."

Given that the courts have taken eight years (and counting) to figure out when a job that's labeled as temporary is actually a full-time position, it's hard to expect Microsoft or any other company to sort out such matters without continued experimentation. In the meantime, Decker thinks that the company deserves some credit for trying harder to make itself hospitable to everyone. "We haven't done a good enough job of telling people what we're looking for and what we're trying to do," she says. "We want temps to be in temporary assignments, and if it turns out that those assignments require long-term work, then we want to make those jobs permanent. We want people to choose to work for us and to like us—no matter what sort of career they're thinking about. We'd like to think that we can offer the best of both worlds."

THE LAST WORD

What an outstanding article on the Microsoft "permatemps" and their battle to get benefits and employment arrangements that they want. I work at the corporate headquarters of a temporary-staffing company, and in our industry we call this "permatemp" phenomenon "flexible staffing."

As a technical writer and as a full-time employee of the world's largest privately held employer of temporary workers, I see both sides of this issue. On one hand, the technology industry just doesn't understand any skill set besides programming, engineering, and (that necessary evil) marketing. Members of the programming corps can be astonishingly arrogant and elitist. They don't like to hire people who don't have "real skills"—but those people represent the very market that the programmers are trying to serve! It's ironic that Microsoft sells its software to more "everyman" customers than any other company, yet its people seem to suffer from the all-too-common techie mentality of believing that its users are stupid.

On the other hand, I just don't buy all of this new-economy hype. The vast majority of people in this country are not able to work in the way that they want to. We must iron out a flexible system that gives everybody what they need.

Name Withheld

"We Take Something Ordinary and Elevate It to Something Extraordinary"

From: Issue 40 | November 2000 | By: Curtis Sittenfeld

An architecture professor at Auburn University, Samuel Mockbee ran a program in which his students built houses for needy families in a rural Alabama community. Sittenfeld, who went on to write the best-selling and critically acclaimed novel *Prep* (2005), brings her novelist's eye to this larger-than-life character in the Deep South and returns with a touching story about the power of design to transform people's lives. Mockbee passed away in late 2001, but his lessons live on.

Around Greensboro, Alabama, everybody knows Samuel Mockbee. They know him down at the Southern Camera store on Main Street, where he sometimes pops in to use the telephone; they know him over at Crispy Chick, where he likes to go for breakfast; and they know him at Mustang Oil Barbecue, where you can get both gasoline and ribs at reasonable prices. Both the postmaster and the district judge know Mockbee, and so does 9-year-old A.J. Harris, who comes running out to the road when he sees Mockbee's truck approach. Even the local prisoners know Mockbee. "If we need something, he helps us out," says inmate Robert Steele.

An architect and a professor of architecture at Auburn University, Mockbee, 55, is known around town partly because, well, he's Mockbee—or, as everyone here calls him, "Sambo." He's big and bearded, he's funny and generous, and he appears to be comfortable with just about anyone. But people also know him because he is changing their community. Despite his playful manner, Mockbee has a serious mission: He uses his art to improve lives. "Architecture has to be greater than just architecture," Mockbee says. "It has to address social values, as well as technical and aesthetic values."

Mockbee's vehicle for addressing social values is the Rural Studio, a small program with big goals. The studio, which is run through Auburn University, addresses problems of racial inequality and of substandard housing in and around Greensboro—and takes a radical approach to undergraduate education at Auburn. Its boldness has attracted some well-known supporters, including the W.K. Kellogg Foundation and, most recently, the MacArthur Foundation, which awarded Mockbee one of its "genius" fellowships in June. Mockbee has been invited to teach at Harvard, UC Berkeley, and Yale, among other schools.

Every fall since 1993, when he and an Auburn colleague named D.K. Ruth founded the studio, Mockbee and two dozen architecture students from Auburn have uprooted from the university's eastern-Alabama campus and headed west to the studio. A farmhouse located two and a half hours from Auburn, the studio is a few miles outside Greensboro in Hale County, in the middle of the fertile Black Belt region. Hale County proudly identifies itself as the catfish capital of Alabama, but it is perhaps better known as the setting for James Agee and Walker Evans's eye-opening chronicle of 1930s sharecroppers, *Let Us Now Praise Famous Men* (Houghton Mifflin, 1941). Today, nearly 60 years after that book was published, Hale County remains one of the poorest areas in the country: Of its 16,870 residents, about 30% live in poverty—1,400 of them in houses that are considered substandard.

To some people, such circumstances might represent tragedy. To Mockbee, they represent opportunity—to help needy families while giving students practical, hands-on architectural experience, and, perhaps even more importantly, to bring together people from drastically different backgrounds. Auburn students are primarily young, white, and affluent; Rural Studio clients are primarily black and poor. But "it's economic poverty, not moral poverty," Mockbee stresses.

"I realized that if I could get students to come and meet these families and help build houses, the students' attitudes about poverty would change," Mockbee says. "This is a community that is black and white, in a literal as well as a metaphorical sense. But when students have an educational experience that exposes them to the realities, rather than the abstractness, of social and political and environmental injustices, they can form their own opinions about it. They can see conditions for themselves—and can try to address them in a positive way."

Each year, second-year architecture students, who spend a semester at the studio, interview several families and then choose one for whom they will build a house. Meanwhile, fifth-year students, who stay at the studio for an entire year while working on their theses, pursue such community-based projects as building a chapel or constructing a playground. Most recently, the Rural Studio created an Outreach Studio program for non-architecture, non-Auburn students.

That entire houses are given away with no strings attached is noteworthy. But those houses, as well as other community facilities, are noteworthy themselves: They are dazzling feats of design. They are made primarily with natural materials, such as hay or rammed earth, or with found materials, such as telephone poles, tires, or windshields. Using such materials keeps the cost of the houses low—most run between $25,000 and $30,000—and gives them a look that is strange, beautiful, and distinctly Mockbee-esque. "My bottom line is, Would I want to live in these houses?" Mockbee says. "And my wife and I would live happily ever after in any of the houses that the students have designed and built."

Justice by Design

To look at the dates and the places of Mockbee's upbringing, you would not necessarily assume that he would be such a tireless fighter for racial equality—which is partly why, in Mockbee's world, assumptions are wrong more often than they are right. A fifth-generation Mississippian, born in the town of Meridian in 1944, Mockbee grew up on the white side of a segregated society. His father contracted tuberculosis during Mockbee's youth; Mockbee, his sister, and his mother were supported primarily by his paternal grandmother, Sweet Tee, whose flair in both her manner and her wardrobe influenced Mockbee at a young age.

Mockbee did not do particularly well in school. "I was an athlete and a daydreamer," he says. Mockbee's school was academically excellent—and all white. "You couldn't buy my education in Meridian from 1950 to 1963," he says. "That faculty was as good as any college faculty today, and it was because money was being spent on white children and not on black children."

Mockbee knew black people, but never as equals. "They came in the back door, and they were maids, or they were caddies at the country club," he says.

It was not until 1966, when Mockbee was drafted by the U.S. Army during his junior year at Auburn, that he was forced to confront his own conflicted feelings about race. For the first several weeks of training camp in Fort Benning, Georgia, he remembers, "Whenever I was standing in line, I'd be sure a white person was in front of me and behind me. When I sat down to eat, I'd have a white person on either side of me and across from me. Then one day I fell asleep in a rifle-range class. When I woke up, I was in the middle of all these black trainees who were also from Mississippi. I was fine, in a nest of equals. I thought, Why have I been worried? I went back to sleep, and the race thing ceased to exist for me."

Since then, Mockbee's liberal viewpoint has not wavered. In conversation, he regularly rails against various forms of hypocrisy and injustice and against those who perpetuate them, whom he calls "Bubbas." Mockbee says, "When my daughters went off to school, I told them, 'You can do anything you want to. Do drugs, raise hell—as long as your grades are good. But don't you come back as a goddamned conservative.'" So far, his daughters, one of whom is in law school at the University of Mississippi and two of whom are undergraduates at Auburn, have complied. "They're all good, liberal Democrats," he says. "All three of them are going to be president of the United States." As for his son, who is 15 years old, Mockbee is less certain. "My wife, Jackie, says that he's a chip off the old butt," Mockbee says, laughing. "I don't know what he's going to be."

Mockbee first combined his social concerns with his love of architecture in 1982. In the town of Canton, Mississippi—where Mockbee and his family still live, though Mockbee himself is away much of the time—Mockbee heard about a Catholic nun named Sister Grace Mary, who was trying to move some houses away from a flood district. Mockbee called the nun (though he's quick to mention that he's not Catholic but "Christian by birth, Buddhist by philosophy, and heathen by nature") and helped her with the project. She then told him about a family that was living—precariously, she felt—in a shack where all seven of the children had been born.

"I said, 'Why don't we build a house using donated labor and materials?' " Mockbee recalls. "And we did: We built a house that was a little more than a thousand square feet for about $7,000. It had three bedrooms, a bathroom, a kitchen, and a loft space." At that point, Mockbee was working at an architecture firm that he had founded in 1977, and he and several colleagues worked on the house for eight months during the weekends. "Having had that experience, I knew that small projects like that were doable by ordinary people," Mockbee says. "It wasn't so complicated that a person of average intelligence couldn't build something. Just because you haven't done something before doesn't mean that you can't get it done. The main thing is, you've got to want to do it."

By then, Mockbee very much wanted to do it. He applied for a grant to build three more houses for needy families in Canton, but his proposal was turned down. Professionally, his life was full—he was working on an acoustics lab and on an observatory on the Ole Miss campus—but his desire to make his work more socially relevant was unfulfilled. In 1990, Mockbee visited an architecture program for American students in Genoa, Italy, that was sponsored by Clemson University. He was taken with the camaraderie of the students, and he found himself wondering whether such a program could exist in the South—a place whose rich history and whose sense of architecture, Mockbee felt, certainly rivaled Italy's. The following year, in 1991, Mockbee began teaching at Auburn. In 1993, he obtained a $250,000 grant from the Alabama Power Foundation and headed to Greensboro with 12 students in tow.

At first, Mockbee planned to stay only a year, in large part because of his family. "But once we did the first year, I realized that I had to stay the second," he says. "And then I realized that I had to see the thing through. The only way to be successful is to make sure you're successful, and you have to stay out on the fringes for that. You've got to leave your family and your home and go to war. You can't do it from your den at home." Along with being apart from his family, Mockbee has also made financial sacrifices. Until receiving the MacArthur fellowship, Mockbee says that he had "lived hand-to-mouth my entire professional life."

Designing Relationships

Once they were in place in Hale County, Mockbee and his students started small. They repaired trailer homes—particularly for families with children, for the elderly, and for the disabled—while they earned the trust of the locals and while they familiarized themselves with the community. "You can't just blow in," Mockbee says. "You don't have to be from here, but you do have to understand the community in which you're going to build. I'm not saying that I couldn't build a house in Spokane, Washington. I would love to do one there. But I probably could do a better one here, because I understand the people and the place."

From the Department of Human Resources in Hale County, Mockbee obtained names of families who were appropriate candidates for both smaller repairs and entire houses. "That office not only introduced us but also vouched for the legitimacy of what we were doing," Mockbee says. "There is a distrust that has to do with the culture of the South. You got a white man from Mississippi named Sambo walking in and saying, 'I want to build you a house. It's not going to cost you anything, and we're not trying to change you. We just want to help you out.' Well, you'd be apprehensive too!"

These days, the Rural Studio is established enough that some people actually come to Mockbee to request houses. (Many of those people, however, do not truly need the Rural Studio's help and are simply hoping for a freebie—though Mockbee generously observes, "I understand that. Hell, I want to build me something.") But persuading community members to work with the studio wasn't always as easy as it is now. One family that needed help was familiar to Mockbee by reputation—for rough behavior and for squalid living conditions. "I didn't want to deal with them," Mockbee says. "But the students wanted to meet everybody so they could pick the family they would work for. We drove down there in a couple of cars. I said, 'Y'all stay right here. I better go knock on this door myself.' So I did, and the man in the family was sitting on the porch. I told him who I was, and I said the social workers were worried about them and thought they'd benefit from us building them a house. He said, 'No, I don't think I'll take one of those today'—as if I was selling Amway."

Mockbee was challenged, rather than discouraged, by the man's lack of interest. "I said, 'Wait a minute, it won't cost you anything.' I wanted him to understand what he was turning down." The man didn't relent right then, but Mockbee had planted the idea, and he planned to return. Mockbee went back to the car, where the students were waiting. "We started driving and got about 100 yards down the road," he says. "Then I got out of the car and got all the students out and said, 'I'm going to tell you something. There is not an architecture agency on the planet that would build a house for that family. They're almost untouchables. If y'all pick them, you would really be doing something wonderful.' "

The students did pick that family, and, with just a bit more persuasion, the man agreed to let them build the house. "We started doing some designs, and we'd show them to him and his wife," Mockbee says. "He started coming around, and then it was like night and day. When we began building, he enjoyed it, she enjoyed it; he enjoyed watching the students and helping them. The chemistry between the students and the family all happened the way that I always hope it will and know it will."

Indeed, the relationships that develop between students and community members are perhaps the most remarkable aspect of the Rural Studio. The students, whom Mockbee has referred to as "my little baby chicks," are often quite sheltered. "They're bright, but they're young," Mockbee says. "They're right out of the mall, and all of a sudden they find themselves in Hale County, Alabama." That can mean, as it did one day last summer, that those students are laying concrete in 105-degree heat. Yet the students invariably rise to the challenge. "These affluent students are working their butts off in order to impress and win the respect of the poorest people in America," Mockbee says. "And the reason they want to win that respect is that there is a certain integrity, a certain honesty these families have. They're wonderful families."

The affection that the students develop for the families is reciprocal. Carlissia Bryant, 16, was in fourth grade when the students built a house for her grandparents, Alberta and Shepard Bryant, who are now in their 70s. At the time, the Bryants—including Carlissia and two of her siblings—were living in a shack with a leaky roof, no indoor plumbing, and no insulation. Alberta, whose legs had been amputated due to poor circulation, had difficulty getting around the dwelling in her wheelchair. Now the Bryants live in an 850-square-foot house with yellow columns, a long front porch, and easy wheelchair accessibility for Alberta.

When it was time for the students who had built the house to leave, Carlissia remembers, "We stood in the middle of the road to keep them from going. My grandmother cried. They told us they were going to come back and visit, and we said, 'Come back all the time.'"

Mockbee, too, finds that his life becomes pleasantly entangled with the lives of studio clients, including the Bryants. Besides his work as an architect, Mockbee is an artist who uses collage, watercolor, and oil paint. (An exhibit was on display at a gallery in New York this fall.) One haunting, somewhat abstract oil painting features Alberta Bryant in her wheelchair, as well as some pet turtles that she keeps in plastic tubs on her front porch. On a more prosaic level, Carlissia reports that Mockbee is fond of napping in a particular chair in the Bryants' living room. When he brings visitors by to see the house, Carlissia says, "he loves to get a little snooze in."

Jeff Johnston and Bruce Lanier, members of a five-person team of students that spent last year building a farmer's market in the nearby town of Thomaston, also became attached to the people they encountered. "Several members of the community came by and helped us out when we needed trailers or trucks," says Johnston, 23. "And they fed us. A guy named Packer was the first person to cook for us. He and his friend Pud brought a fish cooker out, fired it up, and fried catfish for us. We were sitting on the back of a truck, drinking beer and frying catfish."

Community members also opened up their homes to students—to a truly extraordinary degree. The night that Thomaston's mayor, Patsy Summeral, invited the students for dinner after a long, hot day of work, she offered them the chance to take showers before they ate. When he emerged from the bathroom, the 25-year-old Lanier remembers, "she had three sets of clothes laid out—three pairs of shorts here, three T-shirts here, and three pairs of tightie whities here. The tightie whities had come out of her husband's underwear drawer." Though Lanier appreciatively donned a T-shirt and a pair of shorts, he found himself unable to accept the full extent of Summeral's generosity. "I just can't wear someone else's underwear," he explains. "I had to go without that night."

When the market's construction was completed, Johnston and Lanier's work culminated with an opening celebration—including a parade and fireworks—on the Fourth of July. Hundreds of people turned out, and Johnston and Lanier found themselves leading the parade. "All the kids in town were there," Lanier says. "We had a bullhorn and were waving around the flag, and there was some guy driving a four-wheeler with three kids on it waving flags all over. There's only one block to the town, so we started at one end and went to the other end." The brevity of the experience did not detract from its thrill, according to Johnston. "They blocked off the street for us, and it was Alabama highway, so that was pretty cool," he says.

Steve Hoffman, 25, who finished his undergraduate work in the spring of 1997 and who now works at the studio as an instructor, was personally inspired by the work that he and his teammates did with community member Robert Wilson. Hoffman's team, with the help of Wilson himself, built a public pavilion on Wilson's land in the town of Akron, Alabama. "I've never met anyone like him," Hoffman says of Wilson, who is in his late sixties. "He left Akron to work on the railroad when he was 14 years old, and he went all over the United States following work. When he left, Akron had three hotels, the train was coming through and stopping, and there was commerce from the river. Now it's nothing. And his family's land, which was an active farm, is completely overgrown. Robert has had a real broad experience, he's worked hard, and now he's back—devoting himself to reclaiming his family's land. Every day, he's out there at five in the morning, clearing timber, making roads."

Working on the pavilion with Wilson, Hoffman says, "opened up for me the story of this place. And, on a personal level, I look up to him—his sense of hard work taught me a lot. And to see what he's accomplished with his own two hands is amazing. A person from my background is taught how to use your head, so my approach to things was completely different from his. For example, my thinking about concrete was, Where do we get the money to pay for the concrete that we're going to order and that will come in a truck? His thinking was, I know so-and-so who's got some sand, we can buy the cement at such-and-such amount per bag, we can get some gravel from this guy, and we'll just mix the whole thing ourselves."

Studio 24-7

Along with learning from the locals, students also learn from one another—and that learning occurs 24 hours a day, seven days a week. The turn-of-the-century farmhouse that is the studio's headquarters functions as a dorm, a lecture hall, and a cafeteria. "The kitchen is our classroom," Hoffman says. Behind the main building sit four additional housing structures nicknamed—in a nod to the movie *Invasion of the Body Snatchers*—"pods"; the pods are pure Mockbee, with one pod's exterior entirely composed of license plates arranged silver side out, like shingles. The yard is littered with basketballs, soccer balls, bikes, and, for trips on the nearby Black Warrior River, canoes.

"You eat, sleep, and breathe the studio," Hoffman says. "When you get a design critique, it may be over the breakfast table or it may be at 11 o'clock at night when we're teaching class. The schedule is hectic and flexible. We're lucky if we standardize the time for a class and stick to that time every week, because, with the process of construction, when it's not raining, you've got to be building. Or materials might not be available, so you switch things around."

The flexibility of the studio means that many of the best moments occur spontaneously. "If a friend of Sambo's visits, everybody pitches in to help cook dinner," Hoffman says. "We'll go outside, hang a sheet, and the visitor will give a slide show. Then we all will sit around the table, talk architecture, and have a nice meal. That's a social gathering, but it's also a classroom right there."

That such events occur on the fly does not mean Mockbee hasn't laid the groundwork for them. "The closer you can get students together, the healthier I think that is—knowing, of course, there are moments when you have to pull them apart and deal with each individual student," Mockbee says. "In academic settings in America today, you've got a classroom where you go in three times a week and teach for an hour. Then the students are gone, and most of them don't see each other again until they come back to class. That distance doesn't lend itself to discussions and feedback among them. Plus, the students' social development is important. It's important for them to live and eat with a professor so they can see what kind of disposition the professor has and how he handles situations, not just in the classroom but in a social environment as well. In the past, when we've been dealing with a bigot, for example, how to deal with that has become a discussion that everybody wants to participate in and wants to see how it resolves itself. We could talk about something like that in the classroom all day long, but when it really happens, it's a whole different experience."

The same line of thinking is at the heart of Mockbee's approach to teaching architecture. The academic treatment of architecture is notoriously theoretical—so much so that a student can earn a degree yet hardly know how to nail two boards together. To Mockbee, that method of study is absurdly impractical. "Out here, the students have to make decisions and have to live with them," Mockbee says. "It takes a few weeks before they realize that if it's going to happen, they've got to get up and make it happen."

The task of deciding which families to build for—and of building the actual houses—belongs to the students, Mockbee says. "If they dig a foundation ditch for a wall, they do a detail showing how much steel will go in there. Then they have to decide what kind of steel they're going to throw in there, what size steel rebars. They look at us, and we look back at them. I'm not going to tell them; they've got to figure it out for themselves. You put them into responsible positions, and all of a sudden they realize that they have the authority to make those decisions. That's what the program is about. Once they start dealing with practical issues, they take ownership of the project." Though Mockbee always intervenes when he believes that students are doing something truly wrong, he acknowledges that they will make mistakes nonetheless—and he isn't worried. "Every architect makes mistakes," he says. "Frank Lloyd Wright made them. Michelangelo made them. Rural Studio students are going to make them, and they will be in good company."

As for the houses themselves, Mockbee is aware that there are those who might accuse him of a subtle kind of exploitation. The families, one could argue, aren't exactly in a position to turn down the studio's offer of a house—even if the design seems bizarre or unappealing to them. Mockbee rejects this notion. "Some people might say we're aestheticizing poverty," Mockbee says. "I say, Come on down here and spend a week with us—and then say that. The clients are not guinea pigs. We do the preliminaries, we show them a model and drawings, we talk about the materials we'll use. We make sure that they understand everything we're planning, so that if they're uncomfortable with something, they can tell us."

Indeed, for the Bryants' house, students initially wanted to make it two stories, but Shepard Bryant nixed the idea, saying that he was too old to be walking up and down a staircase. Similarly, last summer's students had planned to build a bus stop—but then, after talking to people and learning that the children waited inside for the bus and didn't need a bus stop, they decided instead to make a basketball court. Once the client and the students reach an agreement, however, Mockbee will not apologize for innovation. "We are architects, and we're going to push the envelope," he says. "We're not going to be sentimental or conventional. We're moving ahead."

Nor will Mockbee apologize for the pace at which the houses are built—currently, about one per year. The Rural Studio does not aspire to be Habitat for Humanity, which has built tens of thousands of basic, affordable houses. By contrast, the studio is focused on building houses that have, as Mockbee calls it, a soul. Along with a house for the Bryants, students also built a smokehouse where Shepard Bryant could keep fish and game. The exterior is made of broken-up concrete curbing, with multicolored glass bottles embedded in the walls. The bottles are not there because they are necessary, or even remotely practical, but because they look lovely when the light shines through them.

Mockbee is teaching his students about the things that matter to him. After all, he is a teacher and the Rural Studio is, at its essence, an academic program. "All those houses are homework assignments," Mockbee says. "The students turn in their homework, and I'll be damned, it's a damn house—and a good one too."

THE LAST WORD

Thank you for publicizing the wonderful effort Mockbee and Co. have put into not only enriching society, but the lives of the students that are involved. I was once part of the architecture program at Auburn, so I am familiar with the hands-off approach they use. It's personally challenging, but it was one of the greatest experiences I have ever had. I was a student at Auburn when Auburn implemented the Rural Studies program. I was always impressed by it myself, but am glad that a publication such as FC *has given it the recognition it deserves.*

Jennifer Shannon
Via the Internet

"But Wait, You Promised . . ."
". . . And You Believed Us?
Welcome to the Real World, Ma'am"

From: Issue 45 | April 2001 | By: Charles Fishman

Customer service in the twenty-first century is abysmal. Who among us doesn't have an epic tale (or 10) of inept (or worse) customer service? Particularly when we pick up the phone and try to resolve a problem. Charles Fishman set out to answer the unspoken question: why? His travels are hilarious, chilling, and enlightening, and his discoveries reveal why we're in the mess that we're in and offer a path out. Tragically, things have only gotten worse since this article first appeared, with the explosion in offshore call centers as well as automated systems seemingly designed to do everything possible to prevent a customer from speaking to a human being. Too bad, because the answer to one of the most pressing business queries of our age—how do you delight customers?—is so easy, if only companies would embrace it.

I am in the belly of the beast. I have risen early, traveled far, and overcome lines, rudeness, and indifference. Now, heedless of my chances of coming back without serious psychological or physical injury, I am journeying into a swamp that has become a source of boundless irritation, frustration, confusion—even fury—for tens of millions of Americans. I open the door and step into a customer-service call center. And not just any call center either—one that is exclusively devoted to handling problems with cell phones. It's cool inside and fairly well lit, for a swamp.

I am carrying the very tool itself: a Sprint PCS cell phone. I love my

Sprint PCS cell phone. But God help me when I have to call Sprint PCS. I have sometimes called this very building in Fort Worth, Texas. Often, I'm not even sure that the customer-care advocate I finally speak with after I've been waiting on hold for 17 minutes even knows what a cell phone is.

I have come here at the beginning of a long journey—really, a quest of the sort that was common in antiquity—during which I will cross the continent several times and seek out both oracles and common folk. I am determined to unravel a central mystery of life in modern America: Why is customer service so terrible?

At the Sprint PCS call center, I am soon teamed up with customer-care advocate Chad Ehrlich, a gracious 29-year-old with years of experience delivering service by phone. Chad takes a call from a businessman in Lubbock, Texas. The man is upset about his bill: It was running $60 to $100 a month. Suddenly, it has shot up to $1,600. "I'm not going to pay it!" the man declares.

Chad is reserved. "Let me take a look at that bill," he says. Chad whirls through screens of information. "Hold on a moment for me, sir, I'm going to get a representative from the fraud department on the line." Chad puts Lubbock on hold and dials Sprint PCS's fraud department, where he reaches a familiar recorded message and is put on hold. Lubbock is on hold for customer-service rep Chad, and customer-service rep Chad is on hold for more customer service.

A female fraud rep takes Chad's call. She can see from Lubbock's history that he's complained about this problem before. The conversation between Chad and his colleague in fraud is frisky.

FRAUD: "He thought he was cloned, but he wasn't."

CHAD: "His bills did go from almost nothing to sky-high. . . ."

FRAUD: "We can send him to a cloning specialist and make it 'official' if you want. . . ."

CHAD: "He's denying that he made or received the calls."

The impatient woman from fraud dials the Sprint PCS cloning customer-care department and . . . is put on hold.

Do you ever wonder what's going on while you're waiting on hold for customer service? Really, you couldn't even imagine.

Chad, Lubbock's customer-care advocate, is talking to a woman who is Chad's customer-care advocate. She has called her customer-care advocate, who is busy on another call. So now we have two customer-care advocates on hold waiting for a third customer-care advocate. Meanwhile, a fuming customer from Lubbock (who may or may not be trying to rip Sprint off for $1,600) waits. On hold.

That, right there, is customer service in the new economy. It has become a slow, dissatisfying tangle of telephones, computers, Web sites, e-mail, and people that wastes time at a prodigious rate, produces far more aggravation than service, and, most often, leaves you feeling impotent. What's even worse is that this situation is a kind of betrayal. It wasn't supposed to be this way. One of the promises of the new economy was that the customer would finally be in charge. We weren't supposed to need to call customer care— but if we did, then someone would take our call quickly. (Why not? No one else would be calling.) A customer-service rep would understand our problem practically before we mentioned it, and all would be made right. Everyone believes in delighting the customer.

Don't you spend most of your day delighted? Here's a puzzler. Why do we hear this sentence so often: "We are experiencing higher-than-usual call volumes . . ."? If you're experiencing higher-than-usual call volumes, then why aren't you experiencing higher-than-usual *staffing* volumes? How hard is *that*? What the new economy has done to customer service is exactly the opposite of what everyone predicted would happen. And as chaotic a time as it has been to be a customer, it has been a truly weird time to be delivering customer service. Consider just one example: Five years ago, discount broker Charles Schwab had 1,450 customer-service reps in call centers, and 85% of those reps' time was spent providing real-time quotes and basic company information, and executing trades. Those 1,450 people, sensing the Internet roaring down on them, were worried about their jobs. Rightfully so. At the end of this past year, Charles Schwab's customers did 81% of all of those activities without human assistance. So you would imagine that Schwab could have trimmed its costly battalion of customer-service reps to 1,000, even to 500.

In fact, the number of Schwab reps has tripled to 4,800. But they're not doing what they used to do. Customers have demanded new vistas of service. No one was more surprised than Schwab.

In short, the new economy was supposed to make service better, quicker, and more effective for customers—and easier and cheaper for companies. None of that has come to pass. What happened? I went on a journey to find out.

Bold Promises, Bad Results

AT&T is running television commercials for its Worldnet Internet service. One ad features a series of stand-up comics who are making jokes about the bad customer service of their Internet providers ("My online service is like my husband: I stare at it for hours, hoping it will move").

Cisco is running a TV commercial that opens with a regular guy on a cordless phone who hears, "Your call will be answered by the next available operator." Halfway through the commercial, the man has fallen asleep, phone to his ear.

Mockery is a great cultural barometer. Bad customer service is one of the universal—and unifying—experiences of being an American in the 21st century. You get it at Wal-Mart. You get it at Lord & Taylor. But is customer service really worse than it used to be? A panel of customer-service experts that I assembled couldn't agree.

Don Peppers, 50, of the Peppers and Rogers Group, proponent of "customer-relationship management" and coauthor of the famous *One to One Future*: "I don't think that customer service sucks. I think it's bad. But I think it's better than it was five years ago."

Len Schlesinger, 48, an expert in customer service, previously senior associate dean and a professor at Harvard Business School, and now executive vice president of The Limited Inc.: "Let's see, we've gone from 'meeting customer expectations,' to 'exceeding customer expectations,' to 'delighting customers,' to 'customer ecstasy.' I hate to see what comes next."

Patricia Seybold, 51, CEO of an e-business consulting company and author of the optimistic book *The Customer Revolution: How to Thrive When Customers Are in Control*, which is due out this month: "I agree that customer service hasn't gotten better since the Internet came along. It has gotten worse. But companies are beginning to realize that we're very angry at them. Companies that don't wake up and pay attention to this are going to be out of business."

Well, we can only hope.

Customer service is a notoriously slippery concept—hard to define, apparently impossible to quantify. But there is one guy who knows for sure what's happening to customer service, because he measures it in 65,000 interviews a year with American customers.

Claes Fornell, 53, is a professor at the University of Michigan Business School and an expert on "the economics of customer satisfaction." Fornell is creator and director of the American Customer Satisfaction Index. The ACSI measures how content Americans are with the goods and services that they consume—in the aggregate, and industry by industry, company by company.

Fornell names names! His online data is a carnival for cranky consumers: You can click through and take glee in the lame scores of all of the companies that you love to hate.

First Union, my bank, is down 10.5% in satisfaction ratings since the index started in 1994.

Wal-Mart, my source for diapers, paper towels, and Tide, is down 10% since the index started and down 4% in just the past year alone.

Fornell conceived this herculean undertaking—scores are measured quarterly—because he thought that the U.S. economy was being severely mismeasured. "Eighty percent of GDP is service now," he says. "We have to behave as though we live in a service economy."

The ACSI measures the perceived quality of U.S. economic output—the experience of being a consumer in the United States. In the past five years, the ACSI is down from 73.7 to 72.9. But that number includes everything from Whirlpool appliances to the experience of shopping on Amazon.com.

Here's the amazing thing: Every measured company in the appliance, beer, car, clothing, food, personal-care, shoe, and soft-drink industries is above the national average. Even the cigarette companies have above-average customer-satisfaction ratings.

Not so for airlines, banks, department stores, fast-food outlets, hospitals, hotels, and phone companies.

It's the service that's bad.

"Oh, I think we can say that for sure," says Fornell.

The Hard Truth(s) About Customer Service

I didn't begin my journey through the service jungle at Sprint PCS by accident, or because I think that the company would be a good target for mockery. Sprint PCS is a pure new-economy company. It offers nothing but service—and it's digital wireless service to boot. The company's only product is moving voices through the air. The first time that you could have made a Sprint PCS call was December 1996. From a standing start, in four years, the company has grown to 28,328 employees (10,000 in customer care), 9.8 million customers, and annual revenues of roughly $6 billion. Sprint PCS signs up 10,000 new customers each day.

The company has access to every conceivable technological helper: the Net, automated phone services, and the most-sophisticated call centers. And yet, my own experience dealing with Sprint PCS has been consistently aggravating. In eight years of having BellSouth provide our home phone service, I've only had occasion to talk to them three or four times. I've talked to Sprint PCS more than that since Halloween—always with unhappy results.

Sprint PCS knows the right thing to do. It just can't do it. Faerie Kizzire, 51, senior vice president for Sprint PCS, is in charge of customer service for the company. She's a veteran: She spent nine years at Sprint managing customer service for the long-distance business, then managed customer service for a health-insurance company, and was wooed back to Sprint to create customer care for wireless.

I tell her the story of a call I have just listened to with Chad: Marlene in Ohio has had to call three times just to get a credit for charges that shouldn't have been on her bill in the first place. Before Chad, two customer-care advocates dealt with Marlene by simply telling her that she was wrong. As Chad discovers, Marlene was in fact improperly charged. So why did that happen? Why did two customer-service reps argue with Marlene, rather than credit her? Why does Marlene know more about her calling plan than customer care does?

Kizzire is disappointed. "The complexity of the product and the variations in the product can make that kind of problem very difficult," she says. "We do see some of our people falling on the side of 'I'm right' versus 'I'm going to make it right.'"

Sprint PCS looks as if it's doing all of the right things. The company's training program for reps is 6 to 10 weeks long. Across the call center are exhortations to good service: "Did you dazzle your customers today?" Says Kizzire: "It is true that people who have a little bit of knowledge can be dangerous. We always say, Don't try to dazzle the customer with what you know. These days, many customers have years of experience."

And therein lies a clue to what's really happening to customer service—and why. The secret about customer service in the new economy isn't that it's bad—everyone knows it's bad. The secret is that it's harder to deliver good customer service than ever before. Why? Technology, especially in its early days, is always hard. No surprise there. Why would we expect companies that can't figure out how to run a phone center—talking to real people about problems in their own business—to be really good at using advanced technology to automate the process of taking care of us?

And customers are more demanding. We want good service, quickly. We don't wait at gas pumps, we're antsy in ATM lines, and we pay to FedEx things to avoid standing in line at the post office. Companies have created, nursed, and benefited from this impatience. We are victims of it in our own lives. They are victims of it too. It makes providing customer service brutally unforgiving.

Technology has, in fact, made some things quicker and easier, and it has allowed us to take care of ourselves. I can plunge through the details of my online bank statement more thoroughly in 50 seconds than any automated voice-mail system could permit in 50 minutes, or than even the most patient phone operator would tolerate. This means that when we talk to someone in person, either things are really screwed up, or we are really angry and want to share that anger with a person. Or both. Technology has made the actual person-to-person customer service of big companies much more complicated and demanding.

Despite all of the consultants, gurus, and outsource providers, customer service is hard to deliver in a mass economy. I wasn't on the phones at Sprint PCS for more than a couple of hours, and I can see that the real problem isn't customer service or even culture. No, the real problem is more fundamental: Sprint PCS offers a simple service that is really very complicated. Best tip-off? It takes someone 15 minutes to sell me a phone and a calling plan in a Sprint PCS store. It takes Faerie Kizzire 6 weeks—240 hours—to teach a phone rep to handle any problems that I might have with that phone.

Some Good News: What's the 411?

My favorite example of new-economy meltdown is directory assistance. Directory assistance should be the perfect new-economy product: It's just information—and simple information at that. There is an existing way to bill customers, and, given the swift accumulation of databases, directory assistance should be getting better and better all the time.

"It's gotten so much worse," says customer-service expert Patricia Seybold. "Now you get the wrong number all the time."

I've kept track during the past two months. Over several dozen calls, directory assistance delivered the wrong number about half of the time. Of course, you get charged for the wrong numbers, just as you do for the right numbers. If it's a long-distance number and it's wrong, you pay for that phone call too. As if that weren't enough, here's a moment of customer delight: Call directory assistance and try to get a credit for a wrong number.

"I'm sorry, sir," says the abrupt operator. "We don't give credits."

"I beg your pardon?"

"We don't give credits, sir. You have to call your local phone company. When your phone bill comes."

"At the end of the month?"

"Correct, sir. Is there a number you need?"

So now I've paid once for the wrong number and paid again to be told that I have to call some other company, some other time, to get my $2 back.

Yet one company gives delightful directory assistance—polite, accurate, helpful. It is none other than . . . Sprint PCS. The contrast between cellular directory and land-line directory is as dramatic as the contrast between Sprint PCS directory and Sprint PCS customer care. Ask Sprint PCS for a restaurant's number, and they offer to make a reservation. Ask for the number of a movie theater, and they offer to read you not just the number but also the movies that are playing at that theater, when they are playing, and who is starring in each movie.

Seybold was able to guess exactly what was going on immediately. "It's outsourced," she said.

And so it is. Metro One Telecommunications, a small company based in Beaverton, Oregon, handles directory assistance for Sprint PCS—and also for Nextel and many regional cellular companies. The quality of Metro One's service is no accident. As Seybold predicted, that is exactly what it is selling to cellular companies: good directory assistance.

The economics are great for everyone: Even at what feels like an unhurried pace, Metro One's operators take 50 calls an hour (including breaks, slow periods, and training), which brings in $50 an hour. Half of that goes to Metro One, half is gravy to Sprint PCS. Of the $25 an hour that Metro One gets, operators start at some centers at $9 an hour in straight salary—before incentive pay or benefits. Me, as a customer? I get the right number, for about what BellSouth's wrong numbers cost me.

Metro One has 29 deliberately small call centers: 200 operators or fewer, with 100 or fewer working at any one time. The call center in Charlotte, North Carolina, is lean—spartan compared to Sprint PCS's Fort Worth center. But you can understand the entire place in a single glance. Directory assistance, of course, is child's play compared to helping people with their cell phones. But remember: Standard directory assistance is abysmal.

Heather McCuen, 23, started at Metro One in March 1999, and after nine months, she makes $12 an hour. Calls cascade in on her like a waterfall. "Leith Mercedes." "Larry's Plant Farm." "Start-to-Finish Tattoo Shop." "Just What the Doctor Ordered Restaurant."

"I'm amazed at what people name their businesses," Heather says.

In 11 minutes, she takes 17 calls—38.8 seconds a call. Heather's style is efficient but deliberate. She reads the number slowly to avoid having to repeat it.

What is striking is how little it takes to make people happy, how little it takes to get it right, and how long 40 seconds really is. But what is also striking is how hard it would be to automate this process. To do it right doesn't require much, but it does require a spark of human intelligence on both ends of the transaction.

Even in these brief encounters, the full range of human character is on display. "I'm looking for Shannon Pickering," says a man over a characteristically crackly connection. The Charlotte center serves mainly North Carolina and South Carolina, so the operators are familiar with local geography, but Heather and her colleagues can provide numbers nationwide. Heather patiently searches a couple of the towns that the man mentions, without luck.

"I found someone's day planner in the middle of the road," the man says. "I'm just trying to return it to her." Heather ups her intensity a notch. She broadens her search to all of North Carolina, South Carolina, and Virginia. She tries a variety of spellings for the names. Heather tells the man what she is trying. She is regretful. The man is regretful. The call spills past two minutes. No luck.

Metro One's databases are updated with fresh numbers in real time, all the time. Operators can send along complaints about wrong numbers. All kinds of searches are available. I saw one operator find a particularly elusive residential number by reading through a list of every person who lived on a street.

The Baby Bells shoot for directory calls lasting 17 to 20 seconds, total, compared to Metro One's 33-second standard. That, of course, is the difference. And as trivial as it may sound—what's 15 seconds?—companies know how to do the multiplication. At least, they know how to do it when it's their 15 seconds.

Metro One's Charlotte center handles roughly 275,000 calls a week. The math is easy. If each call lasts 33 seconds, as it does at Metro One, then 275,000 calls require 2,520 hours of operator time. If each call lasts 20 seconds, as it does at BellSouth, then 275,000 calls require only 1,528 hours of operator time.

It takes 50% more people to do it the Metro One way. To do it right.

Secrets of the Amazon: Customer Service as R&D

For all of its struggles—with its balance sheet, its stock, the union drive, and layoffs—Amazon.com has done one thing brilliantly: customer service. I placed my first order with Amazon in 1997 and have been a steady customer since. In four years of making purchases for myself and for others, I've found what I needed, ordered it, received a flurry of e-mails about my orders, and then gotten either thank-you notes or what I ordered. I've never had to contact Amazon about any matter. I have had, in essence, no customer service from Amazon. Put another way, I have had such perfect customer service, the service itself has been transparent. That is exactly what Amazon wants. The goal is perfect customer service through no customer service.

In a very short time, Amazon has set a new standard for customer service, and I went to Seattle to see how. What I discovered is a place that regards customer service as an R&D lab—a way not to help customers, but to help the company.

"We want to make it easier and easier for our customers to do business with us," says Bill Price, 50, vice president of global customer service for Amazon. "We want to have everything go so right, you never have to contact us. To do that, we have to stay tuned up. We have to keep asking, What are the problems?"

Of course, every customer-service VP in America, every customer-service VP in history, would agree with those sentiments. Two things make all the difference at Amazon: the view the company takes of customer service and customers, and the way the company is organized to drive home that view.

Amazon doesn't consider customer service to be the complaint department, or even the quality-control and customer-satisfaction department. Amazon considers Bill Price's outfit to be a research lab for discovering how to adjust and improve customer service. And Amazon considers customer service to be its core business. The company really offers nothing *but* customer service.

So every single encounter with a customer—by phone, by e-mail, even by clicking on Web pages—is considered to be the source of potentially vital information about the course of the entire company.

How does that work?

Well, to start with, the company tracks the reason for every customer contact. It keeps a list of the top-ten reasons why customers contact the company—monitoring the list daily, weekly, monthly—and it is constantly working on ways to eliminate those reasons. For years, the number-one question that people asked Amazon was, Where's my stuff? Now, on every page, starting with the welcome page, there's a box labeled, "Where's my stuff?"

Amazon's operations are so interwoven with customer-driven changes that employees are briefly baffled when you ask for examples.

"Two years ago," says Price, "one common problem was, 'I want to buy five books, and ship them to my five brothers, each at a separate address.' Our system was originally set up so that one order had to go to one address, forcing the customer, in a case like that, to place five separate orders. Now we have a 'ship-to-multiple-addresses' function. And you don't need to get in touch with us to figure it out."

Shortly after its consumer-electronics store debuted, Amazon was deluged with requests for a simple chart that would compare the features and prices of similar products, such as MP3 players and digital cameras. As a result, Amazon has developed a product-by-product "comparison engine" that does exactly that.

Just last year, a customer sent an e-mail pointing out something that had bugged him for years: On the main ordering page, customers are instructed to enter their e-mail address and their Amazon password. Next come two options: "Forgot your password? Click here" and "Sign in using our secure server."

Originally, the options were in that order. If someone simply tabbed from option to option, he would click, "Forgot your password?"—even when what he wanted to do was sign in. Because of that single, irritated e-mail, the ordering page was changed.

Again, though, the head of customer service at any big company could tick off customer suggestions that have drifted up and changed products and operations.

But at Amazon, the notion of customer service as R&D isn't a slogan, it's a structure—an unavoidable force to be reckoned with. Price's division includes a group that does nothing but analyze and anticipate problems and cook up solutions. Indeed, representatives from customer-service project management sit on all launch teams as "the voice of the customer."

The ethic cuts deeper than it would first appear. "You can have a great overall culture," says Price, "with real empathy for the customer and passion for fixing the problems. You can have individual reps who say, 'This customer is *really* upset, and I have to deal with it.' I think we do that.

"What's missing almost everywhere else is, even if you have the empathy and the passion and you address the customer's problem, you haven't really given good customer service in total. You haven't done that until you have eliminated the problem that caused her to call in the first place." Exactly.

It is, frankly, easy to be skeptical of all of this. For such a strategy to work, the entire company has to bend to it. One incident (of many that I encountered) shows how deeply ingrained the attitude is.

The problem materialized during the 1999 Christmas season, the first Christmas that Amazon sold toys. Almost as soon as the selling season began, the company received complaints that were notable more for the level of outrage than for the actual number of problems.

Some toys were big enough to be shipped in their original packing boxes. "They were arriving on people's doorsteps, and the people called and said, 'Hey, we weren't expecting this to look like a Big Wheel. My kid came home from school and found his present! Now I gotta buy another one!'" says Janet Savage, 31, who was a customer-service manager that Christmas. This quickly became known as the Big Wheel problem, and it was Savage's job to resolve it.

It was an interesting moment. One possible response—a perfectly reasonable response—would be to start warning customers about items shipped in original cartons. After all, if you buy something at Toys 'R' Us, you don't complain that it comes wrapped as what it is.

That response was never considered at Amazon. Savage simply started looking for durable, inexpensive wrapping material that would be available immediately and in large quantities. "Our customers were not happy," says Savage. "It was not acceptable to tell parents, Oh well, too bad."

She found rolls of plastic material like the type used in big garbage bags, and Amazon started overwrapping every large toy and a selection of electronics items that were likely to be Christmas gifts. How urgent was it? "I bugged people about it on an hourly basis until we got it resolved," says Savage. "You're either Santa Claus or you're not."

Great Service: Back to the Future

I have a running argument with customer-service experts that may be mostly an argument on my side. It is neatly summed up by *One to One* guru Don Peppers. He offers two key points about service. First, "Service is bad because it's hard to do." Second, "The secret to good service, really, is to treat your customer like you'd like to be treated yourself." Somewhere between point one and point two, I missed the hard part.

The hard part is not the service. The hard part is everything but the service. The hard part is how companies think about what they are doing and how they behave as a result. Why is the service of airlines so bad? Simple: Airlines don't think of themselves as service organizations. Airlines think of themselves as factories that manufacture revenue-seat miles. Airlines have been tuned in to the efficiency of their manufacturing operations, not to the quality of the journey that they provide.

When you spend weeks talking to people about customer service, when you visit people who do it as their livelihood, it is easy to become consumed with the challenges, the technology, and the measurements that obsess the world of customer service.

How much cheaper is it to deliver balances by automated phone menu than through a service rep? How much cheaper is it to deliver balances on the Web than over the telephone? What do people want to talk to a person about? What do they want to do themselves?

How do you create customer satisfaction, customer delight, and customer ecstasy? Most of those questions miss the larger point.

Dan Leemon, 47, chief strategy officer for Charles Schwab, understands this dilemma clearly. Charles Schwab is a brokerage firm, of course. It keeps money for people, has custody of stock certificates, and functions as a bank in many ways. But like Sprint PCS or directory assistance, Schwab is really a pure customer-service organization. Its specialty is financial-services customer service—but it's service all the same. Everything else is record keeping.

"A lot of companies fall into the trap," says Leemon, "of believing that some new customer-service technology will take cost and management burden away and will eliminate the need to have very talented people on the phones and in their retail outlets.

"That has actually never been true," he says. Indeed, the complex demands of customers have increased the length of the typical call to Schwab by 75% during the past five years.

One old-economy sector that is justifiably famous for service is the cruise industry. The high-end cruise lines achieve this by offering training, incentives, and quality facilities. One thing that they do particularly well is suck up customer feedback.

Royal Caribbean Cruise Lines (RCCL), for instance, has 22 ships. When a ship docks at home port at 7 A.M., before it clears customs, someone from RCCL has boarded to retrieve the customer-comment cards distributed to every cabin. The ratings are tabulated, the written comments are transcribed, and the results are returned to the ship's managers before the ship sails again at 5 P.M.

So before the next cruise begins, RCCL's captains, dining-room managers, housekeepers, and entertainers know how the previous cruise went—from praise to serious problems. Imagine what flying the big airlines would be like if you got a comment card at the end of each flight—and the company acted on what it learned.

THE LAST WORD

Why does this sorry state of affairs exist in the first place? Part of the answer is that consolidation has eliminated competition in many industries. If you don't like the service on the United Airlines non-stop from San Francisco to San Diego, well, that's just tough—it's the only nonstop service available on that route.

Meanwhile, where competition does exist, so does decent customer service. For example, Amazon.com competes with scores of online and brick-and-mortar bookstores, so it works hard to provide a great customer experience. Until we take seriously the task of maintaining competition, customer service will probably get worse, not better.

Jeffrey Pfeffer
Thomas D. Dee Professor of Organizational Behavior
Stanford University
Palo Alto, California

Grassroots Leadership:
U.S. Military Academy

From: Issue 47 | June 2001 | By: Keith H. Hammonds

This is the second article in this collection that finds leadership lessons in the world of the military (see also "The Agenda—Grassroots Leadership"). Both happen to spotlight "grassroots leadership" in their titles, yet the articles are very different. Rather than consider one person and how he runs his ship, Keith H. Hammonds analyzes how the U.S. Military Academy, better known as West Point, consistently trains young men and women to lead. Along the way, we meet notable leaders from the world of business whose West Point educations deepen our understanding of how these skills translate to civilian life. This story helps us appreciate what our soldiers know and how they conduct themselves in a time of war, and it's a peek into the future of leadership in this country. The young officers fighting terrorism today will be fighting the competition tomorrow.

"Attention all cadets: There are five minutes to assembly for lunchtime formation. The uniform is battle dress under field jacket." It's 11:55 A.M. It's really cold. About 200 feet above a bend in the Hudson River, the wind rushes across the plain at West Point and slams into the six-story granite ramparts of the United States Military Academy.

This is a massive, fortlike place screaming of history. A statue of General George Washington commands the Parade Ground, flanked by Eisenhower, MacArthur, and Thayer. The stone barracks, square and stark, bear the names of Bradley, Lee, and Pershing.

"There are four minutes to assembly for lunchtime formation." Inside, cadet "plebes," or freshmen, stand at attention, counting off the minutes until the mandatory premeal convocation. Their cues come from clocks mounted every 50 feet or so along the halls.

Students tumble into the sprawling asphalt courtyards between barracks, as they do at least twice each day, every day, year-round. "Fall in!" The command is like an ionizing charge, driving loose bunches into perfect lines and squares—each square a platoon, four platoons to a company, four companies to a battalion, and two battalions to a regiment. "Attention!" Eyes shoot straight ahead.

Formation is a defining experience at West Point. Officially, it is a simple exercise in accountability: From platoon on up, officers must know and report how many cadets are present. But there's more to it, of course. Formation is a nod to the past. Cadets have gathered in this way, on this spot, every day for nearly 200 years. More important, it is a reminder of the primacy of selflessness: Here, the individual yields to the greater whole—to the corps.

On dismissal, the cadets begin marching. The movement looks choreographed—a dozen drab soldier streams flowing in right angles out of the courtyard. In minutes, it's over. A few thousand cadets have removed themselves. The courtyard is silent. And you think, That was one seriously weird exercise. A weird and beautiful thing.

That pretty much describes the whole place.

Leadership Lessons (I)

"The first lesson I learned as a plebe came from an upperclassman yelling in my face. He told me that there were four acceptable answers: 'Yes, sir'; 'No, sir'; 'No excuse, sir'; and 'Sir, I do not understand.' He'd ask, 'Why aren't your shoes shined?' and I'd say, 'Well, it was muddy, and I didn't have time.' He'd be all over me. He was trying to teach me something: If you have to take men up a hill and write letters to their moms that night, there's literally no excuse. If you have to lay off thousands of people from your company, there's no excuse. You should have seen it coming and done something about it."

—James Kimsey, '62, founding CEO, America Online

The "West Point of Leadership"

Each spring, West Point graduates 900-odd men and women, granting each of them a bachelor's degree and a commission as second lieutenant in the U.S. Army. After six-week leaves, they travel to places like Kosovo, Germany, and Guam. Once there, they take on their first jobs as military officers.

This fact alone is stunning: As a nation, we are entrusting to 21-year-olds the safety of our enlisted troops, not to mention the care and deployment of weapons of mass destruction, the keeping of peace, and the occasional waging of war. The corresponding fact is this: By the time they leave West Point, most of these kids are unquestionably up to the job. From the day that they set foot on campus (in early July, before their freshman year), cadets are prepared to take on responsibility, to face challenges, to make decisions under stress, and to pursue the goals set out for them—relentlessly.

The U.S. Military Academy is a factory, and what it manufactures is leaders. Over the years, it has become probably the most effective institution for leadership development in the country. If Harvard Business School is "the West Point of capitalism," well, when it comes to leadership, West Point is the real thing.

Of course, this leadership factory supplies the military. In return for a free college education, graduates are required to serve the U.S. Army for at least five years. After that, however, many spin out into areas like government, education, and, most often, business—where they thrive. "You see them everywhere," says Geoff Champion, a 1972 graduate and a partner at Korn/Ferry. They sit atop Amazon.com, America Online, Commerce One, SciQuest, and many other successful companies.

Why? Understand this about West Point: Everything that we have read and heard about it—the rules, the structure, the rigidity, the conformity—is essentially true. This is a school where students learn, in one class, that "the mortar is your best friend."

But understand this too: There's more to the story. The academy's complex and arcane education hangs on an intriguing tension. Think of it, as West Point's own leaders do, in terms of Athens and Sparta. The structure, the monotonous regime, the rote memorization—that's Sparta, and it's important. Yet West Point also nurtures creativity and flexibility—the Athens.

In the chaos of battle, as in business, leaders can't expect to stick to a fixed plan. They depend on the predictable competence of their subordinates (instilled by all of that training) as well as on their own judgment. Military officers are given orders, but how they get the job done is up to them. "Everything that happens at West Point serves a question," says Ed Ruggero, a 1980 graduate and the author of *Duty First: West Point and the Making of American Leaders* (HarperCollins, 2001): "How do you develop an organization that can thrive amid constant change?"

"This is a unique world, where everyone is trying to develop you," says David Sattelmeyer, a senior, or "firstie," and a battalion commander, one of the highest-ranking cadet positions. "You're constantly watching others to see what works. And people are constantly looking at you. The place keeps pushing you." Everyone is following, and nearly everyone is leading, all the time. Everyone is evaluated—all the time. Every action is taken as an opportunity to learn.

Leadership Lessons (II)

"I had a former roommate who committed an honor-code violation. When he told me what he'd done, I didn't bat an eye. I reported him. Not because I didn't care about him; I cared deeply. But I knew that the principle was more important than his being given a second chance. I was 18, and I realized that my first responsibility was to the principle of honor."

—John Grisillo, '87, president, Compass Group

The Leadership Formula: Knowing, Doing, Being

"People say you can't change someone," says Lieutenant Colonel Scott Snook, "but we're privileged here. We have some of the best and brightest potential in this country, and we have them for 47 months, 24-7. We got 'em at night, on weekends, all summer long."

He is not boasting, exactly. He is marveling at the opportunity. "We have them when they're 18, which is a crucial moment," says Snook, who graduated from West Point in 1980. "They're ripe for change. Not only do we have them, but we're also *empowered* to change them. The country asks us to change who they are!"

Back in rural Pennsylvania, where he grew up, Snook wanted to be a doctor. To his own surprise, he has stuck with the Army for 21 years since his cadet days. He was the executive officer of a company in Grenada, where he was wounded by friendly fire. He earned an MBA and a PhD in organizational behavior at Harvard, where he returns regularly to teach in executive programs.

Snook now heads West Point's Office of Policy, Planning, and Analysis. His mandate is to confront the academy's well-worn apparatus for leadership development and to seek a scientific basis for a system that's rooted in experience and inertia: Why are things done the way they are? What works? *How* does it work? Could it work better?

The first Army leadership manual, written 25 years ago, coined the expression "Be, know, do." It was a neat summation of how effective leaders operate, but it also pointed to the central challenge of leadership development. The capacity for "knowing" and "doing" is relatively easy to build up in a student. It's a function of education and training, which is what most universities are good at.

But knowledge and skills are perishable—both because they're not applied all the time and because they can become outdated. It's the "be" piece—your self-concept, your values, your ethical makeup, *who you are*—that lasts. That's what consumes Snook: What does it mean to be an officer? And how can West Point shape the "be" piece for each of its 4,000 cadets?

Snook really loves this stuff. West Point has devised a mechanism, perhaps unwittingly, that forces 18-year-olds to grow up. Cadets advance by confronting moral ambiguity, by resolving competing claims on their identity. That's how you get at the "be" piece. "We don't know if we have it right," Snook says. "But it happens through experiences, if you're passionately involved. And bottom line, the sorts of experiences that change you are those that get you out of your comfort zone.

"Sometimes," Snook continues, "the biggest window for changing someone's self-concept opens when he fails. That's a fundamentally different way of thinking about development. It might be when he fails a course for the first time in his life or when he commits an honor-code violation. When that happens, he's open to self-reflection."

Leadership Lessons (III)

"West Point is a uniquely humbling experience. I came from a small town, where I was a good student and captain of my sports teams. I showed up at West Point and found that 60% of my classmates were team captains, and 20% were valedictorians. One day you're the local star, and the next you're just one of thousands of bald heads."

—Dave McCormick, '87, senior vice president, FreeMarkets Inc.

To Build Confidence, Teach Humility

The typical West Point cadet looks something like this: male and white (though 15% of students are women, and 25% are nonwhite). Top decile of his high-school class. Jock. Middle-class, middle-American. He came to the academy because it is free, but he is also patriotic on some level.

The norm isn't definitive, of course. Any community of 4,000 people is a community of 4,000 distinctive individuals. But in practice, the cadets who reside in the standard-issue cinder-block rooms of Bradley Barracks look pretty much the same. They say pretty much the same things. Hell, that's part of the deal here: Everyone is part of a team, no individual more important than the mission of the whole.

"Why do we make these kids endure such a spartan four years?" Snook asks. "You stay in stone barracks. You can't put garbage in the garbage cans before 9:30 A.M., and the sinks must be clean and dry at all times. So many rules and regulations. Why?

"Because when you graduate," Snook continues, "you're going to be asked to be selfless. For a lot of hours while in the Army, you're going to suffer. You'll be away from home for Christmas; you'll sleep in the mud. There are a lot of things about this job that make you subordinate your self-interest—so get used to it."

This is the essence of what cadets learn. They hear it in the classroom, but they also witness it around them, every day. The great leaders they see inspire and motivate because they care for their soldiers and because they're willing to do themselves whatever they ask of others. "Look at any leader who's made a big change," says firstie Randy Hopper. "The key is servanthood. You can't lead without making sacrifices."

Hopper, a 22-year-old cadet from Baytown, Texas, is commander of

Company C-2, based in Bradley. There are 32 such companies, each comprised of about 128 students, each with its own nickname (C-2 is the "Flying Circus"), cheer ("Go Circus!"), and culture. The company is the core organizational unit at West Point. It is also the crucible for experiential leadership development. Here's how it works.

Plebes are, as ever, at the bottom. They learn how to follow, absorbing and acting on the orders of their superiors. Second-year students, or "yearlings," are assigned teams of one or two plebes. In this first, modest experience as military leaders, yearlings learn to develop intimate relationships with their subordinates, rooted in mutual trust. They are held directly accountable for their plebes' performance.

Yearlings report, in turn, to third-year students, or "cows" (a long story), each cow responsible for squads of two or three yearlings and four to six of their plebe charges. Cast in the roles of noncommissioned officers of the cadet brigade, cows must exercise indirect leadership. They are accountable for the plebes as well, but they must direct behavior through the yearlings. They must learn to motivate by example.

Firsties run the show. The summer before classes begin, they direct the eight weeks of military training for incoming plebes and yearlings. Come August, they take the roles of commissioned officers in the cadet hierarchy. Platoon leaders report to company commanders and their staffs, who answer to battalion commands, regiments, and the brigade.

Everyone leads, and everyone follows. Everyone models, and everyone assesses. Cadets' formal evaluations of their subordinates' performance count toward final grades. "Everyone's a teacher," says firstie Chris Kane, a platoon leader under Hopper in C-2. "That's what I love about this place. We're all teachers."

In this 24-hour leadership laboratory, students acquire humility. As leaders, they are nothing without followers. "You learn from the beginning that you're not in a position of leadership because you're smarter or better," says firstie and C-2 executive officer Joe Bagaglio. "As soon as you think you know it all, you get burned."

And they must perform under stress. Cadets face a daunting crush of academics, sports, and military activities. The academy's administrators know that there is enough time, in theory, to get it all done; they have studied this. In practice, though, cadets learn to prioritize—what must come first and what can be left undone. More than that, they come to accept that, amid chaos, the only thing that they can control is themselves. Under fire, "you don't ask how to get it done," says Kane. "You just do it."

Major Tony Burgess follows all of this with reactions that range from concern to bemusement to pride. As the tactical officer attached on a full-time basis to C-2, Burgess, '90, is likely the single most influential person in the development of the company's 128 young cadets. He is, as he likes to put it, their "teacher-coach-mentor-disciplinarian-den mother."

Burgess himself is a leadership junkie. The son of missionary parents, he spent his childhood in Mexico and entered West Point with grand visions. "I was going to get out of the Army after five years, and by age 30, I was going to be a millionaire in business," he says. "I didn't know how, but I was going to do it. Then, somewhere along the way, I fell in love with leading."

Burgess has spent 10 years in the infantry, and he will tell you that there is no better job in the world than commanding an Army company. He grew passionate enough about it to start up a Web site, Company Command.com—an unauthorized (but unofficially welcome) resource for company commanders that has attracted many users. With his classmate and best friend, Nate Allen, Burgess has written a book on the same topic, *Taking the Guidon: Exceptional Leadership at the Company Level*, which is available on his Web site.

Among his cadet charges, Burgess radiates intensity and enthusiasm. He is at once approachable and reserved, a buddy and a boss. His success depends on maintaining a fine balance—guiding students' decisions without actually making them, giving students enough rope but knowing when to haul it in. He is the one who must look out for developmental opportunities and failures. He must be ready to influence.

If Burgess succeeds—if West Point succeeds—his cadets will emerge, he thinks, as the "go-to" people. "They'll be the ones who you know will make it happen," he says, "the guys who will do better than we ever imagined possible."

Leadership Lessons (IV)
"I led a team of incoming plebes during basic training. I thought I had to lead the way that I saw others doing it—with stress and shouting, like a traditional drill sergeant. Well, my unit performed very badly. And

they hated me. That experience shook me up. I realized that leadership isn't rule-based. It isn't about stress. It's about inspiration, about setting and communicating a vision. It's about gaining trust. Once you have someone's trust, once you get them on the same sheet of music, they don't want to disappoint you. Then leading becomes very easy."
—Christina "CJ" Juhasz, '90, director in online ventures, Merrill Lynch

West Point's Leadership Curriculum

Until after World War II, there was no explicit leadership instruction at West Point. Back then, the academy was known primarily as an engineering school. How could leadership possibly be taught? How do you teach judgment or inspiration in a classroom?

Hike to the top floor of Thayer Hall, and you will find Lieutenant Colonel Greg Dardis engaging small groups of firsties in discussions of classical-leadership theory, dissecting such leading-edge thinkers as Morgan McCall and Peter Senge. Cadets today can actually major in leadership. And even if they don't, such instruction is deeply ingrained in the curriculum.

In their third year, cadets must take a course called Military Leadership. The timing is significant. At that point, cadets have returned from a summer spent interning with Army units around the world, often temporarily replacing platoon leaders in the field. They have served as team leaders in their cadet company. "They have experience under their belts," says Dardis, who graduated from West Point in 1979 and now heads the leadership and management studies program. "They've observed both good and bad leadership."

The object is to reflect on that experience, to assess it in terms of theory. Early in the course, cadets are asked to write about their leadership philosophy—a graded exercise that forces them to reflect on their talents and weaknesses. They write reflection papers that explain theoretical constructs in terms of their own experiences.

Cadets also take on a raft of case studies penned by West Point faculty, most of them rooted in combat situations. The students also engage in action-learning projects—some of which are distinctly non-military. When Snook taught the class, he would take his students to the elementary school that serves West Point families: "I'd say, 'You all think you're leaders? Well, you're going to lead a recess.' " The assignment: Develop a plan for overseeing seven minutes of playground activity.

Most often, cadets responded by thinking in terms of command and control: First we'll play dodgeball. Then we'll move to the swings. I'll direct every movement of every kid out there.

Then they watched the teacher lead an actual recess. As kids poured out onto the playground, there was chaos. And then order emerged, as the children basically organized themselves into teams. The exact order that resulted was unpredictable—but it was entirely predictable that *some* form of order would emerge.

"I asked them to rate recess," Snook recalls. "Well, they said that everyone had fun, and no one got hurt. So I asked them to tell me about the leader. 'Well, the teacher just stood there,' they said. So, is leading that easy? Is it totally hands-off? No. The way you influence complex, chaotic systems is by setting the starting conditions. You set the starting conditions, the left and right boundaries, and the minimum specifications. The teacher had a fence around the playground, and she established four or five rules. After that, her job was managing by exception."

Meanwhile, the leadership of West Point is thinking about the institution's exceptional past—and challenging future. The academy exists on a razor's edge. To stay effective, it must retain much of what makes it different—yet it also must continuously accommodate changing external demands. "We can't be so different that the notion of being the Army of a democracy fails," says Lieutenant General Daniel W. Christman, the academy's well-regarded superintendent. "We have to reflect what society demands of us."

The 1965 graduate believes that in order to fortify its relevance in the post–Cold War era, the academy must adjust its mission. It must reflect the new ambivalence with which America regards its armed services. That means equipping its graduates less for combat leadership than for "officership"—a vague notion that encompasses any number of the roles that the Army may fill. "We need to educate cadets in a way that doesn't constitute a military straitjacket," Christman says.

That may be so. West Point produces young officers who have been encouraged to act as entrepreneurs, to act quickly and decisively, to operate effectively amid chaos. These are traits that clash with the reality of military service in peacetime. So here's the irony: If the academy's education has become less applicable in the Army, it has grown more relevant in business. "Running a company, especially a start-up, is not unlike a battle," says Mark Hoffman, a 1969 graduate and now chairman and CEO of online-exchange giant Commerce One. "Bombs are going off all around you. The market and the competition are changing constantly. Your stock price is falling. You have to stay calm in the face of strife."

West Point dedicates itself to producing graduates who will, as its mission statement avers, "dedicate a lifetime of selfless service to the nation." The vague wording concerns those who believe that such service should be strictly military. But as a nation, we are short of great leadership in every sector. We may lament West Pointers' abandonment of the military. But guess what? Business has become the new national defense. Service to economy, selfless or not, constitutes service to the nation.

THE LAST WORD

Your profile of the U.S. Military Academy, at West Point, really grabbed my attention. I graduated from the academy in 1956, and I still work in the Army as a civil servant. I agree with those in the article who say that the quality of cadets has gotten better over time. My dad (class of 1928) told me that he would not have been able to enter West Point with the class of 1956. Likewise, I don't think that I could make the grade with the class of 2006. But somehow, both of us were able to meet the standards of our time. West Point has been, and continues to be, the best place in the nation to "grow up" to become a real man or woman.

Maury Cralle
Deputy to the garrison commander
U.S. Army Garrison
Fort Belvoir, Virginia

Boomtown, U.S.A.

From: Issue 59 | June 2002 | By: Charles Fishman

It's no easy feat to make a bomb beautiful. Charles Fishman's tour of McAlester Army Ammunition Plant, a place usually closed to outsiders, does just that. On its face, this is an intimate look inside a workplace—how it operates and who makes it work. But the depiction of the routine processes and the joking banter among workers is jarring. These folks are making, um, bombs! Shouldn't they be more serious? But soon the normality is comforting, and you realize that it's vital to letting the workers achieve perfection. In the end, Fishman paints a remarkable portrait of pride and professionalism in the workplace, with a telling reminder that focusing on whom you're serving (in this case, the men and women of the armed forces) can create that pride much more than pretty surroundings or fat benefits packages.

There is a small town in southeastern Oklahoma where people work in a vast factory unlike any other factory in the United States. The people of McAlester are so good at what they do, and have been doing it for so long, that they have 100% market share in the product they build. And they build an important product—one that is central to America's security.

What these men and women build are bombs—the bombs that drove Saddam Hussein's troops from Kuwait during the Gulf War, the bombs that have pounded Afghanistan. Many of the 850 people at the "ammunition plant," as the one-of-a-kind place is modestly called, are the second or third generation to do this work. For them, bombs are the family business.

To the degree that it's possible to generalize about hundreds of people doing a certain kind of job, America's bomb makers are clear-eyed and sensible about their work. Making bombs is too sweaty and too demanding to be romantic. It is too deadly to allow much daydreaming. It is too vivid to inspire heated philosophizing about foreign-policy goals or America's place in the world. And making bombs is, frankly, too serious to be possible without laughing. Aaron Kilburn is a production-line worker who has been at the plant for 24 years. He is the David Letterman of the bomb lines, always ready with a groaner. "That guy? He's new. His job is using a hammer to test for duds!" *Ba-da-boom.* "If you don't have a sense of humor, you're in trouble," says Kilburn. "Everything we've got out here will kill you, maim you. We're making bombs!"

It's one thing to see, on the television in your living room, the destruction that a single 2,000-pound bomb can do. It's another to stand in a room with an open-topped kettle filled with explosive about to be poured into 10 such bombs. It's something else entirely to come to work in a factory surrounded by dozens of live and soon-to-be-live 2,000-pound bombs, each 8 feet tall. If something were to go wrong, you wouldn't be able to run fast enough. You'd also never know what hit you.

The bombs come from McAlester Army Ammunition Plant (MCAAP), a vast, somewhat dilapidated facility six miles south of the town of McAlester. MCAAP is the source of nearly every nonnuclear bomb that the United States now uses. Although MCAAP is not a secret facility—it shows up on road maps and has a public Web site—it is a closed facility, run by the army, its workers civilian employees of the army. Earlier this year, *Fast Company* was given unprecedented access to the people who work at MCAAP and to the plant's production and storage areas.

The people who make America's bombs do so not only with a tireless steadiness, but also in utter anonymity. A sign on U.S. Highway 69 says simply, "Army Ammunition Plant." A billboard in McAlester salutes the town's prison rodeo and its Italian festival ("Home of cowboys and Italians") but makes no mention of the bomb factory that underpins its economy. No defense secretary has ever been to MCAAP; no president has come to have lunch in the break rooms and thank the men and women who make the tools that give a commander-in-chief his power. It's fine to have aircraft carriers and a vast, agile fleet of fighters and bombers. But an F-18, a B-52,

even a B-2 is worthless without the products of McAlester in its belly or under its wings.

The production of bombs turns out to be an arresting mix of the ordinary and the extraordinary—of disciplined, sometimes mundane work and
unusual risk shouldered every day. The bombs are made in factories that
have changed little since their construction in 1943, and a surprising
amount of the labor is still done by hand. The people at MCAAP make
products that must be perfect, but that they hope are never used. The emotions of bomb making are magnified during wartime, when the consequences of MCAAP's output are breaking news.

Terry Moore, like many of the people at the plant, has work outside
MCAAP. For most, it's on a cattle ranch or a farm. Moore is pastor of Crow-
der Baptist Church. An ordained minister working at a bomb factory. "It
sounds like a contradiction," Moore says. "But we need a strong defense.
This helps maintain the peace. Jesus said to turn the other cheek—knowing
what you have in your arsenal to keep 'em at bay."

Bomb Squad (I)
Larry Lame, 54, a Vietnam War veteran, worked for a number of years
in production at MCAAP and is now an accountant there. His father,
Sammie Lame, died in the last fatal explosion at MCAAP, on January 25, 1971, at the age of 46.

"My father was killed on a Monday. There were six guys in
the building that night. Three were working, three were in the break
room. A guy with a forklift had two pallets of old 20-mm ammunition.
It was real old stuff, black powder back from Vietnam. It went off. It
blew the roof off the building. The three who were working were killed.
The three in the break room survived. They never did tell me why it
blew up."

From the outside, the factory buildings where the big bombs get
made—MCAAP's so-called A-line—don't give away many clues about
their function. In fact, the buildings look desolate. The only hint that
something unusual might be going on inside them is that parts of the
buildings are buttressed with carefully positioned mounds of dirt rising

two stories, and long slides run down these berms from the buildings to ground level.

The slides are kind of an inside joke at MCAAP. If you need the evacuation slide, good luck getting to it. And if you did manage to get to the bottom in one piece, as one employee said with a laugh, "it would just give your body parts a head start"—on the way to kingdom come.

Billy Don Cloud is a supervisor in the building that is at the center of the bomb-making process—the place where gray PBX explosive is poured into steel bomb casings. Cloud has been at the plant for 22 years. "I started here when I was 28 years old," he says. "I came from the oil fields. Is it hard work? Yessir, it is. And dangerous. But you just don't think about it. You block it out—like if you worked at a grocery store, handling groceries every day."

Just inside the building, Cloud and his group are wrangling a big green kettle the size of a hot tub into position. The group of eight look more like bakers than bomb makers. Everyone who works production at the plant wears white coveralls and a brimless white cap. The coveralls are designed to reduce the possibility of static electricity and are laundered in flame retardant. The plant-supplied clothing also protects street clothes from the ingredients of bomb making: paint, tar, and the gooey explosive itself, which spatters around during filling operations.

"Don't get any of the powder on your clothes," says Terry Moore. "You won't ever get it out."

The comparison to baking is not too far off. The enormous kettle, delivered from a mixing building, contains more than two tons of warm PBX, plastic-bonded explosive that is relatively stable and easy to handle. It's the dough used to make bombs; when filled, they will go to a hot room where they will cure for 48 hours. Cloud uses a small motorized cart to move the kettle down the tracks to the filling area. As the kettle rolls along, the wheels set off the occasional pop—tiny flecks of PBX left on the metal tracks, even after clean-up, pop off when squeezed between the wheels and track under heavy pressure. The quantity of PBX in the kettle is enough to flatten this building, as well as the one up the line where bomb casings are prepped— and the one down the line where finished bombs are touched up, inspected, and loaded onto rail cars.

Moore hops up on the moving kettle and with a gloved hand reaches in and scoops up a fistful of PBX. It's a good batch, one that will flow smoothly and quickly. The PBX looks like wet, gray clay. Moore, who has been at the plant for six years, says that the work did make him nervous when he first started. "You look around and wonder, How much explosive is in this one building? You worry."

A grinning Billy Don Cloud cuts in, "That's why we got a preacher!"

"They do try to spread us out," says Moore.

A 2,000-pound bomb does not contain 2,000 pounds of explosive. The prepped bomb bodies themselves weigh 1,500 pounds apiece. Their destructive force, in fact, comes in part from the hundreds of pounds of metal fragments that they generate. MCAAP—which also makes all sizes of bombs filled with concrete for practice—uses a clear designation to ensure that people know what's what. The noses of live bombs are circled by three bright-yellow stripes.

Once the kettle of PBX has made its way to the filling room, the process moves along with businesslike briskness. Except for lifting, everything is done by hand; even at this critical stage, nothing on the production line is automated. (The production buildings are also without air-conditioning. In the summer, inside temperatures reach 100 degrees or more, and everyone is still shrouded in coveralls.)

In the filling room, Cloud's team fastens a pressure lid on the kettle and hoists it up 15 feet. Someone hops onto an industrial tug, like the kind used to move airplanes at airport gates, and pulls a train of bomb bodies under the kettle. Movable platforms are put in place around the bombs, and a couple of people climb up to do the filling.

The kettle has fittings in its bottom; the PBX is squirted through hoses into the bomb casings like toothpaste. Filling bombs with explosive is not as scientific a process as one might imagine. Experienced fillers on the platform use a flashlight to monitor the flow, and they eyeball the right amount of PBX, clipping off the hoses between bombs. It's a bomb, after all: A little more or a little less explosive isn't going to change its quality. Excess PBX is scooped up by hand and set aside in a regular cardboard box for disposal. The filling transforms what is an ordinary steel pipe into a bomb. "It's kind of simple, really," says Cloud. "There's not as much to it as you might think."

Bomb Squad (II)

Donna Kindred, 53, a supervisor, has worked at the plant for 24 years. Many members of her family also have worked, or now work, at the plant: her father, her mother, her husband, her sister, one son, two uncles.

"This place has supported my whole family. I'm proud of the quality work we put out. I wouldn't want our soldiers to be over there and have a dud. I had a son in Saudi Arabia [during Operation Desert Storm]. Some of what he saw there had McAlester Army Ammunition Plant stenciled on it. He could say, 'My mom helped make that.'"

McAlester, Oklahoma, is home to Oklahoma State Penitentiary— Oklahoma's maximum-security prison, which includes death row. The town also has a Boeing plant that produces parts for commercial aircraft, as well as a 200,000-square-foot Wal-Mart. Despite the bombs, though, MCAAP is McAlester's employer of choice. For one thing, salaries in production start at $15 per hour—a figure that Boeing, Wal-Mart, and the prison can't touch. And MCAAP offers relative job security, some chance for advancement, as well as health insurance, retirement benefits, and government vacation and holidays. The plant runs a four-day week, with 10-hour shifts, and that schedule appeals to people who work on farms. Residents often try for years to get hired. Says Kitty Corder, who works for the state employment-services office in town: "If I had 15 people here in the office and one job at the plant, they'd all be applying for it."

And yet there is something reserved about the relationship between town and plant. There is no sign at the town line that says, "Welcome to McAlester—we make the bombs that keep America free!" Not a single business makes even a glancing reference to the ammunition plant. There is no Boomtown Video, no Rocket City Hardware. The high-school team's nickname is the Buffs—short for the Buffaloes. The reserve is an unspoken acknowledgment that making bombs is serious, not something to be brandished about cavalierly.

McAlester Army Ammunition Plant was born in the frantic mobilization after Pearl Harbor. The entire place—nearly 3,000 buildings and hundreds of miles of railroad track and roadways—was constructed in 18 months and opened for production in May 1943. Its dimensions are vast.

The perimeter fence encloses 44,800 acres—three times the size of Manhattan. The plant not only produces weapons for each service as the need arises, it also houses stockpiles of ammunition for all four services.

MCAAP is the Defense Department's largest storage facility. Its buildings have 6 million square feet of space, enough to make six large suburban shopping malls. That space is divided among 2,816 separate buildings. All but a handful of those buildings are ammunition magazines, or "igloos." You don't want too much explosive in a single igloo; you want igloos separated by enough open land that an explosion in one will not set off a chain reaction.

Just inside the plant's front gate is the first of MCAAP's many curiosities: a meandering stream called Peaceable Creek. The name did not come from some military official with high hopes that the bombs would remain in storage for good. The creek had its name long before the bombs arrived.

Alongside MCAAP's main road—even in the heavily trafficked areas— deer, turkey, and geese wander at all hours of the day. In more-remote areas, there are wild pigs, foxes, and bobcats. Just before the second security checkpoint is MCAAP's award-winning day-care facility. It has 41 kids, from 6 weeks old to 5 years old, and a waiting list. Underneath the center is a concrete bunker to protect the children—not from bombs, but from tornadoes. McAlester sits in tornado alley.

Most of the igloos are served by dirt roads and don't have electricity. Every magazine has restrictions of the quantity of bombs each can hold, in order to prevent chain-reaction explosions. To a person standing inside one of these igloos, those limits seem purely intellectual. The air is cool and smells musty. Two-thousand-pound bombs lie on their sides, two bombs to a metal rack, stacked four racks high, 36 rows deep. In a room about the size of a McDonald's, there are 313 bombs, each weighing a ton. In 1985, a car hit a truck carrying such bombs on Interstate 40, north of McAlester. The truck carried no fuses or detonators, but in the fire after the accident, three of the bombs partially exploded and burned. The crater they left in I-40 was 40 feet wide and 25 feet deep.

Bomb Squad (III)
Don Johnson, who works in storage, started at MCAAP in 1985. "Since 9/11, we've hired some new people. A guy was driving a forklift, and he

accidentally knocked over a stack of bombs. I mean, he jumped off that forklift and took off running. I called after him, 'Hey, man! Where are you going? Come back here! You heard the bombs hit the ground, didn't you? If you heard 'em hit, you're gonna be fine. Come on back!'"

Last June, a man working in the finishing room for 2,000-pound bombs was crushed when a bomb fell on him. It was the first fatality at MCAAP in 30 years. In the aftermath of the accident, equipment in the finishing room—where finished bombs are taken from their carts and turned from vertical to horizontal—was automated. The new equipment has safety mechanisms that make it almost impossible to have a repeat of the June accident.

And yet, the new equipment simply sets the bombs—each weighing almost what a Honda Civic does—on a long metal table, where they are rolled along by hand, like so many logs, through the finishing process. The table has no ledges. The work rules just say that before anyone moves a bomb, there is supposed to be a person on each end, to maintain control.

America's bomb-making facility is surprisingly antiquated. As an example, even though parts of the process have been updated, computers are largely irrelevant. And the physical facility itself is beat-up in ways that go beyond the cosmetic. The concrete surfaces of loading docks where ammunition is loaded and unloaded are reduced to gravel in some places. Bathrooms in production buildings are filthy, not because of any lack of care by the employees, but because they're old.

"The buildings are rough," says Billy Don Cloud. "My ranch hands have better bathroom facilities than we do at the plant."

Many of the buildings appear not to have been painted in decades. Indeed, on the glassed-in bulletin boards of one break room in daily use, there are faded news clippings featuring a boxing match between Charley Fusari and Tony Pellone and a U.S. Open in which Lew Worsham beat Sam Snead. Both events happened in 1947. Says one employee: "In peacetime, they don't have the money to fix the plant. In wartime, they're not thinking about the bathrooms or the paint."

The plant's condition is partly a result of the way it is run: MCAAP is, in essence, a business. The base commanders—who typically rotate through on two-year stints—must run the entire facility from the revenue they generate.

"Labor, fire protection, security: It all comes out of the revenue stream," says the current commander, Colonel Jyuji Hewitt. "If I choose to paint the bathrooms—well, it's a zero-sum game. What do we give up to do that?"

So far, the war on terrorism hasn't had a dramatic effect on MCAAP's operations. The military services keep stockpiles of weapons; MCAAP's thousands of magazines—most of which are full—represent additional supply. The plant, of course, was built for World War II, a multifront, multi-year global war. Right now, it runs at a fraction of its full capacity—one shift, four days a week, in only some of the factory buildings. MCAAP will soon add a second shift to replenish the munitions used in Afghanistan.

During World War II, the plant had almost four times the number of workers it does now. Indeed, given what MCAAP is in the business of making, its capacity is truly sobering. Says Dennis Tarron, MCAAP's chief of production planning: "I've seen old work orders from Vietnam where the Navy requested 1.25 million MK-82s [500-pound bombs]. We used to get orders for a half-million routinely."

During the height of the Vietnam War, MCAAP ran three shifts, around the clock, six days a week. "We produced 6,000 finished bombs in a 24-hour period," says Tarron. During the 1980s, says Tarron, that single day's Vietnam-era production "would have been a good load for a year."

MCAAP's staff lives with the plant's condition, much as it lives with the nature of the work itself. Melinda Cook is 25, and she has worked at the plant for three years. Her mother, both sets of grandparents, her great-grandparents, and even a parent of one of those great-grandparents—have all worked at MCAAP. She's fifth generation at the plant. "I try not to think about the fact that we make bombs. I don't really love the work, but I love the people out here," says Cook.

Ron Dugger, 59, has been working at the plant for 18 years. "Do I think about the bombs? I really don't. You concentrate on your area of the production line. You do the best at your job. When I see what's happening in Afghanistan on TV, I think, My Lord, I helped make that. It's kind of a mixed feeling. But I feel like we do make an important contribution. We furnish our military with what they need to fight."

Dugger, a supervisor, is leading a group refurbishing 2.75-inch rockets with fresh fuses. The last step of the process is to put each rocket into a cardboard shipping tube, slide a top on the tube, and tape the top in place.

Oddly, a machine is used for that final step, to wrap the tape around the tube, sealing on the top. The young man operating that machine is careful to fold the end of the tape back on itself, leaving a little shirttail. "We put the tail on so they can peel the tape off easily," he says.

It's the kind of touch that reveals much about the attitude of MCAAP's bomb makers: They're not thinking about whom George Bush or Donald Rumsfeld is going to aim those 2.75-inch rockets at; they're thinking about men and women just like themselves whose very lives might depend on getting the rockets out of their tubes in one hell of a hurry.

THE LAST WORD

I was the Director of Ammunition Operations from April 1980 until September 1982. I was the first USAF officer assigned to the plant. I was really impressed with the work ethic and dedication of the people at MCAAP. I still think fondly of the people that I met and their can-do attitude. There was a wealth of talent and experience put to use every day to keep the operations safe. They truly had pride in their support of our U.S. Armed Forces.

Colonel Douglas C. Robinson, USAF, Ret.
Roxboro, North Carolina

The New Face of Global Competition

From: Issue 67 | February 2003 | By: Keith H. Hammonds

Imagine you witnessed the engine of American commerce rev up in the 1940s and 1950s. Or that you saw Japanese industry commingle national pride and ingenuity in the late 1970s to create an engineering and manufacturing force. That's what Keith H. Hammonds's story on Wipro and the rise of India feels like. He captures a major shift in the evolution of the global economy. Wisely avoiding jingoism and cliché, Hammonds humanizes what's often presented as a faceless threat. Reading the stories of Ganesh Narasimhaiya, Dilis Antony, and Anupam Mukerji, among others, we cannot deny that these talented, dedicated, and extremely hardworking individuals deserve the same things we want for ourselves. Why should they be able to enjoy them only in the United States? Turns out, there's no good answer for that question.

There are certain moments when you can see the future with such clarity it nearly takes your breath away. I went to India and witnessed the future. I am certain of this, because I saw the explosions. I arrived in Bangalore at the start of the Hindu festival of Diwali. Diwali is a four-day-long celebration of wealth and prosperity, of light over darkness. Strings of colored lights festoon every window; even the meanest shanty blazes with candles. In Bangalore, a city of 6 million, children scamper through the alleyways with sparklers. Fireworks burst randomly from tens of thousands of rooftops.

A thousand points of light? Try a billion. India is a nation of 1 billion people, and, despite enormous challenges, it is on the verge of something spectacular. Out of its poverty and chaotic decrepitude erupt a host of small explosions. It is a place crackling with talent and ideas and ambition. It is where a visitor confronts head-on the new face of a global marketplace—and the emergence of a new force in high-tech competition.

Near the center of this phenomenon is a company called Wipro Ltd. On a rooftop at Wipro's Electronic City campus one evening, I joined a few dozen engineers at their team Diwali party. It was like a Silicon Valley beer blast without the beer: Laughing employees played movie charades while a portable CD player pumped out tunes. Diwali traditionally is observed at home with family and close friends, but it's not a holiday that's recognized in America—and these engineers were doing important work for a big American customer. So as the sun faded, they dispersed to their cubicles downstairs and got back to business.

They were toiling on a project for CNA Life, a company 11 and a half time zones away in Nashville, Tennessee. Wipro engineers have been helping CNA reengineer its business processes and improve automated-underwriting performance. This hasn't just involved stringing COBOL code together. Wipro employees have set the strategy, then designed and architected the system. It's high-level stuff, a "mission critical" application.

More explosions: From Wipro's rooftop, you can see a string of holes blown out of farmland nearby. Wipro is excavating the foundation for an 8-acre third phase of its Electronic City facility, the largest of its 10 sites around Bangalore. By 2004, it expects to triple the size of this campus; 17,000 engineers will take on projects for such clients as the Home Depot, Nokia, and Sony.

A decade ago, Wipro was an anonymous conglomerate selling cooking oil and personal computers, mostly in India. Today, it is a $903-million-a-year global company, and most of its business comes from information-technology services. Since 1997, Wipro's revenue has grown by an average of 26% a year while profits have grown by 69%. Its 15,000 technologists write software, integrate back-office solutions, design semiconductors, de-bug applications, take orders, and field help calls for some of the biggest companies in the world. They are as good at doing all of that as anyone in the world. Perhaps better. And they are cheaper—on average about 40% cheaper—than comparable American companies.

It is an irresistible force, and it's on the rise. Three years ago, Bangalore was the software world's biggest body shop, offering coders at $2 an hour. Now Wipro and a few rivals are moving upstream, swinging into such high-value services as consulting, integration, and architecture. Increasingly, Wipro is competing with Accenture, EDS, IBM, and the big accounting firms. And as often as not, it's winning.

Where you stand on all of this, of course, depends on where you sit. Here in Bangalore, Wipro's growth is a matter of tremendous national significance, requital for its loss of high-tech manufacturing and a sign of even bigger things to come. In America, where technology-services companies struggle with weak stock prices and uncertain growth prospects, the rise of a tough, lower-cost competitor is a sensitive subject. That's true even for Wipro's satisfied customers, most of whom declined to speak on the record. (How many American executives want to crow about all of the work they're shipping to India?)

The emergence of Wipro is inspiring and disorienting, a case study in strategic possibility—and a warning of business dislocation to come. So it is with the unforgiving logic of global competition.

The Rank and File: Big Brains, Bargain Prices

If you are an American technology-strategy consultant making $150,000 a year, you should know about Ganesh Narasimhaiya. Ganesh (mercifully, his business card reads simply Ganesh N.) is a friendly fellow. He is 30 years old. He enjoys cricket, R&B music, and bowling, and he lives with his parents in Bangalore. He earned a bachelor's degree in electronics and communications, and he can spin out code in a variety of languages: COBOL, Java, UML (Unified Modeling Language), among others.

In the past three years, Ganesh has worked on high-level projects for Wipro all over the world. He has helped GE Medical Systems roll out a logistics application throughout Southeast Asia. He proposed a plan to consolidate and synchronize security solutions across a British client's e-business applications. For Statoil of Norway, he developed a strategy for transferring legacy system applications onto the Web.

"I want to be on the cutting edge of technology," Ganesh says. The guy is sharp. And hungry. He'll work 18 or 19 hours a day at a customer site. For that, while overseas, he may pull down $7,000 a month. When he's home in Bangalore, his pay is about one-quarter of that—$21,000 a year. By Indian standards, it's a small fortune.

Ganesh is part of Wipro's wedge. The company is massing a small force of high-level strategists, increasingly focused on specific industries, who can compete—with anyone—for any given consulting project. Once Ganesh and his colleagues work their way past a CIO's door, Wipro can play its Trojan horse: offshore outsourcing solutions that dramatically lower clients' expenses.

At that point, your applications developers could find themselves up against Dilis Antony, 30, and her team of four. Antony, who holds the equivalent of a master's degree in computer science, manages a project to build a Web-based customer survey for United Technologies' Otis Elevator Co. division, part of a much broader Web strategy that Wipro is executing for Otis. Antony says that she "wants to grow with Wipro." She has her sights set on bigger management roles. Her programmers average $8,000 a year. She probably doesn't make much more.

Think hard about that. If you are a strategy consultant working for Accenture or EDS in the United States, how do you compete with Ganesh? How does your company compete when Antony's troops can execute Ganesh's solution for perhaps a quarter of the cost of your staff—and execute just as well?

In America's information economy, we have become comfortable framing our competitive advantage in terms of knowledge and innovation. We justify charging premium prices because we have the best-trained talent delivering top-quality information solutions. That's why panic over the overseas migration of manufacturing jobs in the 1980s was short-lived: For all of the talk of a "hollow economy," we remained masters of white-collar brain work. So what happens if brain work can be done anywhere?

The Strategy: The Power of "Power Consulting"

Well, no, it can't be done anywhere. That would understate the enormity of what Wipro is pulling off. The company has been canny enough to understand that peddling a low-cost service can't lead to sustainable growth and profitability. This is the oldest, harshest lesson of the global economy: If what you do can be done by anyone, there will always be someone willing to do it for less.

Wipro knew that long-term prosperity depended on providing services of increasingly higher value. A decade ago, like dozens of other Indian companies, it supplied technical labor on demand. Then it realized that piecework is fine, but relationships are better. So Wipro created development centers within its offices, each dedicated to a single important customer. The idea: to promote relationships that would create annuity revenue.

Today in Electronic City, Wipro hosts development centers for Hewlett-Packard, GM, and dozens of other huge global companies. Lumber company Weyerhaeuser's three centers—one in Bangalore, one in Chennai, and one in the United States—house more than 200 engineers. The engagement began in 1999 with two Wipro employees conducting a modest on-site analysis at Weyerhaeuser's U.S. headquarters. Now Wipro develops, maintains, and supports a broad array of Weyerhaeuser applications from Bangalore.

At the same time, Wipro has embraced quality. In six years, it has trained 7,000 employees in Six Sigma and completed 1,000 quality projects. Six years ago, *Fast Company* profiled a team at Lockheed-Martin that wrote nearly perfect code ("They Write the Right Stuff," Dec./Jan. 1997). The team's claim to fame: It was one of only four outfits in the world to achieve Level 5 certification from the Software Engineering Institute. Wipro has Level 5 certification in three different categories. It's eye-glazing stuff, but an amazing achievement.

Such accomplishments confirmed that Wipro's developers weren't just cheap: They were cheap and very, very good. It was enough to distinguish them from every aspiring dollar-an-hour coder in Malaysia, Russia, and South Africa. But it wasn't enough to allow them to take on the big American firms. To do that, Wipro had to become more like them. "The company has had to let go of the Indian brand and create a global company while maintaining the cost advantage associated with being Indian," says Stephen Lane, research director for IT services at Aberdeen Group.

In 1999, Wipro hired Vivek Paul to run its small technology subsidiary. Paul, an executive with Bollywood-movie idol looks, is Indian by birth. But he made his mark in the United States, graduating from business school at the University of Massachusetts at Amherst and thriving at GE Medical Systems. Among other things, he negotiated one of GE's earliest IT outsourcing joint ventures in India—with Wipro.

Paul headquartered Wipro Technologies not in India but in Santa Clara, California. He saw "a great opportunity to be a player at a company that had a shot at being global." But he also saw a workforce in need of a spark. "The whole ethos was rooted in execution," he says. Indian workers had been raised and schooled to respect authority. They did what they were told to do very well. What they didn't do as well was tell clients what needed doing.

There is a slangy Hindi word, *jugaad*, that describes what Paul was looking for. It implies the ability to think assertively, and work creatively around unexpected problems. "How does one move from being a good pharmacist to being a good doctor?" asks Ranjan Acharya, Wipro's vice president for human-resource development. "A pharmacist cannot add value to a prescription. He can impress with his service but not with a decision."

Wipro needed more doctors. Some of them, it could hire. In fact, it had to. To compete with the big firms, it had to offer expertise in specific industries. If you want to solve a commercial bank's technology problems, you should understand how the banking business works. So Wipro lured Ramesh Subramanian, a McKinsey & Co. veteran who had focused on financial-services clients. It found Aswatha Amarnath, an energy-finance specialist with high-level relationships at big U.S. utilities.

But such high-profile hires still left 15,000 engineers and managers who were thinking like pharmacists. For them, Acharya rolled out a wide-ranging training strategy called Power Consulting. In the United States, a corporate initiative by that name might well be laughed out of the company cafeteria—especially since some elements seem almost insultingly basic. Engineers who are to meet customers, for example, prepare by dressing for a formal lunch and learning to use silverware properly.

But at Wipro, employees accept the training as competitive weaponry. They learn to "understand the context of the relationship," as Acharya says, and to home in on customers' problems. In small groups, engineers practice asking pointed questions about clients' companies, their businesses, and their people. "Our people are accustomed to speaking from Wipro's view," says Acharya. "They must learn to speak from the customer's view."

Employees are taught to analyze situations and to define the scale and

scope of a problem. They learn to "prewire" a presentation, talking to everyone involved ahead of time to prevent nasty surprises. And they are instructed in the fine arts of negotiating and closing a deal. Every new
engineer—and Wipro hired 2,200 engineers in a six-month period last
year—has some consulting perspective built into his 45-day indoctrination.

Where does all of this lead? Up the food chain. Teach engineers to think
like consultants, make them experts in their clients' industries, and you
forge a workforce that will keep pushing the business forward. Wipro expects that strategy consulting will ultimately account for just 10% of its
technology revenue. But those slivers, such as current consulting gigs at
General Motors and Nationwide Insurance, will drive long-term relationships with clients, producing steady streams of outsourcing revenue.

Wipro hopes to win more high-level contracts like the one from Storage
Technology Corp., which this year agreed to outsource the design and engineering of a line of tape-storage devices. By 2004, Wipro employees will
take responsibility for the products' development, supplanting Storage
Technology workers in Minneapolis. And in September, Wipro took over a
whole R&D facility for Ericsson. Beyond accepting the financial risk, the
120-person Wipro team will manage the research process.

Here, then, is Wipro's challenge. New business will come, because in a
global downturn, everyone is looking to slash costs. For Wipro, Power Consulting is all about turning that opportunity into an inflection point. It's
about restructuring straightforward commodity work into high-value partnerships. It's about selling something that no one in the world can replicate.

The Boss: Outsourcing as a Way of Life

Some 8,300 miles from Bangalore, Wipro chairman and managing director
Azim H. Premji slides into the front seat of a Lincoln Town Car for the journey into Manhattan. He is a courtly man, silver haired and impeccably
dressed. This morning, he is pitching some of Wipro's biggest clients and
prospects. He has run late with Verizon Wireless, and he worries now about
making an important appointment at J.P. Morgan Chase.

Premji's story is near legend in India, largely because with a fortune estimated at $6 billion, he is by far the nation's wealthiest individual. In 1946,
his father founded the Western India Vegetable Products Company to

manufacture and distribute cooking oils. The elder Premji died suddenly in 1966, obliging his son to cut short his studies at Stanford to take over the family business. (He finished his electrical engineering degree in 1999.)

Premji proved to be a shrewd opportunist. He diversified into personal-care products and then into lightbulbs. In the early 1980s, after India walled off its economy and shooed away foreign technology companies, Wipro ginned up an R&D lab and produced a passable knockoff of Digital Equipment's PDP11 minicomputer. Within a few years, having concocted its own operating system and semiconductors, Wipro was the leading manufacturer of personal computers, printers, and scanners in India.

When India reopened its gates in 1990, Premji acknowledged that Wipro could not compete with PC imports. But he had his R&D lab, filled with some of India's best talent. So Premji began renting it out to the rest of the world. His engineers designed semiconductors for Texas Instruments, phones for Nokia, and switches and routers for Nortel. Then they started tinkering with software.

Here's what he will tell the executives at J.P. Morgan Chase: "What's happening now in services is what happened 15 years ago in manufacturing. It started in software, in application development. It's moving to software-enabled services. Call centers, legal services, medical. Wherever work can be removed and done somewhere else, it will be done where it's most cost-effective.

"Take a large law firm. The clerks and paralegals could be trained in India, serving partners and associates in the U.S. Salomon Smith Barney has a big research staff here. Why can't 60% of its reports be done from India? Why should they require everyone to be in the United States?" Wipro just signed a contract to interpret radiology images for a major American research hospital. Indian radiologists will, in effect, provide the hospital's second and third shifts.

Why should everyone be in the United States? In his understated way, Premji delights in this question. "I have had meetings in the past year with the top partners of a U.S. accounting firm. One year ago, they thought that the Indian model was not important. Six months back, they raised their target for outsourced jobs to 2,000. Now they're talking about raising it to 25,000. They will get to that number. If they don't, they'll be out of business."

Of course, this is a fair bit of bluster. But a few blocks away, executives at Accenture's New York offices are struggling with exactly the dilemma that Premji proposes. Accenture is more than 10 times Wipro's size. It can take on huge outsourcing projects, such as running a global company's data center, that Wipro won't be able to touch for years, if ever. Still, when Lattice Group wanted to outsource systems integration for its fiber-optic network in the United Kingdom, it awarded the $70 million contract to Wipro.

So Accenture has upped its Indian outsourced workforce eightfold, to 800 this year, even as it has fired partners and cut bonuses in the United States. In November, troubled EDS boasted that it would have 20,000 employees working offshore by 2004. It will spend $100 million to open a new business-process outsourcing center in India by spring and to build up similar capabilities in Argentina, Hungary, New Zealand, and other countries.

Wipro, in other words, is charging upstream into consulting and other high-value services while its bigger American rivals are rushing downstream. Vivek Paul argues that "both ends of the spectrum are racing for the same point. Neither strategy is easy. It's not easy to build a strong global-delivery model, and it's not easy to rent real estate in India and hire engineers. But ultimately, the center point is where the big players will play."

As it nears the center, Wipro is taking pains to seem less, well, Indian. A true global company, Premji reasons, appears to be local wherever it does business. That's one reason why he's sharing his limousine today with Richard S. Garnick, a 20-year technology-sales veteran who joined Wipro last year to head its American field operations. In July, Wipro hired Steve Zucker, a former top U.S. sales executive for EDS, to lead its push into total outsourcing deals.

Within two years, Wipro says, three-quarters of the employees its customers see will be local nationals: American, European, or Asian. It will hire local talent and buy companies that give it instant industry presence. In November, for example, the company paid $26 million for the energy practice of American Management Systems, buying not just credibility but 90 consultants and 50 existing client relationships. And within two years, Wipro will likely begin shipping development work to locations where workers are paid even less than in India. It will itself look offshore, perhaps to the Philippines or Vietnam. This is what a truly global company does. It operates close to its customers, and it constantly seeks opportunities to arbitrage labor markets.

Back in Bangalore, the folks at Wipro are paying close attention to this. Not just Premji and his top executives, and not just the marketing department. Every Wednesday morning, Paul e-mails his "weekly highlights" to every Wipro Technologies group employee. He recounts each contract win and loss, assesses the state of the industry, and lays out Wipro's near-term strategy.

And amid the blond-and-gray cubicles at Electronic City, in the massive lunchroom where servers fill steel trays with rice and curries, employees digest every word. They know all about Accenture and EDS, about the accounting firms and IBM Global Services. And they're not one bit daunted. "We are getting confidence that we're world-class," says Vinayachandron P S, a 35-year-old program manager in Wipro's Oracle practice. "It's a fact now. We know we can beat them."

The Mission: "We Should Be World-Class"

On my last day in India, I flew to Mumbai (formerly Bombay). Mumbai is one of the world's biggest cities: seven islands in the Arabian Sea land-filled together and crammed with 16 million people. There are slums, of course, with people living on top of one another amid mud and garbage. There is wealth too. Or at least the remnants of wealth: spiraling buildings, many now in decay, built during India's two centuries under British rule.

India won its independence in 1947, yet its people are still coming to terms with the result. Arguably, the second most populous country in the world has little to show for the past half-century. It has forfeited leadership in manufacturing to its Asian neighbors, exported many of its brightest minds to Europe and America, and grown poorer.

Imagine, then, that you are a young Indian engineer working for an Indian technology company that is successfully starting to challenge some of the most established service providers on the planet. Yes, you want to make good money and buy a home. But just as likely, your work isn't solely about personal achievement or even your employer's market cap: It's a statement of national identity. "There is the same feeling that I found in Japan many years ago," says Gurcharan Das, the retired head of Procter & Gamble India, now a writer and venture capitalist. "In the 1970s, I visited a factory there; it may have been Toyota. And a worker told me that he was working for the greater glory of Japan. It's the same sense of destiny that is partly driving these people today in India."

There is a young marketing strategist at Wipro named Anupam Mukerji whom I came to know during my stay. Mukerji works tirelessly. He has the Indian equivalent of an MBA, but he could have gone to Wharton and joined an American consulting firm. In one of our first conversations, he revealed some of the emotion that I later heard echoed in different ways throughout the company: "All of us were brought up with the thought that India was once great. We had such a rich heritage. Under the British, we lost a lot of that. Now we're rebuilding.

"Indians are proud and patriotic. Many people feel that we're superior in math and science. We invented the sundial and the numeral zero. So we think that in anything having to do with technology, we should be world-class."

Wipro won't soon stand shoulder to shoulder with Accenture or EDS or Deloitte Consulting. It will struggle to create a brand that truly can compete with those of the big boys. But there is some powerful passion at work here. Wipro's employees are intense and brimming with confidence. They know how good they are. They are enjoying themselves. And really, how long has it been since we could say that about most American workers?

The people at Wipro have seen the future, and it is them. They are the explosions, brilliant and exhilarating (and, yes, cheap). Again, think hard. How will you compete with that?

THE LAST WORD

I was intrigued by Keith H. Hammonds's recent article. One of the first things that struck me was Hammonds's mention of how enterprising Wipro Ltd. was to establish an office in this country. In my opinion, that wasn't a plan to involve American workers but a ploy that many foreign companies use to bring foreign nationals into the United States on LCA-type visas through "intracompany transfers." These workers do not follow a lengthy approval process at the Department of Labor. This is a way for companies such as Wipro to pretend to hire American workers. And since there are many Indians who have obtained citizenship after working here as H-IB workers, such companies hire them and claim that they are hiring American workers! This is an effort to get around the part of the H-IB visa program that is supposed to protect American workers from being replaced by those in the program.

What are American businesses going to do to deal with this phenomenon? How are we going to compete against it? I think that the answer is pretty obvious: Companies such as Wipro will take away all of our jobs if we keep lowering the barriers to entry to foreign companies in the United States and keep giving our work to people from other countries.

C. W. Fletez
Software developer and consultant
Alexandria, Virginia

Adding Value—But at What Cost?

From: Issue 73 | August 2003 | By: Marshall Goldsmith

Why do we always have to be right all the time? That's the curse of the high achiever. The world's top executive coach counsels us that all of our efforts to "add value" may be destroying something far more important.

The two men at dinner were clearly on the same wavelength. One of them was my friend Jon Katzenbach, the former McKinsey & Co. director who now heads his own elite consulting boutique. The other was Niko Canner, his brilliant partner. They were planning a new venture. But something about their conversation was slightly off. When Niko floated ideas, Jon tended to interrupt him. "That's a great idea," Jon would say, "but it might work better if you . . ." and then he would share a different way to tackle the issue. When he finished, Niko would pick up where he left off, only to be interrupted by Jon again. Back and forth it went, like a long rally at Wimbledon.

As the third party at the table, I watched and listened. I do this for a living as an executive coach. I help smart, successful people identify interpersonal challenges that they can improve—and then coach them to get better. I'm used to monitoring people's dialogues, listening for clues that reveal why even the most accomplished people may sometimes annoy their bosses, peers, and subordinates.

Ordinarily, I keep quiet, but Jon was exhibiting classic smart-person behavior. When Niko left the table, I laughed and said, "Jon, perhaps you should just go with Niko's ideas. Stop trying to add so much value to the discussion."

In my experience, one of the most common challenges that successful

198

people face is a constant need to win. When the issue is important, they want to win. When the issue is trivial, they want to win. Even when the issue isn't worth the effort or is clearly to their disadvantage, they still want to win.

Research shows that the more we achieve, the more we tend to want to "be right." At work meetings, we want our position to prevail. In arguments, we pull out all the stops to come out on top. Even at supermarket check-outs, we scout other lines to see if there's one that's moving faster.

In Jon's case, he was displaying a variation on the need to win: adding too much value. It's particularly common among smart people. They may retain remnants of a top-down management style even if they don't want to. These leaders are smart enough to realize that most of their subordinates know more in specific areas than they ever will, but old habits die hard. It's difficult for them to listen to others disclose information without communicating either that they already knew about it or that they know a better way.

The problem is, while they may have improved the idea by 5%, they've reduced the employee's commitment to executing it by 30%, because they've taken away that person's ownership of the idea. Therein lies the fallacy of added value: Whatever is gained in the form of a better idea may be lost six times over in the employee's diminished enthusiasm for the concept. One of my top clients said, "Unfortunately, at the CEO level, my suggestions get taken as orders, even if I don't want them to."

Later on, Jon and I had a laugh over the dinner incident. As one of the world's leading authorities on building teams and instilling pride, he knew the right answer. He was amazed at how often he had said "but." That's how pernicious the need to win can be. Don't get me wrong. I'm not saying that bosses have to zip their lips to keep their staff's spirits from sagging. But the higher up you go in an organization, the more you need to let other people be winners and not make it about winning yourself.

For bosses, that means being careful about how you hand out encouragement. If you find yourself saying, "Great idea, but . . . ," try cutting your response off at "idea." Even better, take a breath before you speak, and ask yourself if what you're about to say is worthwhile. One of my clients said that once he got into that habit, he realized that at least half of what he was going to say wasn't worth saying.

As for employees, be confident about your expertise. Stand up for what you believe in! Years ago, an experienced chocolate maker agreed to produce a sampler box of 12 chocolates for the late clothing designer Bill Blass. The chocolatiers designed a dozen different chocolates for Blass's approval, but sensing that he would resent not having a choice, they seeded the selection with several intentionally inferior pieces. To their horror, Blass liked the inferior chocolates. Blass was a man of great taste in clothes—not candy. After he left the room, the chocolatiers said to one another, "What are we going to do?" Finally, the head of the company, a family business that had thrived for seven generations, decided, "We know chocolate. He doesn't. Let's make the ones we like."

Sweet.

THE LAST WORD

Two things about your article. (1) Getting rid of the "but" and keeping ownership where action is, is very important. Even if the result is slightly different from what you would have created. (2) If the "but" cannot be removed—i.e., the added value springing to mind is very important to add, try saying, "Great idea and . . ." This way, you will be building on top of the idea and not tearing it down.

Anne Daugaard
Denmark

Still Angry After All These Years

From: Issue 75 | October 2003 | By: Jennifer Reingold

When Tom Peters published "The Brand Called You" (included in this collection) and "The Wow! Project," among others, in *Fast Company*, he went from being merely a successful consultant, author, and speaker to being a rock star in the new economy. But who is he? What motivates him now, after the dot-com bust took the new economy with it? We went to Peters's home, an idyllic Vermont farm, to find out why the exponent of the exclamation point is still shouting—and why people are still listening.

It's time to make hay on Tom Peters's 1,400-acre farm in rural West Tinmouth, Vermont. As the farmhands collect bale after bale of fresh hay on this brilliant summer day, the warm sun splashes through the window of Peters's airy farmhouse study, illuminating the entire wall of bookshelves stacked tight with iterations of Peters's 10 books translated into languages from Russian to Japanese. The breeze is calming. The scent of wildflowers wafts through the air. The birds are singing. There's probably even a babbling brook around here somewhere. In short, it's a perfectly idyllic day in what should be the perfectly contented life of one of the world's best-known management thinkers.

"What an ass!" Peters explodes. He's talking about Peter Olson, CEO of Random House, whose Machiavellian approach to management was recently described in excruciating detail in *The New York Times Magazine*. "Someone who takes pleasure in firing like that, it's unbelievable!"

Less than 10 minutes later, the volcano erupts again as Peters talks about his disappointment with a three-book series he published a few years ago. It wasn't the sales that bugged him—he says they hit around 350,000—but how the series was perceived. "I thought it sucked, basically," he exclaims. "It didn't have any impact."

Not to make an impact when you are, among other things, the coauthor of one of the most popular business books ever written (*In Search of Excellence*, HarperCollins, 1982) would certainly be a maddening experience. For a man whose every sentence, including possibly "pass the salt," is uttered with the utmost urgency, it is infuriating. But then fury is something Peters knows how to work with.

Now 60 and a millionaire many times over, Peters could be excused if he wanted to float lazily in his spring-fed pond and spend his days with the sheep, the goats, the alpaca, and the two glorious mountains looming outside his window. Frankly, he doesn't have a whole lot to complain about. But for Peters, getting worked up, annoyed, irritated, steamed, and outraged is the standard MO. It's the way he gets things done. Even his method of dictating the first drafts of his books into a microcassette recorder is to rant. "I'm pissed off at life," he says. "Plus, I happen to believe that only pissed-off people change the world, either in small ways or large ways."

And although he likes to act as if he couldn't care less, changing the world is exactly what he's trying to do in his 11th book, *Re-imagine! Business Excellence in a Disruptive Age* (Dorling Kindersley). The first "big book" he has written since *Circle of Innovation* (Knopf) in 1997, the 352-page tome is basically the unabridged Tom Peters on anything to do with business, from leadership to brands to technology. You've seen or heard about parts of it before, some of it in these pages: ideas such as Brand You and the notion that information technology changes everything in our world. Other aspects, such as the book's beautiful design and Peters's willingness to step back and take a fresh look at the organization in addition to his traditional focus on the individual, are new. Yet this book, coming at a time when many of the New Economy tenets he was best associated with have been discarded, also comes at a critical point for Peters himself. Can his ideas still have impact in a new, far more cynical age?

In *Re-imagine!* Peters envisions his own epitaph, as some 60-year-olds are wont to do. It will read, he fervently hopes:

Thomas J. Peters
1942–Whenever
He Was a Player

"In other words," he continues, "he did *not* sit on the sidelines . . . and watch the world go by . . . as it was undergoing the most profound shift of basic premises in the last several hundred years (if not the last thousand or so years)." The line is vintage Peters, complete with his trademark grandiosity, enthusiasm, and those infernal parentheses. But the epitaph, at least, will prove true, no matter whether you see him as a brilliant thinker who keeps beating the rest of us to the future, a guy who got lucky with his first book and then went off the deep end, or something in between. Tom Peters was—and is—a player.

In person, Peters is far funnier, less pc, more irreverent, and gentler than his uber-punctuated way of writing and public speaking conveys. He still gets mad, obviously, but isn't opposed to conceding a point here or there, or sharing a belly laugh over some of his own excesses. Dressed in a cutoff green sweatshirt, dirty shorts, and hiking boots, Peters, with metal glasses slightly askew, looks more as if he'd spent the afternoon lording it over the weeds in his backyard on a power mower than living the life of "the most influential business thinker of the age," according to his press kit, and the second most prominent business intellectual in the world (after Michael Porter), according to an Accenture study. The refreshing thing about Peters the man is that even if his words are idealistic, he is unabashedly real.

And he is not about to concede defeat. Even as the beautiful future Peters promised us fades in the rearview mirror like a town we never visited, Peters is hard at work repelling the attackers, thrilled, he claims, to be a contrarian again. "So what [if] 98% of the dot-com companies failed? Some of them didn't," he says. "I believe that the New Economy is real. I believe the technology change is just in its infancy." Although he acknowledges that the sort of free agency he championed has become more of a nasty surprise than a liberating choice these days, the notion that you and only you are responsible for your career is more important than ever. "You don't go more than two weeks without seeing that IBM or GE or somebody else is shipping more $100,000 jobs—not $30,000 jobs—offshore," he says. "And so the Darwinian Brand You, every person for themselves, now it's an imperative. It's very different from being cool . . . but the path out is the same whether you got there voluntarily or involuntarily."

True enough. But will people pick up and read a cool, inspirational treatise when the reason they're free agents is that they've been canned? That's the challenge of *Re-imagine!*, which will be published on October 15. It is in some ways a departure for Peters and in other ways a continuation of the same quirks, writing tics, and moments of brilliance that have defined his previous work.

Re-imagine! is most definitely a New Economy book, replete with an unshakable belief that the changes of the past decade or so have permanently transformed the world of work; the book is infused with an optimism that things can and will be better. Those who accuse Peters of lacking relevance and rigor are not going to change their tune this time around. The word WOW isn't as omnipresent as it's been in the past, but it's still there—complete with capital letters, the ubiquitous exclamation points, and the ideology that action beats the pants off sitting around and thinking about action. In Tom's World, it's always better to try a swan dive and deliver a colossal belly flop than to step timidly off the board while holding your nose. Each chapter starts with a "Rant" warning that "We are not prepared" for some massive change—either the coming "stupendous" information-technology adventure or the fact that design will soon be the "Seat of the Soul." Then comes Peters's vision for that theme, such as a new approach to education or a finance department peopled with poets and musicians.

In contrast with such broad visions, Peters's most recent efforts have been focused on narrower subjects. In 1999, for example, there was *The Professional Service Firm 50* (Knopf), a book aimed at energizing the accountants and lawyers of the world. In fact, he originally wanted to do a series of small books, but publisher Dorling Kindersley insisted on starting with the "big think" book, to be followed by a 24-book series. And so *Re-imagine!* is big and unwieldy, trying to tie together the various elements of Peters's thinking, such as the brutally ignored economic power of women, which gets two passionate chapters, and the essential fact that without decent human interaction, none of his inspirational ideas are ever going to work. His view is nothing less than the following: We must destroy virtually all our business organizations and reimagine them, just as Donald Rumsfeld is trying to do with the U.S. military, in order to respond to the new technological and social imperatives of our era. If we don't, he says, we are dead. It's as simple as that.

Although Peters's work reveals plenty of contradictions, most of which he'll readily admit, the one thread binding everything together is passion. Unlike many of his more abstract competitors in the field of management, with Peters it all comes down to one thing and one thing only—the folks. "I like to take the same set of ideas and look at them from the ground perspective," he says. "All these strategy guys—Porter, [Clayton] Christensen—they talk wonderfully about these ideas and then blithely skip over the incredibly boring part called people."

Leadership, and particularly bold leaders who thrive on "paradox" and "the mess," writes Peters, are desperately needed in a post–September 11 world where the virtual organization has gone from consultant-speak to reality in the form of a bunch of Al Qaeda terrorists armed with box cutters. It's the opposite viewpoint of Peters's archrival Jim Collins, whose most recent book, *Good to Great* (HarperCollins, 2001), has hit the perfect tone for this risk-averse age. "It's calming," says Peters, as he fumes about Collins's "stoic, quiet, calm leaders. Wouldn't you like to think that a quiet leader will lead you to the promised land? I think it's total utter bull, because I consider this to be a time of chaos."

What is most obviously fresh and exciting about this book is the design. Irked at Knopf, Peters dropped the imprint for Dorling Kindersley, a London-based unit of Pearson best known for its visually stunning travel and gardening books. "The whole point of what we've been doing is trying to make the medium as interesting as we hope the message is. You can't write about WOW projects in Technicolor times," he says, without presenting the information that way.

It's easy to understand Peters's Technicolor vision when you spend some time in his surroundings. The farmhouse Peters shares with his wife, designer Susan Sargent, is a cacophonous and joyous explosion of color. Sargent's sensibility is all about the feelings unleashed by unusual combinations of unalike colors. Chartreuse meets blood orange meets robin's egg blue in Peters's own household, and that same shock of the visually unexpected makes its business debut in *Re-imagine!* In fact, it was Sargent who first suggested working with Dorling Kindersley.

Visually, the collaboration has been a stunning success. The book looks like a magazine, with arresting photographs of people, buildings, and technologies, plus numbers, exclamation points, and perhaps a few too many shots of Peters expressing a gamut of emotions, from bemused to enraged. His habit of yelling through the use of capital letters is somehow more palatable when they're displayed in cherry red font (the Brand Called Tom's special tint). It is perhaps the first business book that people will actually display on their coffee tables.

Oddly, for a book whose author's name is synonymous with the term "change agent," *Re-imagine!* seems to eschew the notion of personal transformation. Organizations, he says, can be changed if you find and nourish the fringe lurkers and geeks. "FIND THE FREAKS! SIGN 'EM UP! MAKE 'EM YOUR PARTNERS! LET 'EM HELP YOU MAKE REVOLUTION!" he writes. But people, he now maintains, can't be changed. "No, no, no! Never," he says, gathering steam. This is a strange statement coming from someone who gives 70-odd speeches a year—some at $65,000 a pop—on such subjects as "boss-free implementation" and "business excellence in a disruptive age," to the likes of the Equipment Leasing Association and Wal-Mart. "You don't change people. You get damned lucky and catch them at the right moment and they pay attention, but whatever they had when they walked in the door is what they walk out the door with."

The ironic part of all this is that Peters is now on his own quest for change. He has just returned from a visit to Canyon Ranch, that cult of personal transformation that masquerades as a spa. While there, he got a full-scale workup—and the verdict on Peters was as damning as the one he routinely delivers to companies: Change NOW.

Changing his compulsive approach to work, however, is a different story. It goes without saying that being pissed off all the time isn't on Canyon Ranch's recommended list of stress-release activities. "Large doses of adrenaline surging routinely through the system are not good for you," Peters admits. "I'm supposed to be calm now." He now indulges in a deep-breathing exercise that he runs on his computer, and he plans to swap his normal jumping jacks for breath control before he gives a presentation. But he still gives assistants fits by changing everything at the absolute last moment. "There is a moment of truth at 2 or 3 A.M.," he says. It comes when he sees himself "looking into these 3,000 faces who own hardware stores or who are partners at Deloitte & Touche or what have you. And then the whole bloody presentation has to be changed."

Peters becomes wistful when asked what he would do if he didn't have to live life as a human exclamation point but could instead opt to be a simple comma—if he could jettison Tom Peters and start all over. "I don't have a clue," he says. "I've often said I envy Franklin Roosevelt and his stamp collection. And Churchill had his painting. I don't know what I would do. I have no idea." So the quest continues: Find that one person in a thousand. Do work you love. Remain a player. And stay mad at the world.

THE LAST WORD

I find Peters's opposition to Jim Collins's book Good to Great *very interesting. It does seem that Peters's teaching runs counter to the Collins book. My sense is that while Collins's goal is to create great, enduring companies, Peters's is to teach individuals how to be "players." In this view, Peters and Collins don't so much conflict but rather are targeted to have an impact at different levels.*

> David Starr Eckholdt
> Program manager, manager and leadership development
> Intel Corp.
> Chandler, Arizona

How to Give Feedback

From: Issue 80 | March 2004 | By: Seth Godin

Feedback, like love, is something that everyone craves but that can often be hard to share. Best-selling author and marketing guru Seth Godin is here to help. His blueprint for delivering smart feedback is a gem of wisdom sure to make your day—and that of the folks who work for you.

Fast Company readers are far more likely to be asked for their input than the average employee. You're frequently required to approve, improve, and adjust things that are about to become real. And yet, if you're like most people, you're pretty bad at it.

In the interest of promoting your career, making your day at work more fun, improving the work life of your colleagues, and generally making my life a whole lot better, I'd like to give you some feedback on giving feedback. As usual, the ideas are simple—it's doing them that's tricky.

The first rule of great feedback is this: No one cares about your opinion.

I don't want to know how you feel, nor do I care if you would buy it, recommend it, or use it. You are not my market. You are not my focus group.

What I want instead of your opinion is your analysis. It does me no good to hear you say, "I'd never pick that box up." You can add a great deal of value, though, if you say, "The last three products that succeeded were priced under $30. Is there a reason you want to price this at $31?" Or, "We analyzed this market last year, and we don't believe there's enough room for us to compete. Take a look at this spreadsheet." Or even, "That font seems hard to read. Is there a way to do a quick test to see if a different font works better for our audience?"

Analysis is a lot harder than opinion because everyone is entitled to his or her own taste (regardless of how skewed it might be). A faulty analysis, however, is easy to dismantle. But even though it's scary to contribute your analysis to a colleague's proposal, it's still absolutely necessary.

The second rule? Say the right thing at the right time.

If you're asked to comment on a first-draft proposal that will eventually wind its way to the chairman's office, this is not the time to point out that "alot" is two words, not one. Copyediting the document is best done just once, at the end, by a professional. While it may feel as if you're contributing something by making comments about currently trivial details, you're not. Instead, try to figure out what sort of feedback will have the most positive effect on the final outcome, and contribute it now.

Far worse, of course, than the prematurely picky comment is the way-too-late deal-breaker remark. If I've built a detailed plan for a new factory in Hoboken, New Jersey (and negotiated all the variances and integrated the existing landscaping), the time to tell me you were thinking of relocating the plant to Secaucus was six months ago, not the night before the ground-breaking.

The third rule? If you have something nice to say, please say it.

I've been working with someone for about a year, and in that entire time, he's never once prefaced his feedback with, "This was a really terrific piece of work," or "Wow! This is one of the best ideas I've heard in a while." Pointing out the parts you liked best is much more than sugarcoating. Doing so serves several purposes. First, it puts you on the same side of the table as me, making it more likely that your constructive criticism will actually be implemented. If you can start by seeing the project through my eyes, you're more likely to analyze (there's that word again) the situation in a way that helps me reach my goals. "I think it's great that you want to get our quality ratings up. Let's see whether the added people you say this initiative requires are really necessary, and whether beginning your report with staffing needs is the best way to get this past senior management."

Second, it makes it so much more likely that I will come to you for feedback in the future. It's easy to interpret the absence of positive feedback as the absence of any sort of approval or enthusiasm. Finally, being nice to people is fun.

If I haven't intimidated you with my other rules, here's the last one: Give me feedback, no matter what.

It doesn't matter if I ignored your feedback last time (maybe that's because you gave me your opinion, not an analysis). It doesn't matter if you're afraid your analysis might ultimately be a little shaky. It doesn't matter if you're the least powerful person in the room. What matters is that you're smart; you understand something about the organization, the industry, and the market; and your analysis (at the very least) could be the kernel of an idea that starts me down a totally different path.

As always, I welcome your feedback: seth@sethgodin.com. Be nice, but analyze.

THE LAST WORD

Great leaders are either great "feedbackers" or they understand they aren't and they get help from someone who is. Many great companies are run by leader-teams that englobe this vital characteristic. Being good at giving feedback requires both a natural propensity for this (empathy) and mastering the required skills. The latter can be learned, the former not. . . .

Carl Fransman
Brussels, Belgium

And Now the Hard Part

From: Issue 82 | June 2004 | By: Chuck Salter

The benefit of hindsight is that it lets you identify the key decisions that led to the outcome you already know. In this profile of JetBlue, Chuck Salter takes you into the right now, where history gets made. Other promising insurgent airlines have grown to the size of JetBlue, but couldn't get over the hump to become major players. Salter takes advantage of his extraordinary access to capture a company preparing for the future, revealing the usually unseen work involved in kicking things up a notch in business. The result is a rare portrait of a company at a critical juncture.

He's flying, but not the way you imagine the CEO of an airline flying.

Instead of sitting aboard a new blue-and-white jet in leather-upholstered comfort, David Neeleman is piloting a dirt-caked Chevy Tahoe, doing a Dale Earnhardt Jr. through the dark streets of Queens. It's five before 9, his night flight to Salt Lake City departs at 9:25, and Neeleman, the CEO of JetBlue Airways, is 15 minutes from the airport. You do the math.

"I hope we make it," he says with a laugh, gunning the Tahoe into an open lane. "If there's an accident up ahead, we might not."

He could have left the office earlier, but that's not like him. Or he could have left the driving to someone else, but he's not that kind of CEO. He may run an airline with more than 6,000 employees and 57 twin-engine jets, and he may be, as a new book about him claims, "arguably the most innovative figure in modern-day aviation." But he prefers to drive himself, just as he does every morning on the nearly hour-long commute from Connecticut. If the vehicle suggests anything, it's practicality; he and his wife, Vicki, have nine children. Kids' clothes litter the backseat. An empty water bottle rattles amid discarded newspaper pages in the foot well.

As Neeleman races toward John F. Kennedy Airport, darting and weaving through evening traffic, it's clear that he's doing what comes naturally and what he happens to do so well: flying by the seat of his pants.

It's worked pretty nicely so far. At a tough time for the U.S. economy, JetBlue has quite literally soared. While much of the airline industry was crippled by September 11, and while United Airlines and US Airways fell into bankruptcy, JetBlue has been a dramatic example of what can happen when the right entrepreneur with the right idea—low fares and popular frills such as satellite TV and leather seats—comes along at the right moment. Founded in 1999 and flying since 2000, JetBlue has put together 12 consecutive profitable quarters. It enjoys among the industry's best operating margins, the highest percentage of seats filled, and one of the top rates for on-time arrivals.

And Neeleman has an even grander flight plan for JetBlue: He aims to vault his start-up airline into the ranks of the majors, with 290 planes and 25,000 employees within seven years. Although it hit almost $1 billion in revenue last year, JetBlue is still tiny compared with American Airlines, with $17.4 billion, or United, with $13.7 billion, or Delta, with $13.3 billion. And for all its meteoric growth, JetBlue still operates just 220 flights to 23 destinations a day. Compare that with industry leader American's 4,200 daily flights to 250 cities in 40 countries. Now JetBlue is about to embark on a steep climb: In the next 12 months, it expects to hire between 1,700 and 1,800 employees. It's introducing a new plane every three weeks—and next year will be adding one every 10 days, including a second type of aircraft.

Clearly, Neeleman will have to fly by more than the seat of his pants. The airline industry is littered with great start-up airlines that never made it to the big time, all founded by ambitious and imaginative people. Neeleman is already running a company bigger than anything he's ever run before, and its organizational and competitive issues are increasingly daunting. This is, of course, the test all entrepreneurs face if they're lucky enough: Can the genius that helped them create a successful company from nothing be redirected to the very different challenges of running a vast enterprise?

But there's a special twist in JetBlue's case. Much that's distinctive about this airline—from the enthusiasm of its employees to its relentless customer focus to its hip, slightly countercultural image—is precisely the sort of thing you can pull off when you're small, and that becomes far tougher the bigger you get. Can JetBlue maintain those qualities as it morphs from nimble start-up into the bureaucracy that's required to manage a vastly more complex operation?

It's a question that applies to many truly innovative companies these days. Call them postmodern corporations, perhaps. If they pull off this transition, they become big, but remain in important ways the antithesis of bigness—think Starbucks, Dell, and Amazon. Like JetBlue, they depend on flexibility, speed, and a sense of intimacy with employees and customers alike. Put another way, the challenge JetBlue now faces is this: Is small scalable?

As Neeleman rushes into the terminal on this February night, it sure looks as if the answer could be yes. JetBlue is still the sort of outfit where the ticket agents at JFK call out, "Hey, David!" It's 9:15, but there's no need to panic. There's a slight delay. On his way from ticketing through security to the gate, Neeleman takes his time, chatting almost nonstop with employees. It could come across as patronizing, all fake smiles, glib lines, noblesse oblige. The difference here is that the boss knows many of these employees by name. He asks about their job, their kids, a spouse undergoing chemo.

At that moment, JetBlue still feels truly intimate. But then, as Neeleman heads down the jetway, the pilot of the plane teases, "So you really do exist." Turns out, it has taken him two-and-a-half years to finally meet the CEO. It's the hint of danger, the serpent in the garden. JetBlue isn't even that big, and already there's a pilot who has worked here since 2001 and can joke that Neeleman is just a myth.

For all his hands-on entrepreneurial brio, it's clear that Neeleman has been thinking big since the very beginning. For one thing, the bench of executives he's assembled to run the airline every day has depth that would be the envy of any other young company. And Neeleman and his team have carefully laid the groundwork for growth. Some things that start-ups usually wrestle with, like sophisticated technology, are already in place, years ahead of schedule. Pilots, for example, store their flight manual on laptops, so it can be updated instantly. It's the industry's first paperless cockpit. And Neeleman has other resources that will come in handy—like money in the bank, about $600 million in cash and cash equivalents.

He'll need it, because this is one vicious business. A new airline hasn't managed to join the ranks of the real majors in a long time. Since deregulation in 1978, in fact, only a handful of start-ups (such as AirTran and America West) have survived out of the more than 100 launched. For good reason. Planes are damn expensive, and it takes a lot of people to run them.

And Neeleman's start-up has gotten big enough to draw serious competitive fire: In just the last year, two major airlines have started their own versions of JetBlue, Delta's Song, and United's Ted. In December, JetBlue pulled out of Atlanta, its first retreat, after Delta and AirTran flooded the market with new cheap flights. And in January, JetBlue announced that its usually stellar profit margin had dipped three percentage points to 13.3% in the fourth quarter of 2003, largely due to price-cutting by the majors.

Then there are the inevitable growing pains—pains that, in this business, can be lethal. For now, JetBlue enjoys the lowest costs in the industry, just over six cents per passenger seat mile. But any start-up with new planes would have lower costs. The jets don't need major maintenance yet. They will. And none of the staff have worked at the airline more than a few years, so the pay scale is fairly low. It will rise. The point is, large airlines fork over more money to run their business, and the reason why isn't just unimaginative management. That's another price of being big.

Before JetBlue has to worry about the problems of bigness, of course, it has to last long enough and grow fast enough to face them. And Neeleman, 44, has one hole in his resume: He has never run a large company, or even worked at one for very long.

His forte has been launching businesses. While at the University of Utah, he started a travel business and dropped out to run it. Later, he teamed up with the owner of a local travel agency to launch Morris Air, a regional airline, which was eventually purchased by Southwest Airlines, a company he had long admired. Neeleman went along to take his dream job, executive vice president, but lasted less than six months before he was fired. "David didn't understand the nuance of the organization," says Ann Rhoades, a Southwest vice president at the time. "He needed to walk, not run." He went on to help create the company that developed Open Skies, the software for e-tickets, and started and departed from his second airline, WestJet, a thriving low-cost carrier in Canada, by the time he started JetBlue.

But if he's not a big-company guy, Neeleman knows how to attract and adapt mature talent to an immature company. Dave Barger, president and COO, ran Continental's Newark, New Jersey, hub. John Owen, CFO, was treasurer at Southwest. And the head of HR was none other than Rhoades, who had helped show Neeleman the door at Southwest. He has learned a lot since then, she says—including how to practice the sort of restraint that can come hard to strong-willed company founders. "He realized that if you hire A-players, you don't have to sit on them and tell them what to do," she says.

Neeleman and Barger are an impressive duo and a bit of an odd couple, the excitable entrepreneur and the detail-oriented, highly organized, even-tempered son of a United pilot. "They're yin and yang," says Dave Bushy, who recently joined JetBlue as vice president of flight operations and who once held the same title at Delta.

Neeleman doesn't dwell on minutiae, doesn't dissect problems; Barger spends hours poring over operational matters, ironing out glitches such as too few wheelchairs at a gate. Neeleman skims business books, looking for nuggets; Barger reads them cover to cover. While Neeleman can't leave the office until a half hour before a flight from JFK, Barger leaves an hour-and-a-half early. They're alike in the ways that matter most, though. They share the same down-to-earth style and unrelenting work ethic (read: 12-hour days). They believe the best bosses practice "servant leadership," helping others do their jobs better.

If there's one airline that serves as a cautionary tale for JetBlue, it's People Express Airlines. Back in the early 1980s, it revolutionized air travel, offering dirt-cheap fares, preaching customer focus, and priding itself on an energetic staff. Its charismatic and boyish fortysomething founder, Donald Burr, was featured on magazine covers and on TV. The airline reached a billion dollars in annual sales in less than five years. Sound familiar?

Then, at approximately the same point JetBlue finds itself today—on the verge of becoming big—People Express stretched too far. Its systems couldn't handle rapidly increasing volume, and it also choked on an acquisition. People Express wound up with a one-way ticket to oblivion just a year later. "I lived it," says Chris Collins, who was a team manager at People Express and is now JetBlue's vice president of systems operations. "For five years, we were the best thing going. A year later, we're [gone] because we couldn't sustain growth. You want to know what keeps me up at night? Figuring out what we're going to need not next year but five years from now."

To get big, JetBlue's team knows, it's sometimes necessary to act big. For instance, Barger understands the processes and tools needed to drive consistency through the operation—the often mundane details and numbers that seem to elude so many entrepreneurs. Early every morning, he and members of the operations team review the previous day's flights. On Mondays, they review the past week. At their fingertips: things like takeoff and landing times, and when the last bag hit the belt (the goal is no longer than 20 minutes after the plane reaches the gate). "The 45 minutes you wait for your bags is your last impression," Barger says.

The program also produces a list of "focus flights," the 10 worst delays, which the team deconstructs. Since people have such low expectations of low-fare carriers, Barger says, JetBlue wants to differentiate itself through reliability. Two of the most important performance numbers are the completion rate (the proportion of flights that aren't canceled), in which JetBlue led the industry last year, and on-time arrivals, in which it ranked second.

One of the latest tools designed to help JetBlue as it grows is an "operational recovery system." During any disruption—weather that grounds some flights, for example—it allows planners to select various goals before rerouting planes. No canceled flights or delays beyond three hours? The software produces a solution and calculates its cost. It factors in each plane's maintenance and fuel needs, and the flight crew's experience and availability within FAA rules. With the current fleet of 57 planes, the program is a perk. Down the road, with 100 or more planes, it will be indispensable.

As it manages growth, the airline must also standardize many other things it does to avoid starting from scratch every time. For example, JetBlue has developed a checklist of what has to happen whenever it enters a new market. Everyone involved has access to the list on the corporate intranet. Each department sees what has been done, what remains to be done, deadlines, problems. Currently, the checklist makes launches that occur months apart more predictable. But before too long, it'll make simultaneous launches, unthinkable early on, manageable.

These efforts also improve efficiency, which will be critical in the years ahead as JetBlue tries to offset rising costs for aging planes and more-senior employees. And low costs remain an obsession. JetBlue's reservation agents, for example, work from home rather than in an expensive call center. At the same time, Neeleman is looking to widen profit margins again. A new 100-seat regional jet fleet being added next year will tap relatively uncontested—and so more profitable—markets.

In many ways, the question of whether JetBlue can do all this—grow and standardize and automate—while still preserving its personal touch comes down to this: Can Neeleman be scaled?

He's certainly trying tonight. As the plane heads toward Salt Lake City, he works his way down the aisle talking to customers. He meets someone who knows his father. He meets a fellow entrepreneur. For an hour-and-a-half, Neeleman chats and collects business cards. He has an ease with people of all types—been that way since he worked as a Mormon missionary in Brazil.

In some sense, the plane is his personal focus group. He asks customers what they like and don't like, what the airline should do differently. He jots down suggestions. Almonds, the newest snack, are being introduced in May after passengers asked him for a low-carb item.

Neeleman's real audience, however, is the flight crew. He works alongside them, creating "the JetBlue experience," great service that fosters loyal customers. "I want them to know that I value what they do," he says. "I value it so much that I'm not too good to do it. I fly with 8 to 12 crew-members a week, but the other 1,200 flight attendants know about it."

Neeleman likes to say that the airline's TVs are overrated, that the real secret weapon is the employees, all of whom are called "crewmembers" to emphasize the companywide sense of teamwork. If you treat people well, the company's philosophy goes, they'll treat the customer well. "There is no 'they' here," says Al Spain, senior vice president of operations. "It's 'we' and 'us.' We succeed together or we fail together."

JetBlue's staff isn't unionized. While insisting that he's not against unions, Neeleman makes it clear that he would prefer to avoid them. If management and crewmembers trust one another and if people feel they're compensated fairly (last year's 17% profit sharing certainly helped), he believes that there's no need for a third party. And the crewmembers are more likely to stick by the company in tough times.

One challenge for a rapidly growing company is stoking the fires of new and old employees, the ones who are just joining the company and haven't been exposed to the culture and the ones who have been with the airline for years. You keep both groups excited, Barger says, by making them realize how much their contributions matter.

Take the pilots. At most airlines, they're seen as one-dimensional technicians, says Bushy, the VP of flight operations. He prods JetBlue pilots to participate in the business. One pilot creates elaborate airport diagrams to help orient colleagues. Another pitches in doing financial analysis for the company. And another is making an inventory of her fellow pilots' skills in hope of identifying other abilities that might be useful to the airline.

One of the reasons Neeleman and Barger have been so effective at building a dedicated staff is that their visibility is no gimmick. They're not making pronouncements from the corner office. David and Dave, as they're known to crewmembers, are out cultivating and championing the culture on the front lines. In addition to flying JetBlue most weeks, they appear together at nearly every first day of orientation for new hires. They conduct monthly "pocket sessions," informal Q&As with crewmembers.

As JetBlue's planes and cities multiply, though, Neeleman and Barger will no doubt seem less visible, simply because they can't be everywhere. To combat creeping management anonymity, each officer is assigned one of the airline's destinations, a "Blue City." Once a quarter, he or she visits that operation to meet with crewmembers and work alongside them. The visits help employees in the field form working ties to executives at headquarters. "Not many companies have the kind of culture where you're a customer-service rep and you can pick up the phone and call a VP at the company and get their ear right away," says Vinny Stabile, vice president of people.

All this effort isn't just to make employees feel good (or even to keep them from unionizing). Ultimately, it's about building a system that consistently delivers a better experience to passengers. And that may well be critical to JetBlue's survival. Despite plenty of evidence that the cost of a ticket is what matters most to airline passengers, Neeleman believes that JetBlue can compete on more than price. In some markets, its passengers are willing to pay fares that average $20 more than on American and Song. Ordinarily, upstart carriers duke it out in bare-knuckled price wars. Neeleman's betting his airline that good service, delivered by passionate employees, will give JetBlue a lasting edge.

But as JetBlue grows, it relies more and more on employees who weren't there in the beginning, when the entire staff could fit in one room. They weren't in the crisis center on September 11, scrambling to find shuttle buses and hotel rooms for stranded passengers. They weren't at JFK during the blackout in 2003, when employees armed with little more than flashlights worked around the clock to make sure most flights took off. They haven't been through the experiences that bind a staff together.

That's why preserving the culture increasingly requires conscious effort, starting with orientation. On the first day, Barger explains the JetBlue brand, and Neeleman teaches how the company makes money and how each employee contributes to the bottom line. "Our people have business literacy," says Bushy. And they care, in large part because the numbers affect their profit sharing.

He's supposed to be on vacation. That's what Neeleman tells the few dozen employees gathered in a training room at JetBlue University in Forest Hills, New York. He had promised his family a long weekend in Florida. When he drove them to the airport, though, he put them on a plane and headed to work. He'll join them tomorrow. Neeleman doesn't want sympathy. He simply wants the group to know how important he considers them and their training. On the first day of the program, Principles of Leadership (POL), Neeleman leads a session called "Why are you here?" It also explains why he's here.

POL is a sort of midflight correction—a response to some troubling evidence that JetBlue's culture was already starting to stray off course. In a 2002 staff survey, one-third of respondents voiced unhappiness about their supervisors. To their dismay, Neeleman and Barger discovered they were promoting people without teaching them how to manage. Employees griped about bosses whose abrasive style and favoritism undermined the environment that David and Dave had nurtured.

The answer was POL, a five-day program taught by senior executives for managers at every level, from VP to first officer. The idea is to reinforce and transmit the key elements of JetBlue's culture by teaching attendees to practice the five primary principles: "Treat your people right," "Communicate with your team," "Inspire greatness in others," "Encourage initiative and innovation," and "Do the right thing." "POL is designed to create leaders that understand what I would do if I were there," says Spain, the operations chief. "They're not clones, but I want them to understand the foundations of the business, the principles we built the company on, and the leadership principles."

JetBlue's senior leaders tell stories to illustrate those principles—stories that often have to do with flexibility or circumventing barriers. When is it okay to break the rules? Spain describes how a JetBlue pilot bought a couple of dozen McDonald's Happy Meals for kids when his plane was stuck on the ground. The fast-food run may have been unorthodox, but he did the right thing.

Make no mistake, though: POL is all about helping JetBlue scale. Graduates become "anointed proprietors of the culture," says Stabile. "Instead of 25 officers, you have 800 people in leadership positions throughout the company who believe in this culture." Most carry a copy of the principles with their ID badge. "It's our crewmembers' bill of rights," says Neeleman.

And it's values like those taught in POL that, in turn, attract people like Bonny Simi. She's one of the hardest sort of people for JetBlue to sign on, an experienced pilot working for a major airline. If pilots switch airlines, they start over, at the bottom rung of seniority. But Simi, a captain at United for 12 years (and three-time Olympic luge slider), wanted to be more engaged with an airline, more inspired.

Wary of a young, unproven airline, she researched the company for six months. The values mirrored her own, but she wanted to be sure they weren't just talk, and that it would be worth taking a big pay cut. She read business-school case studies and SEC filings. She contacted Michael Lazarus, then chairman of JetBlue's board, and grilled him. "This is the next 20 years of my life," she says. "I had to be sure."

Several months into the job, Simi routinely sends Bushy ideas on how to improve safety and standardization. Recently, she walked into the office of Collins, the vice president of system operations, without an appointment to pitch an idea on pilot reports. "Did I feel valued that I had an idea and a vice president here said, 'I like it'? Definitely. That was so cool. Does that inspire me to come up with other ideas to make this a better airline? In a major way."

At half past midnight in Salt Lake City, Neeleman looks as grounded as you could get. Dress shirt untucked, eyes rimmed red, he's coming down the aisle of the Airbus A320, his arms wrapped around a bundle of blankets and pillows. All JetBlue employees help clean a plane when it lands. Another cost averted: no cleaning crew. But like other practices at JetBlue, it serves a symbolic purpose as well. The work transcends job titles. Pilots don rubber gloves to empty seatbacks. Staffers traveling on their day off pitch in, too. And so does the visiting CEO.

In his own way, Neeleman does scale. Like JetBlue, he's retaining certain qualities while evolving. He's not the brash, impatient thirtysomething entrepreneur who thought he had all the answers at Southwest. He's a 44-year-old big-company executive in the making.

He's still a man on a mission—to continually improve the product, the JetBlue experience—and he still has an uncanny ability to rally other people to that mission. But he also says he's not as hands-on as he used to be. He understands his role. "I'm not the guy to oversee the day to day," he says. "That's Dave Barger. He loves that. I'm looking for the new deal, the new technology. My passion is making sure our product stays fresh and exciting and that we keep our costs low."

Not day to day, perhaps. But Neeleman can't resist checking, tweaking, reaching out. He logs on to the airline's Web site and books a flight to Buffalo to find out if the extra leg room is being promoted enough (it's not). He calls the operations department to find out what's being done for passengers on a plane that was struck by lightning and delayed for six hours (not enough). He also makes time to call a flight attendant he knows who collapsed on a flight the day before (she's fine).

Neeleman's one-on-one leadership may seem quaint and overmatched in a large company, but it has ways of rippling out, of moving people to feel passion about his vision and their work at JetBlue. "I would walk through a burning building for him," says Tom Krizek, the pilot of the Salt Lake City flight. He's the same pilot who met Neeleman for the first time five hours earlier and spent the last hour of the trip talking with him about family and life and flying after Neeleman moved to the cockpit. The pilot who had greeted him, "So you really do exist."

And after 1 A.M. (3 A.M. his time), Neeleman stands in line at the Hertz counter. As he waits, he talks to a few passengers who have just gotten off his flight. He asks about their upcoming ski trip, tells them about plans to expand JetBlue to new cities. When they're done, he steps forward and hands over his premium club card. He didn't have to stand in line for his car. He could have whipped out the card and been on his way, but that would have meant jumping ahead of JetBlue customers. That's not his style.

THE LAST WORD

Last year, we took our kids down to Florida to visit Grandma and Grandpa on JetBlue. Traveling with three children under the age of four is intimidating enough, but imagine getting them through an airport and on and off a plane—not once but twice.

The folks at JetBlue were amazing. They helped carry all of our paraphernalia on and off the plane, made sure our children were all settled in, and even offered us an early snack run. They didn't have to cater to us and the other families on the plane. But they did, and it made our experience all the better. It's that sort of service that made us JetBlue customers for life.

David Parmet
Pound Ridge, New York

The Toll of a New Machine

From: Issue 82 | May 2004 | By: Charles Fishman

In this award-winning story, Charles Fishman considers the latest generation of self-service kiosks, already ubiquitous in airports and rapidly
emerging in other venues such as fast-food restaurants. Rather than
merely reviewing the technology and profiling the company behind it, or
lamenting how the kiosks are putting people out of work, Fishman cleverly
analyzes the productivity such technology truly creates. The kiosks not
only present opportunities to do more with less but also more with more.
You can rethink the jobs of the people who once had to spend their days
doing the repetitive tasks the kiosks do best. You can redeploy talent to
address the additional transactions you can now handle. In a delightful
twist, the kiosks could create more interesting jobs—and give customers
better service.

The intersection of Interstate 4 and Florida's Highway 27 is a well-known
spot, the point where the clutter of Orlando's theme parks exhausts itself
and the old Florida of citrus groves and sandy ridges picks up.

There is a McDonald's at this intersection, and in a booth on a recent
Friday, Don Vaughn is having lunch with his daughter-in-law and grand-
daughter. They've driven 12 miles to this McDonald's, drawn by the power
of a dawning technology.

"It's fantastic," says Vaughn, a local. "I love it. It's the new age."

"We tell [the machine] the way we want it," says Chrystal, Vaughn's
daughter-in-law, "and we know it's done right." Done right, in Chrystal's
case, means no onions.

The liberating new-age technology in use right there inside the

McDonald's—a pair of kiosks bolted to the floor near the front counter—allows customers to use a touch screen to order their Big Macs and Happy Meals exactly the way they want them. Vaughn, Chrystal, and Heather drove to this particular McDonald's—as they do regularly—just to order their food on the touch screens themselves.

In the tumult of lunchtime at a busy McDonald's, and in the tumult of the U.S. economy, the slim, silver machines would be easy to overlook, though each is as tall as a person and sports a colorful screen. There are just 85 of them, installed in 48 franchised restaurants, all without the help of McDonald's itself.

The company quietly putting self-ordering computers in McDonald's is Kinetics Inc., whose self-service technology has already swept through the airline industry, with results that have amazed executives and customers alike. Every day, hundreds of thousands of airline customers check themselves in, cheerfully doing work that used to be done by thousands of airline ticket agents. Kinetics' self-service vision could have the same impact on the fast-food business as it has had on airlines—and fast food and airlines are just the start. Besides checking ourselves in for flights at the airport, we may soon be checking out rental cars at our destinations without talking to anyone, and then checking into hotels at a lobby kiosk that, first, displays a diagram of all the rooms available and then, after we choose one, pops out a room key.

If you look at the dozens of Kinetics self-service machines lined up at Delta's terminal in Atlanta, or Northwest's in Minneapolis, or Continental's in Houston, you'll begin to understand the role they're already having in a powerful economic trend: the ability of U.S. businesses to do more and more with the same, or fewer, workers. Labor productivity grew at an astounding annual rate of 9.5% during the third quarter of last year, the largest quarterly leap since 1983. That's an unsustainable pace (and it dropped to a more typical 2.6% in the fourth quarter), but it is part of a steady trend that has productivity increasing in the past two years at more than twice the historical pace. Crudely put, the numbers mean the work that required 100 people in 2000 requires just 89 people today.

Kinetics and its kiosks are capitalizing on this productivity trend and driving it. The company, which makes about two-thirds of the nation's airport self-check-in machines, is an all-but-unknown Lake Mary, Florida, outfit. Although Kinetics does everything itself—from designing and manufacturing its own machines to servicing them in the field—it is tiny. Last year, tens of millions of airline customers checked themselves in on machines that were designed, produced, and supported by just 67 employees.

But the impact of Kinetics and its kiosks isn't as obvious or as scary as the sensationalist headline those numbers might suggest—"67-Person Company Puts Thousands of Airline Employees Out of Work!" True, airlines have been shedding jobs in the past few years, but that's largely due to industry woes that have nothing to do with automation. And it's unlikely that these machines will mean the end of ticket agents, rental-car clerks, or the front-desk staff at hotels. Instead, those jobs will change—and eventually, there may be more of them, not fewer, because of self-service. That seems counterintuitive, but employment has actually grown in other service businesses that have been automated. At the dawn of the self-service banking age in 1985, for example, the United States had 60,000 automated teller machines and 485,000 bank tellers. In 2002, the United States had 352,000 ATMs—and 527,000 bank tellers. ATMs notwithstanding, banks do a lot more than they used to and have a lot more branches than they used to.

Instead, the story of Kinetics offers a glimpse of the continued power of computers, automation, and the Internet to transform our lives as both workers and consumers—a power that, far from having plateaued, is only just getting started. Information technology hasn't touched lots of things that are just waiting to be automated, computerized, or kiosked. That they will be automated seems inevitable. But the results aren't so clear. Will all these smart machines create more jobs and free workers to tackle more rewarding, more complex tasks? Or will we gradually see the disappearance of a whole category of frontline workers? Will kiosks leave customers feeling well cared for and more closely linked to the businesses that use them, or frustrated and trapped in a real-world version of voice-mail hell? The answers have a lot more to do with how a company uses such machines than with the technology itself.

Kinetics, which delivered its first machines to Alaska Airlines in 1996, has transformed a kludgy, aggravating part of the air-travel experience that has long resisted improvement. In December, 70.3% of Northwest Airlines' passengers checked themselves in for their flights, the majority using Kinetics' kiosks, the rest online, a function made possible by Kinetics' software. That's up from 50% in May and 20% in 2001.

Entering an arena dominated by muscular global players such as NCR, Diebold, Siemens, and IBM, Kinetics has consistently beaten the giants in head-to-head competition for business. Kinetics' technology is running not just the self-check-in machines of Alaska, Continental, Delta, and Northwest, but also AirTran, Hawaiian, and Frontier. In March, Kinetics won the business of United Airlines, which had been using IBM. United plans to begin installing Kinetics' machines immediately. The company's software makes possible the newer Internet check-in process for many airlines; it runs the ticket-issuing system for Orbitz; and, along with its hardware, is spreading to gates at many airports to speed boarding.

Unlike many information-age companies, there is nothing virtual about Kinetics. The company takes pride in doing everything: Employees write the software, design the hardware, and staff a storefront factory in Lake Mary. A field group of 12 technicians keeps the airport kiosks running at what Continental says is 99.5% reliability. And CEO, president, and founder David Melnik says privately held Kinetics is profitable and has been so almost since its first contract. "Companies multiples of our size don't have the impact on culture and business that we do," he says. "That's a pretty radical thing. I think it's pretty cool."

At Continental Airlines, 66% of U.S. passengers check themselves in at Kinetics kiosks. "We never thought it would go above 25%," says Scott O'Leary, Continental's senior manager in charge of airport self-service for passengers. As for the lines that used to bedevil even business travelers, says O'Leary, "We are essentially queueless." And once customers are standing at a kiosk, he says, "the mean check-in time is 66 seconds. For customers with no bags, it's 30 seconds." At big airports, your plane is more likely to stand in line to take off than you are to check in.

Self-service has begun to pop up in so many places—photo-processing kiosks in drugstores, self-testing kiosks to renew driver's licenses, automated toll payment—that the technology has quickly gone from novel to unremarkable. But self-service often feels like the opposite of service, or it feels as if the customer has been made an involuntary, unpaid worker. Whatever the efficiency of pumping your own gas, doing so doesn't make the experience of filling your tank any better; depending on the weather, doing it yourself is often downright unpleasant.

But here's something every airline passenger knows: Kinetics' machines actually improve the task they automate. They don't just make the experience quicker, they make it better. Jeffrey Lammers, who used to design nuclear weapons and until February was Kinetics' head of hardware engineering, says, "You won't find anyone who flies a lot who won't just hug these machines."

The self-service kiosk shows you a seat map of the plane you're boarding—you see where your seat is, you see what seats are still open, and you're free to pick one you like better. And only you know that after your first choice—aisle, far forward, but not bulkhead—and your second choice—window, far forward, but not bulkhead—your third choice is any row where there's an empty middle seat. Except not farther back than row 20, because you don't want to wait 15 minutes to get off the plane. And then there's your fourth, fifth, and sixth choices. No ticket agent has the patience to walk through this with any passenger, let alone every passenger. The kiosk handles it in seconds. And it can be programmed to operate in 12 languages. "It's the end of the 'veil of secrecy' at check-in," says Continental's O'Leary. "It's a quick, informative check-in, instead of standing in line for customer service." When this kind of automation is done right, Kinetics' CEO Melnik says, "People don't perceive it as technology, they perceive it as an enabler in their life."

Melnik, 39, is one of those smart, restless souls who stumble into entrepreneurship because it makes so much more sense than working for companies that are too big, too slow, and too hesitant. A college dropout whose real passion is marine biology (for a while, he performed as "Flipper Boy," cavorting with dolphins at the Miami Seaquarium), he started the company that became Kinetics in 1988 after working as a sales agent for a Tampa travel agency. The experience of selling and delivering airline tickets to small businesses got him wondering why those tickets couldn't be handled more like money in ATMs and less like a special product that had to be "produced" at a travel agency. "I got interested in this, and it hooked me," he says.

Melnik worked with NCR on several projects, including plans to bring an early kiosk to the Trump Shuttle in New York's LaGuardia Airport. He worked with Siemens on a project for Lufthansa. He also worked as a waiter, accepted start-up funding from his mother-in-law, and lived for several years off the teacher's salary of his wife, Cindy. He can write software, and he can "bend metal" to make kiosks.

It took nearly eight years of persistence for the technology, the airline mind-set, and the customers to catch up with Melnik's vision. He sold Alaska Airlines on those first machines, called Orcas, using a cardboard mock-up.

How this kind of simple but powerful self-service technology ripples through businesses and the economy always looks easier to predict than it is. The first passenger elevator in the world, created by Elisha Otis, was installed in a New York department store in 1857; it wasn't until 1950—nearly a century later—that the Otis Elevator Co. came up with the technology for self-service elevators. In 1955, 500,000 people in the United States were working as elevator operators, jobs that were almost all gone less than 10 years later.

But as it turns out, the impact of even the most pervasive self-service, on productivity and on customers, is easy to misinterpret. Kinetics' machines improve the productivity of airline ticket agents—but not by allowing the ticket agents to do more work, more quickly. They allow the ticket agents to preside over more work being done—in this case, by the customers. And it may be this sort of productivity improvement that helps make possible the "jobless recovery," in which companies manage to grow without hiring new employees or without recalling those who have been laid off.

Indeed, when you use a self-check-in machine, you can't help but wonder about the thousands of airline employees who have lost their jobs since September 11. Last year, Northwest flew 12% fewer passengers than in 2000. But it did so with 25% fewer employees. If Delta had been staffed in 2003 the way it was in 2000, it would have employed 2,500 more people. Since the end of 2000, Kinetics' three biggest customers—Delta, Northwest, and Continental—have shed some 37,000 employees, enough people to run all of Northwest today.

Of course, the airlines are a complicated case—their business was out of

whack before the September 11 attacks, and the attacks hit the airline business harder than any other. But even where the impact of such machines
looks obvious, labor tends to squirt around the economy in unpredictable,
even counterintuitive, ways. Although Continental now has 780 kiosks in
130 airports, with the machines handling the vast majority of passengers,
the airline has reduced the number of airport agents by only 4% since September 11.

Melnik likes to say that each Kinetics self-check-in machine, at an initial
cost of between $6,000 and $10,000, takes the place of two and a half ticket
agents, because the machine is available (at least) from 6 A.M. to 9 P.M.,
seven days a week—or about the number of hours that many agents would
work. But that both understates and overstates the machines' impact.

Kinetics has installed 3,800 self-check-in machines for airlines—but
9,500 ticket agents have not lost their jobs. At the same time, at airports in
Atlanta and Houston, where there are banks of dozens of check-in machines, the kiosks handle surges of passengers easily and quickly. No airline
can have 50 or 100 ticket agents waiting to take bags and issue boarding
passes; but many airlines have that many check-in terminals in individual
airports.

At Continental, O'Leary acknowledges that the airline is using Kinetics'
technology to grow traffic without adding staff and costs. "It's absolutely
true that before self-service, we were adding staff and [airport] real estate
like you wouldn't believe," he says. "Once you have self-service deployed,
you can absolutely contain those costs. But we still argue we are getting better productivity and service out of our existing agents."

O'Leary is sensitive to the perception—from both staff and passengers—
that Kinetics' kiosks take jobs. But he argues that they're really just eliminat-
ing tedious, repetitive work and freeing agents to deliver real customer
service to passengers who don't like the machines, or have more complicated issues. "My position has evolved," he says. "Watching anyone do cleri-
cal transactions over and over again just looks like wasted time. Having [a
ticket agent] punch the same combination of 122 keys over and over and
over again—that's just wasted effort in the 21st century. It's not the society I
think of as productive."

* * *

Here's how persuasive the self-service machines were to Gary and Kim Moulton, who own the McDonald's at the intersection of Interstate 4 and Highway 27 in central Florida, and five more McDonald's in that area. The day in early 2002 when the very first machine was delivered and hooked up, the Moultons ordered nine more. "I said, 'Tell us when you can install the rest of them,'" says Gary.

For the Moultons, the self-service ordering machines have been one surprise after another. "The first surprise was, the first day it went in, customers said to us, 'It's not just fast, it's not just accurate—this is fun!' " says Kim. One college girl was so amazed by the machines, she ran up and hugged Gary. "She said, 'Thank you, this is the greatest,' " he recalls, still amazed at the reaction. (The Moultons' favorite customer response comes at their highway store, from tourists: "We don't have these up north.")

The Moultons expected the kiosks to handle 25%, maybe 30% of their volume; the average across all six stores after two years is 45%, and at a couple of them, more than 50% of customers order themselves. People routinely stand in line for the kiosks, even when the counter is clear, with people ready to take orders.

These machines are the work of Todd Liebman, who started a company called Quick Kiosk, which he sold to Kinetics last year. Liebman is now head of a Kinetics division targeting "quick service" restaurants. Fast-food machines are both simpler and more complicated than the airline machines. They are simpler because they don't have to constantly and quickly access vital, secure databases such as passenger manifests. They are more complicated because even a McDonald's lunch menu offers many more choices than an airplane seat map. You can specify the elements of your burger—cheese, lettuce, ketchup, mayonnaise—in a range of choices from none to extra. Everything from breakfast to dessert has a picture.

The machines have actually increased the Moultons' labor costs—in two ways. Volume overall is up so much that they have had to add kitchen staff to make more food. And the Moultons have added "kiosk representatives" to greet customers and help them with the machines. "We've basically had to add two people per store," says Gary. "One in the kitchen, one for the kiosks, and we haven't been able to take anyone off the front counters." But if labor costs have gone up, the Moultons' cost of labor as a percentage of sales has dropped. "We've outpaced the labor costs with the increase in sales," says Gary.

That's the double-reverse flip of the productivity improvement: The kiosks make everyone at the Moultons' restaurants so much more efficient—customers, kitchen staff, counter staff (who still take all cash payments and deliver everyone's food)—that the Moultons have used the machines to increase their payroll. During the breakfast and lunch rushes, the kiosks give the Moultons all kinds of headroom to keep customers flowing and lines down.

In fact, unlike the airport, where you've already picked your airline before you face check-in lines, the kiosks in a McDonald's can quickly increase business. One of the key factors in picking a fast-food lunch spot is the wait. The front counter is a choke point. "I had a customer come up to me in one of our city stores recently," says Gary. "She said, 'I love these kiosks, but it sure is hurting your business, because there are no lines at lunch anymore!'"

The final surprise is that customers who use the kiosks spend more money. Because the Moultons' volumes are so high, and have remained that way for so long, they know this is not some quirk of self-selection. On average, customers who use the machines spend $1 more per check. "With the size of our typical order, that's a 30% increase," says Gary. "That's huge."

The Moultons have a couple of ideas to explain why kiosk checks are bigger. The color kiosk screens are a great sales tool—you can put the new McDonald's premium salads right in the center; 20% of customers who initially don't order a drink and are offered one (with a picture) buy it. Then there's the embarrassment factor. A substantial customer might be reluctant to upsize the fries, or order two Big Macs, or an extra apple pie, from a counter person. The kiosk can't snicker, even to itself.

In some ways, the job issues are less stark at fast-food restaurants than at airline ticket counters. "You are always going to need a substantial number of people to run a McDonald's," says Liebman. "You aren't going to automate the cooking of the food, you aren't going to automate the delivery of the food, not any time soon." The McDonald's kiosks take payment by credit card; for cash, in terms of speed, it's still much quicker to have a customer step to the counter and hand over money to a person than feed bills and coins into a machine. And although it's easy to lament the steady erosion of personal contact in commerce, McDonald's is rarely the source of richly satisfying service encounters.

Kinetics CEO Melnik has been working on travel kiosks for more than 10 years and sees the kiosk business as a graveyard of silly ideas. "We are an industry built on failures," he says. "People are enamored with kiosks. There are kiosks all over the place that no one uses: kiosks at the mall for shopping, kiosks for community information, kiosks for job listings."

Kinetics has been successful, Melnik says, because it isn't trying to trick-up an ordinary experience with a "multimedia experience." "We focus on transactions that already exist," he says, and he wants machines that make those transactions steadily simpler. "I think that 10 years from now, serving yourself will be the default, versus now, where it's the exception," he says.

And when you raise your eyes from the airline business—where Kinetics has had a dramatic impact while selling 1,341 machines in 2003, manufacturing an average of just 5 a day—the market size, and the potential for transformation, is stunning. Kinetics is already talking to rental-car, cruise-ship, movie-theater, and hotel companies. The fast-food business alone could keep Kinetics busy for years. The top five fast-food chains by revenue—McDonald's, Burger King, Wendy's, Taco Bell, and Subway—have 48,000 restaurants in the United States.

It's easy to envision the typical fast-food restaurant installing a couple of kiosks inside. But for impact, the real key is the drive-through lane, where a Kinetics touch-screen kiosk, mounted on a pole and weatherproofed, could solve a problem that has confounded engineers for 40 years: our inability to be heard through the drive-through speaker when we shout, "No mustard!"

THE LAST WORD

Automate me? Why yes, please and thanks. I appreciate innovative integration, valuable technology, and speedy service. Machines aren't rude and I get it just the way I like it. I say, change or be changed.

Cynthia Nevels
Dallas, Texas

The Thrill of Defeat

From: Issue 83 | June 2004 | By: Bill Breen

Drug development is R&D at its most extreme. The stakes—life and death, the end of suffering—are gigantic, as are the challenges. It can take decades to crack the code of an illness, which means that some brilliantly talented scientists may go their entire careers without sharing the success of a blockbuster drug like Lipitor or Zoloft. Bill Breen visited Pfizer's Groton, Connecticut, labs, the hub of what may be the largest R&D effort in the world, to learn how these folks stay motivated through extreme, prolonged failure. His chronicle of Pfizer's 30-year-plus effort to develop a drug to treat diabetes complications will make you think twice about just what it takes for a pharmaceutical company to create a successful medicine. And you'll also never feel the same way about setbacks in your own work.

Nancy Hutson is a whip-smart, outspoken 55-year-old biologist who joined Pfizer Inc. as a research scientist in 1981. She spent the next 15 years in drug discovery at Groton Laboratories, and put 35 medicines into development at a total cost of billions. Despite all that time and money, not a single one of Hutson's new-drug prospects ever made it to market. Nothing that she touched, in other words, was a success.

So has Hutson found another line of work? Is she, perhaps, a biology teacher? Or maybe a consultant, that ultimate refuge for someone with a record of relentless commercial failure? Hardly. Since 2000, Hutson has been senior vice president of global research and development at Pfizer and the director of Groton Labs, the largest drug-discovery facility on earth. And before that, she held a series of increasingly important management posts at Pfizer's Central Research Division.

Hutson's ascent in the face of what would be, by the standards of most other industries, a catastrophic series of disappointments, tells you a lot about the rarefied world of pharmaceutical R&D. Drug discovery is a costly slog in which hundreds of scientists screen tens of thousands of chemicals against specific disease targets. After a remorseless round of testing, most of those compounds will prove to be unstable, unsafe, or otherwise unsuitable for human use. Pfizer spends $152 million a week funding 479 early-stage, preclinical discovery projects; 96% of those efforts will ultimately bomb. In today's show-me-the-money corporate world, drug labs like Groton may be unique: Because drug-development projects are parsed out over years and sometimes even decades, and because their rate of attrition is so horrendous, these labs are prisms through which conventional notions of success and failure get stretched and squeezed into strange new shapes. They're also a world in which many of the typical emotional incentives for coming into work each day—the chance to be part of a winning team, to launch a hit new product, to beat a sales target—simply don't apply.

Any business that's developing new products or tackling new markets— any business worth its salt, in other words—faces setbacks; they are the price of ambition. And we're all exhorted to dare to fail. Still, the assumption is that our defeats will be only occasional setbacks—instructional blemishes on our otherwise untainted records of success.

Pfizer's drug-development efforts are failure at its most extreme, and they demand persistence at its most heroic. Want to know how to motivate people to take on almost impossible odds, and then how to lead them through disappointment and loss? Ask Hutson. Drug discovery's high-risk, high-reward model means that she must steel both herself and her talented and ambitious researchers for lifetimes of chronic futility. "As leaders, a big part of our task is to keep the best and brightest minds in research connected to the mission," she says. "At the same time, we have to help them understand that only a tiny minority of them—over their entire careers— will ever touch a winning drug." Within Pfizer, in fact, the scientists who have actually invented a successful compound are viewed as near-mythic figures because there are so few of them. And for the rest? "We have to lead them through failure," Hutson says.

*   *   *

Make no mistake: Groton Labs isn't some academic hothouse where a few eggheads are allowed to toil fruitlessly forever. This is a vast commercial enterprise, and one on which Pfizer depends for much of its future success. More than 4,000 people work on this sprawling campus built on what was once a submarine shipyard in southeastern Connecticut. In Building 220, a massive complex of glass and steel, more than 750 chemists, biologists, and drug-metabolism specialists take on an endeavor that's among the most ambitious of human efforts—to invent medicines that will stop cancer, diabetes, Alzheimer's, and other chronic, long-term diseases. Pfizer might well have the biggest R&D operations of any company in the world. Working out of 16 facilities stretching from California to France and on to Japan, its army of 13,000 research scientists is more than four times the size of IBM's R&D staff. Pfizer's research budget of $7.9 billion is nearly five times that of the world's largest consumer-products company, Procter & Gamble.

And despite the odds, Groton Labs has had a long and storied history. It has previously produced three blockbuster drugs: Feldene, Zoloft, and Zithromax. What's more, it is well positioned for the future: Four vaults, hidden behind a series of alarmed doors in Building 118, contain a priceless armamentarium of 600,000 compounds invented at Groton. Pfizer hopes that at least one of those substances might prove to be the building block for the next Viagra or Lipitor.

Yet for all that, if the previous occupants of this patch of shoreline had designed and built submarines the way its current denizens develop and test new drugs, whole fleets would have slipped to the bottom without a trace. To help her team deal with the daunting odds that face them every day, Hutson has forged a community of people with a common sense of mission. "You can see how people react to her when she walks the halls," says Richard Leider, Hutson's executive coach. "People love her. This is her family, and she treats them that way."

Pfizer's future may well depend on how well Hutson's "family" manages disappointment. A year ago, the company said it would bring an unprecedented 20 medicines to market by the end of 2006. Pfizer chief Hank McKinnell has staked the company's performance—and mostly likely his career—on the ability of the drug giant's scientists to produce new therapies for treating an array of ills, from epilepsy to nicotine addiction to high cholesterol.

Of the thousands of drug-development programs at Pfizer that have ultimately floundered, one quest exemplifies both the tantalizing promise and the daunting odds of those efforts: the 32-year attempt to develop a medicine to treat the devastating complications of diabetes. It is the longest drug-discovery odyssey in Pfizer's 155-year history; it might well be one of the most futile pursuits in the annals of modern drug development. It is also the effort that taught a young Nancy Hutson how to survive a broken heart.

To Make One Life Better

When Hutson arrived at Groton Labs some 23 years ago, Pfizer was a third-tier drug company, and the campus consisted of three buildings. After studying biochemistry at Vanderbilt University and completing a postdoctoral stint at the University of Oxford, Hutson could have spent her career in academe. Instead, she surprised her fellow academics by opting for the hurly-burly of experimental drug discovery. "I wanted to make a difference in people's lives," she says, "and the only way for me to do that was to apply my science in the U.S. pharmaceutical industry, where 99% of the world's drugs are discovered and developed."

When Hutson joined Pfizer in 1981, its pursuit of a drug to treat diabetic complications was already nearly a decade old. The company had predicted what has now come to pass: that diabetes would become a global epidemic. Currently, there are an estimated 151 million diabetics worldwide; that number is expected to increase by 46% within the next six years. So Pfizer's diabetes program long ago passed the first hurdle for any major drug-development effort: the certainty of a huge and growing market. The program also had a particular personal appeal to Hutson: Her husband, Ian Williams, a fellow postdoc whom she met at Oxford and who was hired along with her at Pfizer, has had type 1 diabetes since he was 11 years old. "It was almost my fate to work in diabetes," Hutson says.

Pfizer's research into diabetic complications began in 1972, after university scientists and investigators at the National Institutes of Health identified an enzyme, aldose reductase, that seemed to play a critical role in the slow destruction of diabetics' nerves, eyes, and kidneys. Pfizer scientists scanned the company's library of new molecular entities against the enzyme. They eventually found a molecule that blocks aldose reductase. Other companies were soon trying to develop their own compounds. But within four years, Pfizer synthesized sorbinil, the chemical name for the first orally active aldose-reductase inhibitor.

When Hutson arrived at Pfizer, sorbinil was just entering large-scale human trials. "Those were enormously heady times," she says. "There was a woman in the sorbinil trial who suffered from diabetic neuropathy—the nerves in her feet were so damaged, she couldn't tell whether she was standing on carpet or a tiled floor. But after she tried sorbinil, she regained sensation in her feet. Once I heard that story, I was hooked. To make one life better—that's the most exciting occupation that anyone could have. You have to be indefatigably optimistic to survive in this business. And we were."

It's a refrain you often hear when you probe Pfizer scientists about what enables them to persist. There's a quality of unabashed idealism to what they do, and the hope that a successful project may ultimately save or improve lives can be so awe-inspiring that repeated setbacks seem somehow less significant.

Peter Oates, an expert in glucose metabolism, has harnessed that hope to sustain him through 19 years of work on Pfizer's diabetes project. His mantra: The patients are waiting. "If you have ever massaged cream into the stumps of a diabetic's legs, as I have, or known someone who's died from diabetic renal failure, as many of us have, this is not an empty slogan," says Oates, whose uncle lost both legs to diabetes. "They're not only waiting, they're counting on us."

Still, Pfizer scientists are tackling an obstacle that has thus far proved insurmountable: Diabetes is a chronic, degenerative disease that develops so slowly that it can take years to determine whether an experimental drug is having any impact. After almost a decade of tests—and vast amounts of data that delivered mixed but encouraging results—sorbinil hit a wall. A small percentage of patients in late-stage trials developed a potentially fatal allergic reaction to the sorbinil molecule. It was then that John Niblack dubbed the entire effort a "Vietnam project."

"It was a quagmire," says Niblack, Pfizer's former chief of global R&D,

who retired two years ago. "The regulators and our clinical people were extremely worried. And the results from the trials were still unclear. Some people argued that we were closing in and winning. If we stopped, we'd have to write off millions and millions of dollars. Do we soldier on when some patients are getting sick or do we surrender?"

The decision: surrender. "That's the way it is in this business," Niblack shrugs. "Most of your labor is in vain."

It was a searing disappointment for the researchers at Groton—"a death in the family," Hutson says. Some scientists had spent a decade working on the project; when sorbinil crashed, more than a few switched gears and moved into other research programs. "It was the right decision, but I was heartbroken," says Hutson. It was also a watershed moment for her. "Losing sorbinil taught us that you have to keep some of your emotions in reserve," Hutson says, adding that the defeat transformed her into a professional drug developer, tempering her original starry-eyed optimism with a new sense of realistic, if diminished, expectations. "We were just as determined as ever. But did we still believe we'd change the world overnight? No. That dream was over."

Holy Spaces

While sorbinil's death cost Pfizer tens of millions of dollars and more than a decade's worth of time and talent, it still didn't quash the company's quest for a breakthrough antidiabetes drug. Even as sorbinil entered late-stage clinical trials, a Pfizer team of medicinal chemists had synthesized a second aldose-reductase inhibitor. Dubbed zopolrestat, it proved to be 40 times more powerful in the test tube than sorbinil.

Early-stage human trials showed that patients tolerated zopolrestat well, but Pfizer's executives were understandably reluctant to once again lay siege to diabetic complications. They were finally swayed by the old cliche: You can't win if you don't compete.

As with sorbinil, more than a decade of tests and trials followed for zopolrestat. With diabetic rats, zopolrestat halted nerve damage and in some cases even reversed it. By early 1999, the results from human trials were encouraging enough for Pfizer to select a brand name for what it hoped would be its first-ever antidiabetes drug: Alond, the runner-up name for the pill that came to be known as Viagra. That January, Forbes predicted that zopolrestat would be one of a new generation of blockbusters to emerge from Pfizer's lab. But as the months progressed, biopsy data showed little difference between patients who received zopolrestat and those who got a placebo. It had taken years of testing to make clear that the drug couldn't do in humans what it had done in rats. On August 12, most of Groton's scientists heard the news at the same time Wall Street did: Zopolrestat was dead on arrival.

After two spectacular flameouts in two decades, it looked as if Pfizer's antidiabetes program was finished. But once again, Pfizer had hedged its bets. Back in 1985, as zopolrestat was heading out of the lab and into clinical trials, Hutson had asked Oates to take a final look at their aldose-reductase research. His brief: Unless he found a new pathway that was worth pursuing, he was to close the program.

"I badly wanted a winner," Hutson says. "Peter would turn over every stone, and if there was another way for treating diabetic complications, he would find it. I told him, 'Just follow the science.' And he did."

Following the science, in fact, was what Oates lived for. A large photograph dominates a wall in his small, spartan office, just off the diabetes lab in B-220. It looks like a swirling galaxy of stars, but it's an electron micrograph of a human cell, magnified 44,000 times. Oates's blue eyes widen as he points out the cell's DNA. The photograph shows what he and other diabetes investigators are really trying to accomplish: to see into an invisible world and take on diabetes at the molecular level. "I've spent my life in that cell, trying to understand the fundamental biomechanisms of diabetes," he says. "This work is exciting, it's draining, it's daunting. We're on a journey into inner space, and there are false leads and unexpected insights all along the way."

The photograph also offers a glimpse of what motivates Oates and his colleagues: the sheer intellectual challenge of this pursuit. With his wire-rimmed glasses and starched white lab coat, and his talk of finding his life's calling in the cytoplasm of a cell, Oates is every inch the pure scientist. His world revolves around the lab and the lab bench—"holy spaces," he calls them, "and I have to breathe that holy air to fully stay alive." He has come to accept that his work may never produce a marketable product, but the scientific insights gained in the holy spaces are enough. "When you look at a glowing cell under a microscope, you're looking at life itself," he says. "It's a mystical experience. That stuff transports me."

For nearly 10 years, Oates and a colleague kept the aldose-reductase program barely alive. It was a classic skunk-works project—offline and largely unfunded. "Their work was an open secret, but we didn't flaunt it," recalls John LaMattina, chief of Pfizer's worldwide R&D operations (and Hutson's boss). "Some people would have been less than thrilled to learn that we were still going forward with this effort."

As he worked through the data, Oates began to build the case that high sugar levels inside the cells of diabetics cause damage primarily because of increased oxidant stress. What's really needed, he concluded, is a new generation of superpotent inhibitors that can block the sugar-linked production of oxidants and so slow the ravages of diabetes on sensitive tissues.

In 1993, Oates, working with other scientists and robot scanners, screened Groton's entire library—at the time, more than 250,000 compounds—against the new target. They found a single compound, CP-131337, that showed a glint of promise. After still more years of testing, Oates was convinced they had come up with a powerful agent that should be declared a candidate for a medicine. Once again, Pfizer would have to decide whether to commit to another antidiabetes drug-development program that would take years and millions. "Declaring a new-drug candidate is a pretty big deal," says Oates. "Some powerful people didn't want to move forward."

In the end, Oates's team prevailed. Despite all the years of failed tests and trials and accumulated data, Pfizer was swayed by a question that has thus far proved to be irresistible—as well as unanswerable: What if this one is the winner? To find out, the compound, known as CAN (for "candidate") 809, is now in early development.

Small Victories

Will CAN 809 finally be the brass ring for Pfizer's diabetes research? Hutson and Oates have long ago stopped investing themselves in such hopes. Sure, he'd like to develop a product that ultimately makes it to market, Oates says, "but that's beyond success. That's supersuccess. That's winning the lottery." Instead, they live for the small victories, the incremental steps that may, someday, pile up one on top of the other to put the ultimate prize within reach. Hutson, for example, has made sure that when a researcher publishes a paper, or when a lab gets some positive results on a new therapy, it's trumpeted throughout the organization. "Science folks don't live for the big day when a drug makes it to market," she says. "They live for the small moments when you see exciting results in journals. Small victories help them to deal with the reality that, in all likelihood, there will be no big victory."

There's another fact of scientific life that helps researchers endure so many failures: Ultimately, theirs is a collective effort. A global village of scientific colleagues is dedicated to the effort to unlock the secrets of diabetes. And as the years have passed, the researchers at Pfizer have come to take comfort in the sense of scientific fraternity. "We all know that diabetes is such a tough problem, we can solve it only by cooperating," Oates says. "Even though a colleague or I may disagree strongly over an interpretation of scientific data, each of us knows that the other individual has also committed his or her life to achieving the same objective. Over time, you grow to love and respect these dedicated, hardworking brothers and sisters in arms." It would be great, Oates says, if Pfizer is the one to solve the problem. "But we would be happy if anyone succeeds, because it hasn't been done yet."

It's unlikely, Hutson points out, that their CEO shares the same magnanimous point of view. And she's right, of course. Three years ago, in an effort to stanch the alarming flow of failed R&D projects, Pfizer dispatched 600 of its top scientists to determine why so many compounds flunked in clinical trials. This Attrition Task Force fanned out across Pfizer's worldwide labs, interviewing researchers and compiling their findings in a vast database of doomed projects. The goal, then and now, is to cut the labs' failure rate to 92%. While that number still seems wildly excessive, it represents a doubling of Pfizer's R&D survival rate, from 4% to 8%.

LaMattina, the chief of worldwide R&D, believes the task force has already helped R&D leaders to rebalance the company's portfolio between high-risk efforts like the antidiabetes program and safer bets, such as a next-generation Lipitor. But he warns that it will take another five years to determine whether there's a major, sustained difference in the survivability of Pfizer's compounds. And even then, Pfizer and the rest of Big Pharma will still be stuck with the same brutal model, since they're at a loss to come up with a better way. "We just love spending hundreds of millions of dollars on every new medicine we develop," Hutson says with a heavy dose of sarcasm. "Don't you think that if we knew how to produce drugs cheaper and faster, we'd do it?"

Of course, there is an alternative model: that of the smaller, nimbler biotechnology companies, which focus narrowly on a few promising areas of research. But John Niblack, for one, rejects that approach. "If the biotech formula is so successful, why has it produced so few innovations?" he asks. The one way to improve your chances of a breakthrough, he suggests, is Big Pharma's equivalent of a human-wave attack, in which hundreds of project teams operate simultaneously in multiple therapeutic areas. Only very few giants like Pfizer can absorb the losses of such an effort—and still continue to invest in the program year after year.

And so how does one judge the diabetes effort? With no marketable drug after decades of trying, is it time to call the program a failure? Niblack is unsparing. "We've learned a lot about diabetes complications and about how to run complex clinical trials, and perhaps that knowledge will serve us well in other areas," he says. "But the pharmaceutical industry is not in the business of publishing white papers. Our job is to invent important new medications that are needed by patients and that pay off for us and our shareholders. Judged by that standard, the program is a failure."

Oates doesn't see it that way, and neither does Hutson. In those inevitable dark moments, when all of the hard work seems futile, Oates recalls a remark that's been attributed to another irrepressible warrior, Winston Churchill: "Success consists of moving from failure to failure without losing heart." The program is progressing and so is the science—and that, in itself, constitutes a victory. Just as time and crushing pressure can transform carbon into diamond, the weight of vast amounts of money and the passage of decades at Pfizer's Groton Labs have turned what most of us might see as failure into something much brighter.

THE LAST WORD

Most of us have a fairly negative view of such huge pharmaceutical companies as Pfizer. I am not prepared to acknowledge them as altruistic giants, at least not in their corporate mentalities, but your wonderful illumination of the people who are working every day to try to improve and save lives lends a whole new human aura to the names on the stock ticker. The next time I pop a pill, which will be all too soon and frequently, I'll think of the people like Dr. Oates and Dr. Hutson and feel a twinge of gratitude for their efforts on our behalf.

Mark L. Chien
Wine-grape agent
Penn State University Cooperative Extension
College of Agricultural Sciences
Lancaster, Pennsylvania

A Design for Living

From: Issue 85 | August 2004 | By: Linda Tischler

Good design has the ability to make a simple, everyday object a work of art. No artist exemplifies that idea better than Michael Graves, the man who made the teakettle sing and the toaster smile. But the legendary architect and designer's greatest creation may be the team that will carry on his ideas long after he cannot. Linda Tischler spent months reporting this inspiring portrait of the artist as a wonderful leader.

Maybe it was the stack of screaming yellow Hazmat buckets in the corner that gave Michael Graves the will to live. Or the big gray barrel emblazoned with the warning: ambulance waste. Or possibly the view of the Soviet-style concrete parking garage across the driveway from the hospital.

All Graves remembers from one terrible afternoon last December was that as he lay, critically ill, on a gurney in the University Medical Center at Princeton's ambulance bay waiting to be transported to New York, one overpowering thought gripped him: "I do not want to die here, because it's so ugly."

Graves delivers this line to an audience of staffers sitting around a conference table in his Princeton, New Jersey, office. They laugh merrily, although the joke has a practiced feel, as if it had been trotted out regularly to mute the painful reality of Graves's current situation. In late February 2003, the man who helped rescue architecture from the chilly geometry of mid-century modernism, and revolutionized product design with his affordable creations for Target Stores, began a struggle with an illness that, if it didn't kill him, threatened to rob him of the very thing he lives for: his work. Eighteen months later, Graves has emerged, disabled but still in command of his craft and his two firms, Michael Graves & Associates and Michael Graves Design Group. What's more, his companies have had a wildly successful year, with a flurry of new product-design deals, a slew of new architectural commissions, and the gala celebration of the fifth anniversary of their partnership with Target.

Much like Tom Sawyer's delicious glimpse of his own funeral, Graves's near-death experience has given him something few of us are afforded: a first-hand taste of his own legacy. If he ever doubted it before, he must know now that he is a seminal figure in architecture and design, and that his career stands as a testament to the value of a lifetime well spent on good work. But the catastrophic events of the past year have revealed an even more remarkable achievement. Graves has built something larger and more enduring than himself—a team that will carry on his life's work without him. That's highly unusual for any leader whose unique creativity and vision are the essential life force of an organization. Think of Martha Stewart Living's prospects with Martha in jail, or Apple's years in the wilderness without Steve Jobs. But far from faltering in his absence, Graves's firms have thrived. This great designer's greatest design may turn out to be collaborative organizations that could replicate, amplify, and extend his genius.

True, a mere 105 architects and designers will have a tough time matching the accomplishment of a single Graves, whose witty creations—from a singing teakettle for Alessi to the Dolphin and Swan hotels at Disney World—have become true American icons. It's a remarkable record of achievement that dates back to a childhood in Indianapolis, when Graves's mother told her drawing-obsessed child that if he wasn't as good as Picasso, he'd starve. She suggested he become either an engineer or an architect. When he discovered what engineers did for a living, he picked the alternative. He followed that calling from architecture school in Cincinnati and at Harvard to the American Academy in Rome, to a professorship at Princeton, to an array of brilliant buildings, to the National Medal of Arts in 1999, and the American Institute of Architects' Gold Medal in 2001—the highest award the 63,000-member body can confer on an individual.

But now, strapped in a bulky wheelchair, dressed in a cable-knit sweater in his trademark slate blue, and shadowed by his beloved yellow Lab, Sara, Graves is confronted daily with his losses, both large and small. There is, for example, no wheelchair access to his book-lined former office at 341 Nassau Street, a charming old yellow-brick building that dates back to the late 1700s and once served, he loves to tell visitors, as the town brothel. Instead, he has had to relocate down the block to a functional but prosaic building that can accommodate his chair. An inveterate globe-trotter, he now finds travel difficult and exhausting. An urbane, cosmopolitan man who loves being around people, he is now dependent on others reaching out to him. And an avid golfer, he's now forced to find a way to practice his sport from the seat of a golf cart.

Still, Graves is grateful to finally be back at work full time. And to those who would try to write him off because of his condition, he has one defiant message: Don't count him out. He notes the array of citations and tributes he has received this year with rueful ambivalence. "In the last six months, I've been getting an award a week," he says. "You're made to feel that this is a lifetime achievement award, and you haven't finished living yet."

Paralysis and Growth

A year earlier, that was not so certain. Graves's *annus horribilis* started innocuously enough, with a sinus infection that was more of an annoyance than a cause for alarm. In February 2003, Graves and three members of his team headed to Frankfurt for Ambiente, the giant international consumer-goods fair. Graves, a notoriously indefatigable 68-year-old, seemed uncharacteristically tired. His traveling companions chalked it up to a combination of a nagging head cold, the rigors of covering the vast show, and jet lag from an itinerary that had sent him ping-ponging around the globe.

"Michael cleaned me out of Sudafed," says David Peschel, a product-design director who had come along. Graves's doctor had given him two vials of medicine for the trip: one an antibiotic, the other a decongestant. Thinking it was just a double supply of the same medicine, Graves took only the decongestant. His symptoms eased, but the infection remained. After Frankfurt, Graves continued his breakneck travel schedule, stopping to see a client in Geneva before heading back to New York.

Five days later, back at his office in Princeton, his condition worsened. "He was sitting at a meeting that Monday morning with his head in his hands, and said, 'I've got to go home,' " says Karen Nichols, who is one of the firms' principals. "That was only the second time in 17 years that I'd heard him say he didn't feel well enough to work."

At home that night, Graves, who lived alone, phoned his neighbor to ask if she would call an ambulance and take care of his dog. Doctors at the Princeton hospital were baffled by his symptoms, which included a low-grade fever and excruciating nerve pain in his back, a sensation Graves has described as a dentist's drilling a tooth without novocaine. Nichols and Susan Howard, another partner at the firms, spent the night at his bedside. "During the night, he kept screaming in pain," says Nichols. "No amount of painkiller could do anything. It was awful." At about 3 A.M., Graves said he couldn't feel his legs. Given all the morphine and Demerol he had received, the doctors were not especially alarmed. But by morning, they realized there might be real paralysis.

Graves was rushed to New York–Presbyterian Hospital, where the paralysis was temporarily arrested. He was there for six weeks before being moved to the Kessler Institute for Rehabilitation, a clinic in West Orange, New Jersey, that had served as the rehabilitation facility for fellow Princetonian Christopher Reeve. The exact cause of the infection has never been resolved—it may have been transverse myelitis, a viral infection, or bacterial meningitis. In April, Graves's condition began to worsen, with the paralysis creeping perilously up his spine and threatening to compromise the use of his hands—and his ability to draw. He sought out a doctor in Miami who specializes in spinal-cord injuries, and who stopped the paralysis from spreading. Since the first of the year, Graves has been in and out of various hospitals as his health has waxed and waned. Most recently, he has been back in the office, supervising projects, accompanying his architects on new business pitches, and making the occasional trip to New York to collect an award, or to Minneapolis to visit Target.

Stunningly, while their founder and guiding spirit has been sidelined, Graves's firms have had banner years. In July 2003, the product-design practice was spun off into a separate business, Michael Graves Design Group. Over the past 18 months, it launched more than 100 new pieces for Dansk's tabletop china line; rolled out its first collection for Delta Faucet Co., a line of 60 products, including kitchen faucets and showerheads; produced 19 area rugs for Glen Eden, the carpet company; delivered two collections of chairs and accent pieces for furniture maker David Edward; and created more than 100 products for Target, ranging from a souped-up toilet brush to a dartboard. In fiscal 2004, total retail sales for the group's products are estimated at $174 million, up from $95 million in 2003. Meanwhile, the architectural practice, Michael Graves & Associates, has won a variety of new projects, ranging from a library in Beacon, New York, to a hotel in Beirut, Lebanon, to a courthouse in Nashville, Tennessee, and business schools for both Temple University and the University of Miami (a deal Graves brokered from his Florida hospital bed). It now has more than $800 million in projects under construction or on the boards.

"Despite Michael's illness, the practice has had its most expansive year ever," says Nichols. "We've always relied on the diversity of our services and product lines as part of our business model, but this year we tackled new categories and made a commitment to growing new areas of the practice."

Graves has no plans to retire, but six years ago he arranged a succession plan, naming six partners whose average tenure at the firms is 20 years. When crisis arose, the plan had an unexpected dry run. "When Michael got sick, the partnership immediately stepped up to the plate," says Linda Kinsey, senior director of product development.

Communication had always been a challenge, given the firms' four separate buildings, two of them Colonial-era houses. The partners dispatched regular e-mail messages to the staff, reporting on Graves's condition, and held small meetings in the individual studios to plan client communications and coverage of the work. While the firms did not go public with the news of Graves's condition until he entered rehab, clients were quickly informed, and the architecture practice's principals divided up Graves's responsibilities—from lectures to client visits to accepting awards—to make sure the public face of the company remained visible and vital.

Back in the studios, Graves's decades-long investment in teaching his staff his distinctive aesthetic paid off. "We can all kind of channel Michael," says Peschel, "but occasionally, I'd have one of those 'What would Michael do?' moments. That's when I'd wish I could put something in front of him, because I knew he would do something special that I couldn't do on my own. Luckily, we have people here who have been around so long that you could still get there, even if he wasn't available."

In many ways, Graves's absence made visible a structure that was already implicitly in place. "Our discipline is inherently collaborative," Nichols says. "It never was a one-man show. Michael never thought of it like that." Indeed, he didn't. Graves recalls that painter Chuck Close, whose paralysis is so severe that he has to hold a brush between his teeth, called while he was in rehab. "He said, 'You'll have to get used to people helping you more and sharing your very personal work,' " Graves says. "I didn't say anything, but that's what we already do. That wasn't an issue for me—that sharing."

Once Graves had entered Kessler, about an hour's drive from the office, teams were organized to visit several times a week, bringing food, providing companionship, and rigging up Rube Goldberg–like creations to overcome the facility's design flaws, such as out-of-reach light switches and maddeningly distant drawers. Graves is a notorious workaholic and famously private man; his colleagues are the closest thing he has to family in the immediate area. Twice married, he has lived alone since the mid-1970s. His daughter, Sarah, and three grandchildren live in Calgary, Alberta; his son Adam lives in Indianapolis; his 18-month-old son, Michael Sebastian, lives with the child's mother in Florida. His brother, Tom, lives in southern New Jersey.

When Graves was well enough to work, caravans of designers laden with sketches and prototypes began regular treks between Princeton and West Orange, and Graves began working his magic again. Typically, a design team will develop sketches. Then Graves will work with them to add his special touch. "Whether it's turning your drawing upside down, or doing some little sketch on it, it's this great alchemy thing that happens," says Peschel.

Graves is often characterized as a witty designer, and certainly, in many of his designs, that is true. The whistling bird at the tip of his Alessi teakettle, a Bakelite steak knife with a shark's-grin blade, the 19-foot dwarves holding up the pediment at Disney's corporate headquarters in Burbank, California, come to mind. But wit is just one point on the spectrum of emotions that characterize Graves's designs. They are also comforting, playful, charming, inspiring, and evocative—in short, unfailingly human. "It's really about intuition," says Nichols. "Michael insists that you be able to understand intuitively how to use something, or approach something, simply by looking at it."

Smiley Toasters

Waiters are clearing the remains of the chicken lunch when Ron Johnson, the man behind the widely heralded Apple retail stores, steps to the stage to deliver his keynote speech at the seventh annual Success by Design Conference in Providence, Rhode Island. Johnson reaches for a mouse and clicks on the first slide of his presentation. Instead of a shot of a gleaming Apple store, a black-and-white photo of Graves beams down. The tribute is apt; a year earlier, Graves was to have delivered the same keynote when he got sick.

But this is not just another lifetime-achievement tribute. Prior to joining Apple, Johnson had been a Target vice president. He was the first to suggest that Graves try designing products for the discounter. And that collaboration has taught Johnson the true power of good design.

"In the mid-1990s," he tells the assembled designers and educators, "products based on design didn't exist for everyday people with everyday budgets." Johnson had long admired Graves's Alessi teakettle, the world's best-selling designer teapot at the time. But its $150 price tag limited sales to the well-heeled. When the two finally met, Johnson suggested that Graves try designing for a broader audience. He jumped at the chance. His biggest frustration, Graves told Johnson, was that his students at Princeton couldn't afford to buy his products. "I would love to democratize design," he said.

While good design at low prices is now fairly ubiquitous, the concept was radical in the mid-1990s. "People thought he was crazy," says Johnson. "A lot of designers thought he was selling out for a quick buck, that he would reduce design quality and make design trivial. But because of how well his products were executed, it did the opposite."

Not only did Graves prove that it was possible to deliver great design at affordable prices with the homeliest of objects, but also that design could be a differentiator in the marketplace. Johnson drives the connection home for his audience: "What I learned from Michael Graves is that by creating a great teakettle, we could create an identity for Target that set it apart in its industry."

If the collaboration with Graves changed Target's standing in the retail industry, it also expanded the public understanding of the range of things that architects can do. "With his work for Target, Michael reached out into an area where angels fear to tread—or architects dream of being transgressed," says Robert A.M. Stern, dean of the Yale School of Architecture. Stern says the move prompted plenty of sniping in the more pompous architectural circles. "You stick your neck out, and somebody tries to chop it off," he says. "But Michael is very good at these smiley toaster things. It was a brilliant business move, and he did a great job."

For Graves, designing everything from a toilet brush to an office tower is not dilettantism. It's an outgrowth of a philosophy that doesn't discriminate between what's homely and domestic and what's grand and public. "In the last couple of years, we have taken it upon ourselves to say, we would like to do furniture, we would like to do wall coverings, we would like to do fabrics and faucets and everything," says Graves. "And we have. All those things are part of our domestic view of the world."

"You Have to Let Go"

Despite Graves's medical problems, sources at Target say his firm never missed a beat during the year. "To be honest, it's actually gotten a little better," says Steve Birke, a VP and general merchandise manager at Target. "Because he hasn't been traveling overseas as much on his architectural commissions, Michael's staff has had more face time with him."

To make Graves's life in rehab more comfortable, Birke personally sent him a DVD player, and the company donated a set of Graves-designed games for the facility's recreation areas. To accommodate the designer's restricted mobility when he returned to work, Target helped select video-conferencing equipment for the firm's conference room, enabling Graves and his staff to meet with their Minneapolis clients without having to travel.

The architecture side of the business has been a little more difficult to handle. If clients are hiring a firm for a multimillion-dollar project, they often want to see the man behind the brand. With projects ranging from a retail and restaurant building on the Bund in Shanghai to that courthouse in Nashville, Graves used to be on planes more than 50% of the time. Tweaking drawings takes you only so far. "Most clients have been understanding, but the ones that are difficult are where they expect personal services and for him to go to meetings," says Nichols. "The name on the door is the one they want to see."

Graves himself acknowledges that some in the industry have used his disability to their own advantage. His voice trembles slightly as he describes an encouraging note from architect David Child. "It was the sweetest letter," he says. "Other people might say, 'Michael can't design buildings anymore. He's always in the hospital; he's not in the office. So you don't have to consider him.' That's how cutthroat it is."

Still, the architecture practice seems to be thriving, with a variety of new commissions. Graves is both delighted and chagrined. "I'll tell you what's got me worried: when these guys go out to an interview and I'm not there—and they get the job!" he chuckles.

But for such a private man, the personal limitations of his disability may be the hardest thing to bear. He has had to install an elevator and wheelchair-accessible shower in the exquisite house he designed two blocks from his office, and adapt to the constant presence of a live-in caregiver. He confessed to *The New York Times* that he now wishes that he had a life partner.

One bitterly cold Saturday this past winter, he confides, he found himself at home with no commitments, no company. "A lot of people are hands-off on me now, because they don't want to bother me," he says. "Nobody dropped by. I realized I either have to get used to this privacy, or I have to make plans if I don't want to be stuck. It's a funny in-between time for me."

The loss of mobility has also been difficult for Graves to accept. He rails at the size of his wheelchair, which maneuvers like a bulky SUV and, he feels, sticks out. "It makes you such a visual guinea pig, to be in a big thing like this," he says. He is on a quest to find a smaller version. When asked if there's something he'd still really like to do, the answer is simple: He'd like to walk.

"I feel like I've paid my dues, I've done a year," Graves says quietly. "I know what it's like. Now let me back." He pauses, and his voice gets softer. "I looked up the other morning and said, 'If He would give me just 15 minutes a day, a half an hour a week, a day a month.' But you have to let go."

The Simple Life

The party at the Chelsea Art Museum looks like a typical downtown fashion-crowd affair. The bar is teeming with Cosmo-swilling partygoers and a CBS-TV crew roams the room with lights and a boom. Along the walls, arrayed on pedestals like precious objects from a lost civilization, are the latest products from the Michael Graves Design Group's spring collection for Target: a cocktail shaker with a green olivelike rubber stopper, a Yahtzee game, a mantel clock. Tables and chairs are set in the corner, ranged around board games, including a Monopoly set with Gravesian-themed game pieces: a toaster, a clock, a blender, a teakettle, and hotels that look suspiciously like a Graves-designed foreign ministry in the Hague.

Graves, resplendent in a tweed jacket and blue shirt, happily surveys the scene from his wheelchair, while the stereo blasts "Give Me the Simple Life."

The event is a combination party, celebrating both the publication of Phil Patton's book, *Michael Graves Designs the Art of the Everyday Object* (Melcher Media, 2004), and the fifth anniversary of Graves's partnership with Target. John Remington, a Target vice president, hushes the crowd and raises a glass of champagne for a toast to the collaboration: "To an incredible icon of architecture and design—and a really good friend."

Then Graves takes the mike and, in a voice that begins a little hoarse then becomes increasingly strong, speaks for five minutes about the importance of design. For a moment, the events of the past year fall away, and Graves is once again in command, the center of his design universe, the master of all he surveys. It feels good. The applause ends, the music starts back up, and Graves drums a happy beat on a copy of the book in his lap.

I think back to our conversation in Princeton. On that afternoon, as Graves, visibly exhausted, prepared to go back to his house, I asked what message he would want people to know, based on his own experience with a disability.

He looked at me then with a mixture of frustration and resignation. "There should be no downtime," he said. "Sitting in front of the tube isn't in the cards anymore. You've got to be doing something. That's how I would plan my life if I got my legs back. I'd make use of every f—ing minute." Then he rolled away.

THE LAST WORD

Life is beauty and worth fighting for. This is a sentimental first line, but it resonated while I was reading your story, which I very much enjoyed. Most of all, your story provided inspiration. The protagonist, Michael Graves, is ultimately a practitioner of design as a life force. He's transforming the sentiment of the first line into a way of life, which must remain design's drive and destiny. Thank you for a meaningful and warm piece of writing for all practitioners of not only the discipline of design but of living.

Nate Burgos
Principal
Nate Burgos Inc.
Chicago, Illinois

In Search of Courage

From: Issue 86 | September 2004 | By: John McCain

The senator from Arizona, war hero, and renowned straight talker evaluates the character trait of courage and rescues the word itself from the overuse that's leached it of some of its meaning. His essay should be kept on the desk of every politician or business leader as a handy reference, because, as McCain notes, leadership isn't possible without courage.

Over the past 30 years, American culture has defined courage down. We have attributed courage to all manner of actions that may indeed be admirable but hardly compare to the conscious self-sacrifice on behalf of something greater than one's own self-interest. Today, in our excessively psychoanalyzed society, sharing one's secret fears with others takes courage. So does escaping a failing marriage. These are absurd examples of our profligate misidentification of the virtue of courage. There are many other closer calls. Is the athlete's prowess and guts on the playing field an example of courage? Is suffering illness or injury without complaint courageous? Not always. They may be everyday behavior typical of courageous people. They may be evidence of virtuousness. But of themselves, these acts, admirable though they are, are not sufficient proof of courage.

Courage is like a muscle. The more we exercise it, the stronger it gets. I sometimes worry that our collective courage is growing weaker from disuse. We don't demand it from our leaders, and our leaders don't demand it from us. The courage deficit is both our problem and our fault. As a result, too many leaders in the public and private sectors lack the courage necessary to honor their obligations to others and to uphold the essential values of leadership. Often, they display a startling lack of accountability for their mistakes and a desire to put their own self-interest above the common good.

That means trouble for us all, because courage is the enforcing virtue, the one that makes possible all the other virtues common to exceptional leaders: honesty, integrity, confidence, compassion, and humility. In short, leaders who lack courage aren't leaders.

Lack of courage is not the exclusive failing of political leaders, but our failings as well as our virtues set a national example. We may have learned important lessons from the intelligence failures that preceded the terrorist attacks of September 11 and the fruitless search for weapons of mass destruction in Iraq. But I'm not sure we set a reassuring example to the rest of the country by declining to punish anyone involved in those failures. Not one person was fired or was moved by his or her conscience to resign. Similarly, the prisoner abuse scandal at Abu Ghraib has occasioned much soul-searching but little in the way of personal accountability. The enlisted people responsible for the abuses are facing courts-martial, as they should. But others higher in the chain of command have yet to face serious disciplinary action or offer their resignations. No one has had the courage to stand up and say, "It's my fault, I'm going to resign."

When no one takes responsibility for failure, or when responsibility is so broadly shared that individual accountability is ignored, then failure in public office becomes acceptable. It's hard to see how that serves the country.

The same holds true for the business world. Corporate America has taken significant blows to its reputation, because too many executives don't have the courage to stand up for what they know is right. The perception among many is that corporate leaders are committed only to their own self-enrichment. In 2002, Leo Mullin, the former CEO of Delta Air Lines, received a bonus of $1.4 million plus $2 million in free stock, even as the airline laid off thousands of employees. He left Delta with a huge severance package that was in no way justified by his performance. More recently, we've learned how Enron's traders bragged about gouging California ratepayers during that state's energy crisis. Those traders weren't executives, but they were inspired to behave the way they did by the "me first" climate of self-aggrandizement that Enron's leaders had created. When there's an absence of courage, greed and selfishness take over. And it's not without consequences. There's a growing disdain—if not contempt—for much of corporate America. And that's not healthy for the country's future.

If courage is in scarce supply, then demand is down as well. We are a strong, mostly lawful, prosperous country. We don't have as much to fear as we did in the past—despite the events of September 11 and despite the ongoing war in Iraq. Approximately 200,000 Americans went to Iraq to destroy the regime of Saddam Hussein. From a country of 270 million people, that's less than 1% of the population. Very few of us are called upon to test our courage in the crucible of fear and hard moral choices. And yet, courage still matters—more than we think.

Without courage, all virtue is fragile: admired, sought after, professed, but held cheaply and surrendered without a fight. Winston Churchill called courage "the first of human qualities . . . because it guarantees all the others." That's what we mean by the courage of our convictions. If we lack the courage to hold on to our beliefs in the moment of their testing, not just when they accord with those of others but also when they go against threatening opposition, then they're superficial, vain things that add nothing to our self-respect or our society's respect for the virtues we profess. We can admire virtue and abhor corruption sincerely, but without courage we are corruptible.

Courage is not always certain, and it is not always comprehensible. As courage demands great sacrifice, so does it demand great economy in its definition. General William Tecumseh Sherman defined courage as a "perfect sensibility of the measure of danger and a mental willingness to endure it." That seems to me as apt a definition as any. Courage is that rare moment of unity between conscience, fear, and action, when something deep within us strikes the flint of love, of honor, of duty, to make the spark that fires our resolve. Courage is the highest quality of life attainable by human beings. It's the moment—however brief or singular—when we are our complete, best self, when we know with an almost metaphysical certainty that we are right.

One thing we can claim with complete confidence is that fear is indispensable to courage, that it must always be present for courage to exist. You must be afraid to have courage. Suffering is not, by itself, courage; choosing to suffer what we fear is. And yet, too great a distinction is made between moral courage and physical courage. They are in many instances the same. For either to be authentic, it must encounter fear and prove itself superior to that fear. By fear, I mean the kind that entails serious harm to ourselves, physical or otherwise, the kind that wars with our need to take action but which we overcome because we value something or someone more than our own well-being. Courage is not the absence of fear, but the capacity to act despite our fears.

In the past, I've been able to overcome my own fears because of an acute sense of an even greater fear—that of feeling remorse. You can live with pain. You can live with embarrassment. Remorse is an awful companion. And whatever the unwelcome consequences of courage, they are unlikely to be worse than the discovery that you are less than you pretend to be. I can recall all too well those times I've avoided the risk of injury or disappointment by overruling the demands of my conscience.

One such time came during the 2000 campaign for president, when I failed to say that the Confederate flag that flew over the state capitol of South Carolina should be taken down. I rationalized, in a moment of cowardice, that that decision should be left to the people of South Carolina. After the campaign, I returned to South Carolina and apologized, which didn't mean much since the apology came after the fact. The lesson that I took from that experience was this: In the long run, you're far better off taking the courageous path. I don't know if I would have won South Carolina, but taking the position I did, I lost. Maybe I would have lost by more if I had spoken out—so what? At least my conscience wouldn't have bothered me long after the disappointment of a lost election had worn off.

If fear is a condition of courage, so too is love. It is love that makes us willing to sacrifice, love that gives us courage. And it was love that helped me endure five years of captivity in a Hanoi prisoner-of-war camp, the love and compassion that came from my comrades. Whenever I was down, my fellow prisoners picked me up, many times at risk to themselves. I learned what I didn't want to learn: that I had failings that required the assistance of others. The great privilege of my life is to be associated with men of courage who tried to impart their own courage to me.

Love makes courage necessary. And it's love that makes courage possible for all of us to possess. You get courage by loving something more than your own well-being. When you love virtue, when you love freedom, when you love other people, you find the strength to demand courage of yourself and of those who aspire to lead you. Only then will you find the courage, as Eleanor Roosevelt put it, "to do the thing you think you cannot do."

If you do the thing you think you cannot do, you'll feel your resistance, your hope, your dignity, and your courage grow stronger. You will someday face harder choices that very well might require more courage. And when those moments come and you choose well, your courage will be recognized by those who matter most to you. When your children see you choose, without hesitation, without remark, to value virtue more than security, to love more than you fear, they will learn what courage looks like and what love serves, and they will dread its absence.

We're all afraid of something. The one fear we must all guard against is the fear of ourselves. Don't let the sensation of fear convince you that you're too weak to have courage. Fear is the opportunity for courage, not proof of cowardice. No one is born a coward. We were meant to love. And we were meant to have the courage for it.

THE LAST WORD

I really don't know much about John McCain aside from his presidential run and his TV appearances. But his article ("In Search of Courage") in your September issue sums up courage perfectly, especially for a young businessowner like myself who is hesitant to focus and do what has never been done in my industry. Remorse is definitely an awful companion—one that I do not want to live with, and certainly one I do not want my son to live with.

Hank Hurst
Web/Visual F/X designer
4 Advanced Media Inc.
Tampa, Florida

Balance Is Bunk!

From: Issue 87 | October 2004 | By: Keith H. Hammonds

———————

The rising demands of work and life keep encroaching on each other to the point where now we don't even blanch when a cell phone with e-mail capability is a constant companion on weekends and vacations. Perhaps the only thing worse is our efforts to keep the two spheres of our lives in balance. That provocative, counterintuitive notion is the thesis Keith H. Hammonds puts forth in this deeply reported, keenly observed piece. Hammonds goes further than just noting that our efforts to attain balance are making us miserable and more out of balance. He offers us a radical solution, one that enraged the "balance" industry that tries to help us have it all, but one that just might be crazy enough to work. And give us back our lives.

———————

It may be that you recently had a week that defied sanity. You faced an impossible deadline at work. You were expected at your daughter's dance recital, at a soccer game, and at a meeting with the kitchen contractor. Then another big project landed in your lap (thanks, boss!). You were exhausted, and your spouse was miffed. And your job? Well, at 11 one night, you finally bailed on that deadline.

And you wondered, What's wrong here? Whatever happened to balance?

The truth is, balance is bunk. It is an unattainable pipe dream, a vain artifice that offers mostly rhetorical solutions to problems of logistics and economics. The quest for balance between work and life, as we've come to think of it, isn't just a losing proposition; it's a hurtful, destructive one.

This is not, of course, what many of us want to believe. In the last generation, balance has won huge cultural resonance. No longer mere cocktail conversation fodder, it has become something like a new inalienable right, creeping into the American ethos if not the Constitution: life, liberty, and the pursuit of balance. Self-actualization and quality time for all!

This hopeful premise, born of the feminist movement, has been promulgated relentlessly since the 1980s by writers like, well, me. (At one point, in the name of balance, I actually diapered my infant daughter on CNN.) The froth fed a sort of industry, as consultants rushed to help businesses help employees balance work and life. That's the point of on-site day care, of breast-feeding rooms, of flextime and telecommuting and take-home dinners from the company cafeteria—and, more notorious, in days of dot-coms past, of take-your-pet-to-work policies and foosball tables.

But the balance movement is fatally flawed. For those of us trying desperately to keep up with everything that needs doing, it poses two mythical ideals. If we work hard enough at it, one goes, we can have everything. Or if we cut back, we can have just enough to be truly content. The first obliges us to accomplish too much, often at too high a price; the second doesn't let us accomplish enough. Either way, balance is a relic, a fleeting phenomenon of a closed, industrial economy that doesn't apply in a global, knowledge-based world.

There's a better way to think about all this, one that requires us to embrace imbalance. Instead of trying to balance all of our commitments and passions at any one time, let's acknowledge that anything important, and anything done well, demands our full investment. At some times, it may be a demanding child or an unhappy spouse, and the office will suffer. At others, it may be winning the McWhorter account, and child and spouse will have to fend for themselves. Only over time can we really balance a portfolio of diverse experiences.

For now, the balance mania persists: Media mentions have soared in the past five years, and executive coaches say their clients are as consumed by the problem as ever. Employers, meanwhile, are trying desperately to say the right things: Accenture, the big professional-services firm, knows "how important it is for our employees to strike a balance between their work and personal lives." Google offers workers a slew of benefits (On-site dental! Dry cleaning!) billed as "balance enhancers."

But this passion and fury is misspent. All our striving for balance is only making us crazy. Here's how to think about living in a postbalance world.

The Happy Workaholic

Sigmund Freud suggested it first: Imbalance is part of the human condition. The father of psychoanalysis observed that anxiety is a crucial "signal" function, a response to danger—either external physical danger or internal psychological danger.

That is, anxiety is a central part of our existence. It is a source of creativity and drive; it spurs us to accomplishment. Great leaders, serial innovators, even top sales reps may be driven by a kind of inner demon—the need to prove themselves, to achieve for fear of being worthless (or, as Freud postulated, for fear of castration).

But it's hard to argue with the result: Such people are incredibly productive. They drive change. And that cuts to the problem with a reductionist view of balance. Simply cutting back on work inevitably fails, because in real life, success in work is predicated on achievement. In a competitive business environment—which is to say, every business environment—leadership requires commitment, passion, and, to be blunt, a lot of time.

This isn't a cynical argument in favor of clocking the hours—though let's face it, in some organizations, that pressure is all too real. Rather, building something great, leading change, truly innovating—"it's like falling in love. You have to abandon yourself to it," says John Wood. "There's the risk of inherent contradiction between wanting to do something entrepreneurial and wanting to have balance."

Wood is 40 years old. He helped build Microsoft's business in Asia until 1998, when, trekking through Nepal on vacation, he saw villages with few schools and bookless libraries. In response, he started Room to Read, a not-for-profit group that builds schools and libraries and provides books and scholarships to Asian children.

Wood isn't married, though he does date. He loves biking, running, and the annual trek that he takes with friends through Southern Asia. Mostly, though, he loves Room to Read. He'll do 11-hour days in his San Francisco office, have a working dinner, then check e-mail late at night. He works seven days a week, year-round.

But here's how he thinks about it: "I don't look at balance as an ideal. What I look at is, Am I happy? If the answer is yes, then everything else is inconsequential. If you look at the number of hours I work, it's probably extreme. But those hours talking with an adviser over dinner—is that work? Well, yeah, but it's also stimulating.

"At Microsoft, my definition of balance was getting a decent number of hours outside the office and off e-mail. Now I don't care about that, because the e-mail I check at midnight may come from a person who says he wants to endow a school in Vietnam. So I can't help but read that e-mail, because it's a chance to change a kid's life."

Most achievers don't work hard just at work. They think about their work a lot of the time outside the office. Even if they acknowledge the value of paying attention to their families or their health, they're consumed—and thrilled—by the task at hand. Stewart Friedman, a professor at the University of Pennsylvania's Wharton School, and Sharon Lobel of Seattle University have a term for such folks: "happy workaholics."

Friedman, who has long encouraged business leaders to pursue "whole" lives, thinks it's possible for leaders to be "poster children for balance," as he says. But he also agrees that conventional arguments for balance devalue the work half of the equation. "Work is an experience through which much of life's rewards and opportunities for service can be realized," he says. "Creating value for the world, for the next generation, all our high-minded ideals—much of work has the potential for giving voice to that sort of aspiration. And most executives are passionate about what they do.

"So if people are fulfilled through their work, why do we question that?"

Balance Is for Fat People

Pavan Vishwakarma is a 25-year-old freelance Web and e-commerce software developer. He lives and works in Bhopal, India, but he has done work for companies in Illinois, Nevada, and Canada. And he has, as he advertises, "no working hours limitation. I can work up to any stretch of time."

You want balance? Vishwakarma doesn't, particularly. He wants to work, and he'll work cheap—a lot cheaper than you will.

The global economy is antibalance. For as much as Accenture and Google say they value an environment that allows workers balance, they're increasingly competing against companies that don't. You're competing against workers with a lot more to gain than you, who will work harder for less money to get the job done. This is the dark side of the "happy workaholic." Someday, all of us will have to become workaholics, happy or not, just to get by.

Tom Patterson has spent the last year setting up a technology operations center in Hyderabad, India, for MarketTools, the Mill Valley, California, marketing-research company where he's senior vice president of technology and operations. And he has been stunned by what he sees there.

"I'm amazed at the work ethic," he says. "People are hungry, entrepreneurial, and willing to do whatever it takes at great sacrifices. These kids are working for a change in economic status. Things that we take for granted like housing, health care, vacations—this is what they're looking at. And the difference to them between $6,000 a year and $10,000 is huge."

Protest, if you like, against labor exploitation or unfair competition. The reality is, workers in India, China, Brazil, and, inevitably, everywhere else aren't stopping long to worry about it. They make our developed-world notion that workers actually are entitled to balance seem quaintly dated.

For years, work-life advocates have held up as a model the "work to live" ethic of Europeans, who historically have toiled fewer hours than Americans. But those would-be paragons are failing, too. The French government is reconsidering its decision in 2000 to reduce the national workweek to 35 hours. And two of Germany's largest companies, Siemens AG and DaimlerChrysler, have (with popular support) won union concessions that will force longer hours for employees.

If you're competing against Pavan Vishwakarma—and ultimately, we all are—you can't have both a big paycheck and reasonable hours. The laws of economics won't allow it. If we want time with our families, time to give back to our communities, time to stay slim, we're going to have to accept a pay cut—and even then, we'll have to work darned hard. Hungry beats fat, every time.

The Superman Trap

For many, the great fallacy is not that we aspire to accomplishment but that we aspire to everything else, too. Unwilling to prioritize among things that all seem important, we instead invent for ourselves the possibility of having everything.

In part, this is the inevitable result of the rush of women into the workforce and the proliferation of two-income families. Can any couple facing two full-time jobs, kids, aging parents, groceries, the dog, the bills, and telemarketers at dinnertime expect anything but all stress, all the time?

But it's not just demographics; it's also desire. If women's inner voices in 1963 were saying, as feminist writer Betty Friedan surmised then, "I want something more than my husband and my children and my home," then today many (and many men, too) are saying something different: "I want it all."

So it is that Tina Sharkey, AOL's senior vice president of life management and community, finds herself on a plane two or three days a week, taking photos of her meal, the flight attendants, everything, so her two young kids will know what she does.

Sharkey's routine seems, to many who know her, mind-boggling. She and her husband, fully employed entrepreneur Seth Goldstein, live with their kids in New York. But many of her 250 employees are at AOL's Dulles, Virginia, headquarters. So she spends one or two nights a week at a hotel nearby. Even at home, her workday is a whirl; she typically breaks at 6 P.M. to go home but is back online from 10 P.M. to 1 A.M. As "chief everything officer" of her family, as she puts it, Sharkey coordinates the children's care and family meals, and participates in what school functions she can.

She is an extraordinary woman who evinces both intensity and empathy. But her regimen poses a trap for the rest of us. If we work hard enough, we imagine, we can do anything—and, therefore, everything. "Balance is misleading people," says Laura Nash, who with Howard Stevenson surveyed hundreds of professionals for their new book, *Just Enough: Tools for Creating Success in Your Work and Life* (John Wiley & Sons, 2004). "The problem is, they're looking for a magic bullet, a one-stop solution." It is a peculiarly American quest for perfection, for "a solution in achievements."

You've seen supermen and superwomen: They're the ones at their kids' baseball games, half-watching while tethered to their cell phones (been there). Or they're on the phone at work, sorting out child-care schedules and meal assignments with their nannies and spouses.

The problem, as Nash points out, is that while success at work is largely rooted in achievement, success outside of work mostly isn't. The things most of us say we value in our nonwork lives—simply caring and being there for others—aren't a function of accomplishing anything per se. Contentedness in that realm is less a matter of doing more than of cutting back.

Obvious enough, isn't it? Life is about setting priorities and making trade-offs; that's what grown-ups do. But in our all-or-nothing culture, resorting to those sorts of decisions is too often seen as a kind of failure. Seeking balance, we strive for achievement everywhere, all the time—and we feel guilty and stressed out when, inevitably, we fall short.

The Book of Life

Do we throw up our hands then? We can't do everything, but neither can we retreat from the things that are important. How do we make work and life happen on our terms?

The short answer is, we don't entirely. But there are saner ways to confront the problem. One is rooted in the short term. In their interviews and surveys, Nash and Stevenson learned that successful professionals who were also happy had found ways to "switch and link"—to switch the focus of their full attention with lightning speed among activities and people in different realms.

David Zelman, a psychotherapist and executive coach, sees this as a crucial skill successful people must learn. "Can you leave the office in the office? Can you give someone outside the office the same attention you gave your CEO? If you can give your children or your spouse 100% of your attention, even for a brief period, it goes way longer than compromising and giving them some time because you think you should."

The other solution is more about structure. It forces us to take a long-term view. Give up on the promise of balance at any point in time. Instead, consider a life and career as a portfolio. In each chapter, we have different responsibilities and priorities: children, home, travel, aging relatives. We face a corresponding variety of roles and opportunities on the job: a big project, moving up the managerial hierarchy, consulting, a start-up, a top leadership role.

Balance, for what the word is worth, then becomes a lifelong quest—

balance among chapters rather than within each chapter. "It gets in people's heads that the ultimate goal is a 50-50 split between work and life," says work-life consultant Cali Williams Yost. "But there are times when I've happily devoted 80% of my time to work—and other times when I couldn't." The tough part is recognizing the chapters for what they are—just temporary episodes that together make up a coherent and satisfying whole.

That's why Sharkey finds her current manic lifestyle acceptable—because, she says, "this is just one chapter in my life." The opportunity to fix and build a business at AOL—and to create something that brings lasting value to women and families—is, she believes, worth the frenzy and the compromises. "I feel like I have so much to contribute. I have to leverage myself and contribute in the way I can."

Consider it an exercise in continuous redesign, in adapting to ever-changing circumstances and priorities. For couples, this also requires constant rebalancing of roles and responsibilities: You got the promotion, so I'll telecommute for now—until my next big opportunity comes up. Those who succeed, says Zelman, are "the people who learn to dance with change, who create and ride the wave." They don't make decisions once or twice, but all the time.

And here's what's crucial: With each decision, these people invest themselves, their passion, and their time in what is most important to them. They also agree to give up something important; a portfolio life doesn't excuse them from the need to make trade-offs. The decision to reject the mirage of balance requires the discipline to continually prioritize and compromise.

Is that balance? Only in the sense that, over time, things more or less balance out. But that doesn't make it perfect, or easy. In some ways, it's counterinstinctual. It forces us to think differently about our careers and about the contributions we make in all realms of our lives. And it gives us a plan that's valid only until the next baby, project deadline, layoff, or illness.

But all things considered, it could prove a lot saner.

THE LAST WORD

It's 10:20 p.m. I'm working in my office at home, catching up on e-mail. I'm buried in my Fast Company, *reading "Balance Is Bunk!," when at my door*

appears a little 3-year-old visitor. "C'mon, Daddy, isn't it time for bed?"
There's no doubt that the pull of competition—personally, within our organi-
zation, or across the globe—is strong. But then I think of my little late-night
visitor, and I have to wonder: What is it all for? I may not know how to bal-
ance, but I sure know where the priorities need to be. Time to sign off and go
to bed.

Matt McElrath
Chair of human resources
Mayo Clinic Scottsdale
Scottsdale, Arizona

The Accidental Guru

From: Issue 90 | January 2005 | By: Danielle Sacks

The most influential thinker in business isn't a businessperson. In fact, he's a writer for *The New Yorker* magazine. And Malcolm Gladwell makes the most surprising of gurus. The self-effacing Canadian has grabbed the attention of the business world with the power of his prose and the contrariness of his thinking. With every story and book, he forces his readers to consider: What if everything we accept as true about this subject is wrong? Leaders have responded by making him a best-selling author and sought-after speaker. They even want him to be a consultant. But Gladwell was largely unknown beyond his writings, until this article looked past the pen to find the personality who may end up being the twenty-first century's pre-eminent business thinker.

"I really like that term 'momentary autism,' " a woman says softly into the mike. She is in the back of the Times Square Studios speaking to a room of some 200 people, and more important, Malcolm Gladwell, who's standing solo onstage. It's the second day of the fifth annual *New Yorker* Festival, and Gladwell has just finished a detailed reprise of the seven seconds that led to the infamous 1999 fatal shooting of Amadou Diallo. Minutes before, every eye in the room was locked on him as he unspooled the nanodecisions that misled four New York cops into thinking the innocent Guinean immigrant was an armed criminal, resulting in 41 shots, 19 to the chest.

As the woman repeats the phrase to the crowd, you can hear her digesting it as if it has just become a part of her. It is a term Gladwell introduced to the group only moments earlier when describing what happens when our ability to read people's intentions is paralyzed in high-stress situations. Cocking his hands back in a gunlike position, he had explained in a tone that was part sociologist, part Shakespearean actor, how the cops misread a "terrified" black man for a "terrifying" black man. "They didn't correctly understand his intentions in that moment, and as a result they completely misinterpreted what that social situation was all about," he said. "I call this kind of failure 'momentary autism.' " It's only one of many neatly packaged catchphrases Gladwell sprinkles throughout his new book, *Blink: The Power of Thinking Without Thinking* (Little, Brown, January 2005). There's "rapid cognition," "thin-slicing," and the "Warren Harding error," but "momentary autism" is the one that you can quickly imagine this woman using, explaining to her boss why she froze during the new business pitch.

No one in recent memory has slipped into the role of business thought leader as gracefully or influentially as Gladwell. Soon after his first book, *The Tipping Point: How Little Things Can Make a Big Difference* (Little, Brown, 2000), fell into America's palms, Gladwell made the leap from generalist staff writer at *The New Yorker* to marketing god. Since then, Gladwell has oscillated between pen and mike, balancing lengthy *New Yorker* articles with roughly 25 speaking gigs a year, his current going rate some $40,000 per appearance. Last year, he spoke at such highbrow conferences as TED and Pop!Tech and was invited to share his wisdom at companies including Genentech, PricewaterhouseCoopers, and Hewlett-Packard. His *New Yorker* articles have become required reading for B-school students. *The Tipping Point* spent 28 weeks on *The New York Times* best-seller list and more than two years on *Business Week*'s, and today there are almost 800,000 copies of Gladwell's trend-mapping bible in print. Mention his impact, though, and he modestly tries to brush it off—leaning, like any good journalist, on data points to support his argument. "Remember," he points out, "even a book that's a best-seller still is only read by less than 1% of the American public."

But as the expert in social epidemics knows better than anyone, it's not how many people you reach, it's whom you reach. Gladwell and his ideas have reached a tipping point of their own, and evidence of his impact can now be found in all corners of our culture, from politics (Donald Rumsfeld used "tipping point" to describe the war in Iraq) to entertainment (legendary hip-hop group The Roots used it as the title of their latest album).

But nowhere is Gladwell's influence being felt more than in business. Starbucks' Howard Schultz publicly attributed his company's success to the tipping-point phenomenon. The public-relations agency Ketchum created what it infelicitously named an "Influencer Relationship Management" database that emulates Gladwell's model of connectors, mavens, and salesmen. One tech company even named itself TippingPoint Technologies Inc. The mere mention of his name to creative directors or product developers results in nouns not typically associated with business thinkers: He's a rock star, a spiritual leader, a stud.

Now Gladwell's back again in bound, written form, this time exploring how first impressions affect decision making. In *Blink*, he argues that by distilling the first few seconds in which we interact with a person, product, or idea into what is useful information and what is misleading, we can learn to make better decisions. "We talk endlessly about what it means to think about a problem, deliberative thinking and rational thinking," he says. "But we spend very little time talking about this other kind of thinking, which is happening in a split second and which is having a huge impact on real-world situations."

The more Gladwell discusses his next big idea, the more it becomes apparent that his drive is both intellectual and practical. He understands that in order for change to happen, he must package his ideas in a language that people can use to discuss them. The curious journalist who sees himself as nothing more than a "conversation starter" has earned himself a greater responsibility than that. To the business world, he's now a corporate sage, a 21st-century Peter Drucker.

A Genre of His Own

When you see Malcolm Gladwell for the first time, standing barefoot at the entrance of his breezy Tribeca apartment, you are struck by how young he looks. He's 41, but seems closer to 30. His slight build is that of a high-school runner, his halo of bushy brown hair evokes Lenny Kravitz. You notice his relaxed stance, his jeans and fitted white T-shirt. If you were going to rely on your own uncanny ability to nail first impressions, you would probably never guess that this is the guy so many people claim has changed the way they do business.

From an early age, Gladwell was drawn to the written word.

Raised in a home with no TV, the youngest son of two published authors was reading the Bible by age 6, and by 16 won a writing competition for a story in which he interviews God. A track star as well, "he was very, very competitive," says his father, Graham, a math professor. "In fact, he was obnoxiously competitive." While he was clearly precocious, Gladwell describes his Canadian upbringing as "very mellow," attributing it to Canadians' general nonchalance toward the American ideal of success. "There isn't this big fretting about getting into college," he reflects. "It seemed like a very easy and warm way to grow up, and by comparison, sometimes I feel like things seem to be a lot more at stake in America."

This combination of a laid-back demeanor with an inner ambition has turned out to be his competitive edge in journalism. He got his inauspicious start in high school publishing a 'zine: *Ad Hominem: A Journal of Slander and Critical Opinion.* "The rule was, in every article you had to attack somebody," says Gladwell, smirking while noting that only about four issues ever made it to press. While he dabbled in journalism, "it never occurred to me you could actually make a career out of [writing]." So the self-described "slightly lost" University of Toronto grad with a history degree tried breaking into advertising—to no avail—and on a lark landed an editorial gig at the conservative magazine *The American Spectator.* He was later fired, probably, he says, for his penchant for oversleeping. Gladwell eventually found a home at *The Washington Post,* where he worked for nine years, migrating from the business beat to science and medicine to New York bureau chief. He gravitated to business writing for the same reason he gravitated to science—because they are about real things that have tangible consequences.

Since joining *The New Yorker* in 1996 ("It just kind of happened," he says), Gladwell has, as his editor Henry Finder puts it, "essentially invented a genre of story." A "Malcolm Gladwell story" is an idea-driven narrative, one focused on the mundane rather than the bizarre. It takes you on a journey in and out of research through personal, social, and historical moments, transports you to a place you didn't know you were going to end up, and changes the way you think about an idea. The result is articles such as "The Talent Myth: Are Smart People Overrated?" published in 2002 and still circulating today. In it, Gladwell uses psychology and case studies to demolish the "star" talent system that McKinsey & Co. lauded—and its client (the then-bankrupt) Enron epitomized. "They were there looking for people who had the talent to think outside the box," he writes. "It never occurred to them that, if everyone had to think outside the box, maybe it was the box that needed fixing."

The business community's fervor for Gladwell and his work, particularly *The Tipping Point*, stems from this potent mix of the entertaining with the perspective-shaking. In *The Tipping Point*, Gladwell reveals a map for how ideas, products, and behavior become contagious within a culture. He traces the word-of-mouth life cycle through the people who start and then accelerate it, whom he dubs "connectors," "mavens," and "salesmen." "I bought books for my whole team, my whole family, and all my friends. I probably bought 30 copies," says Nikki Baker, a marketing analyst at Pepsi who tested the concept for the Aquafina Essentials product launch in 2002. A year after the beverage giant was busy pitching its bottled water to yoga instructors (deemed "key influencers"), its more irreverent competitor, Glaceau (maker of Vitaminwater and Smartwater), began seeding 500 influencers across the country. Matt Kahn, Glaceau's director of corporate marketing, now makes *The Tipping Point* required reading for his 35-person marketing team, starting from the point of hire.

Other companies have built entire practices around his ideas. After Simmons Market Research's team read the book, it created the Tipping Point Segmentation System—syndicated research its clients can use in order to understand how to reach the 12.5% of the U.S. population that falls within Gladwell's classification of tipping-point segments. One of its clients? Gladwell's own employer, *The New Yorker*. Its sales team applies the data to its 950,000-plus subscriber list to help convince advertisers of the magazine's "influencer" following. Gary Warech, a vice president at Simmons, puts it plainly: "It was a great book. It became the bible, the must-read in business circles. Our guys read it and said, 'This is great. We can operationalize this and help our clients.'"

In the Blink of an Eye

The impetus for *Blink* started with Gladwell's hair (as did his brief splash in the gossip pages when he got "a little too close to some candles" and it ignited during a recent literary event, according to the *New York Post*'s Page Six). For most of his adult life, he had worn it closely cropped, but several years ago decided to let it grow out into a woolly Afro. "The first thing that started happening was I started getting speeding tickets. . . . I wasn't driving any faster than I was before, I was just getting pulled over way more." Then there was the day Gladwell was walking around New York and cops surrounded him, mistaking him for a rape suspect. "I'm exactly the same person I was before," recalls Gladwell, who's half black (his mother, a therapist, is Jamaican). "But I just altered the way someone makes up very superficial, rapid judgments about me." Rather than merely grouse—legitimately enough—about prejudice, Gladwell, who has the tendency to look in on his own life as a case study, was inspired to try to understand what happens beneath the surface of rapidly made decisions. "The idea that something that is extraordinarily harmful in society could be exactly the same in its form as something that's incredibly useful is really interesting to me."

The "useful" that Gladwell advocates in *Blink* is the idea that we can teach ourselves to sort through first impressions to "figure out which ones are important and which ones are screwing us up." While most of us would like to think our decision making is the result of rational deliberation, he argues that most of it happens subconsciously in a split second. This process—which Gladwell dubs "rapid cognition"—is where room for both error and insight appears. Many of the snap judgments we make are based on previously formed impressions and are competing with subconscious biases such as emotions and projections. Once we become aware of this, Gladwell argues, we can learn to control rapid cognition by extracting meaning from a "thin slice" of information.

Hiring is one area where we tend to fall into the "dark side" of rapid cognition, says Gladwell. He conducted a study to showcase how we often succumb to what he calls the "Warren Harding error" (Harding being, he says, "one of the worst presidents in American history," who nevertheless radiated "all that was presidential"). Polling about half of the Fortune 500 companies, Gladwell discovered that the vast majority of their CEOs were at least 6 feet tall (only about 14.5% of all American men are 6 feet or taller). What does this say about the way we hire? "We have a sense of what a leader is supposed to look like," he writes. "And that stereotype is so powerful that when someone fits it, we simply become blind to other considerations."

Similarly dangerous is how first impressions cripple breakthrough ideas and innovation. Gladwell tells the story of furniture maker Herman Miller

Inc. in the early 1990s, when it created a new office chair. It was made of plastic and mesh, and while it was created as the "most ergonomically correct chair imaginable," he says, it was just plain ugly. Focus groups, facility managers, and ergonomics experts all despised it. Why? "They said they hated it," writes Gladwell. "But what they really meant was that the chair was so new and unusual that they weren't used to it."

Gladwell argues that it's a mistake to rely on the first impressions of customers who are inherently biased against the unfamiliar. Herman Miller execs went against the market research, stuck with their instincts, and created the Aeron, which eventually became the company's best-selling chair ever. "What once was ugly has become beautiful," he writes. Unless you're willing to take that kind of leap, he says, you're condemned to doing knockoff, me-too chairs.

For every Herman Miller "going with your gut" success story, though, there are 100 flops by companies that didn't listen to customers. Gladwell acknowledges this, but notes, "only by accepting the risk of failure will [a company] ever hit a home run." Relying on the good judgment of your staff, he believes, is the key ingredient for a new kind of decision-making environment, and judgment is what companies should be screening for when hiring. With the right people in place, companies can liberate themselves from their obsession with data-driven decisions.

While the notion is provocative, the road map *Blink* offers corporate America gets fuzzy from there. (For example, Gladwell never explains how Herman Miller's execs overcame their concerns about the Aeron's ugliness.) Gladwell offers much more insight into how those in rapid-decision-making professions (such as firefighters or ER doctors) can slow down a moment or create an environment where spontaneous decision making can take place. That's less applicable in the white-collar workplace. You can learn how to untrain yourself from making the Warren Harding error, but you're more or less on your own in rewiring your thinking.

This raises the primary criticism of Gladwell's work—that he sometimes stretches his colorful stories to make them apply to business issues. And he admits it. "I'm just trying to get people to start a conversation, even if the conversation is, 'Well, that's interesting, and that's not, and that's sort of bulls—t.' . . . I'm much happier getting criticized for overreaching than I would for being too timid."

In effect, that's exactly the leap he wants companies like Hewlett-Packard to make. For a company of numbers-driven engineers, steering away from data is downright frightening. "We want to innovate and break out, but we don't have the instinct for it, really. It scares us a little," says Shirley Bunger, HP's director of brand innovation. So as part of her mandate to help HP's 145,000 employees think differently, she brought Gladwell in last June to share the Aeron story.

Bunger recalls watching reactions around the room as Gladwell's presentation erupted into a vibrant discussion. "There were some people who just had this sense of relief and connection and then other people with this sense of 'Oh my God, this man is completely challenging everything I believe in,'" she says. At one point, someone asked Gladwell if he believed in focus groups, and he replied, "I think we would all be better off if focus groups ceased to exist." While this idea and others in *Blink* aren't revolutionary, they're exactly the kind of thing that can spark change. And who better to hear them from, argues Bunger, than Gladwell?

Guru or Scribe?

Companies like HP are still vying to "bring in Gladwell in a way that he could really shape some of our work," says Bunger. Add it all up: a passionate following, companies eager to sign him on as a consultant, some accessibly packaged books, and a knack for addressing a room full of businesspeople with the intimacy of a dinner-party chat. It sounds like the beginning of Malcolm Inc.

"Oh God, no," Gladwell laughs, shielding his hazel eyes with his hands. "I can't imagine anything more horrible." While he is flattered by how many diverse groups have been drawn to his work and he enjoys speaking to companies, formal consulting would be a breach of his first commitment—journalism—and he claims he'll never do it. Yet when you ask Bunger, she says Gladwell was very receptive to the idea of a formalized working relationship. And he's already well entrenched in the pantheon of business prophets: Gladwell is number 27 in Accenture's ranking of "The Top 50 Business Gurus," above the likes of Jack Welch (34) and Richard Branson (45).

Gladwell's reluctance to accept the trappings of gurudom reflects his professional DNA: He's more Peter Drucker than Tom Peters. Like Drucker, he doesn't come from the usual feeder pools of consulting or academia, and his MO isn't prescribing the solution but sparking more questions. "I was definitely surprised that he didn't have all the answers and he didn't care about it," says Nikki Baker, the marketer at Pepsi who saw Gladwell speak at *The New Yorker* Festival last October. "He was just a thinker."

She doesn't mean that as faint praise, of course. But not everyone holds Gladwell's thinker credentials in such high regard. "When [Gladwell] talks about mavens or connectors, in my neighborhood we call them 'gossips,' " says Mario Almonte, who heads the PR practice for Herman Associates, a marketing communications agency. John McGrath, a psychiatrist who's also the vice chairman of a public-affairs firm, believes marketers became starry-eyed over Gladwell's first book because he props up the elusive with the quantifiable. "You tend to think, 'Oh wow, this is really science-based stuff.' Well, it's new language, but it's not science." In fact, the tipping-point concept has been around for decades. The idea was first deeply explored by the economist Thomas Schelling (as Gladwell acknowledges in his original tipping-point article), and marketers have been practicing these ideas without Gladwell's vocabulary for years. "It's one of these things that's kind of obvious but nobody said it," says Henry Mintzberg, the management guru and a Gladwell admirer. "You know, thousands of psychologists spend lifetimes studying these things, and here, one guy kind of waltzes along with a really interesting idea."

Gladwell's real gift is packaging these ideas in a way that makes them palatable. "[He] acts almost like a translator between the scholarly world and the practical world," says Frank Flynn, an associate professor of organizational behavior at Columbia Business School, who uses many of Gladwell's articles in his MBA classes. Gladwell deflects the charge that he's just a savvy marketer of ideas, standing by his earnest intentions to help frame people's thinking. "When I was writing *The Tipping Point,* I realized that in order for people to talk about something . . . they need some way to describe and name things," he says. "So I always like to try to come up with simple, sort of catchy ways of capturing complex ideas."

While Gladwell's newfound role in the business spotlight might be entirely accidental, he sees himself as part of a greater movement. "I feel like there's been a kind of intellectual awakening in the business world in the past 20 years or so, where people began to realize that there was an enormous amount to be learned from the world outside of business," he says. "I think of myself as one of the many people who are trying to feed that curiosity."

As CEOs and marketers and R&D teams immerse themselves in Gladwell's new notions of decision making, and as he gears up for a new flurry of speaking gigs, Gladwell admits he hasn't given much thought to what's next. "I don't think that far ahead," he says, his eyebrows perking up like bookends. "Yeah, I don't really have high expectations about much. It's a good psychological position to be in, because that means I'm usually delighted by what happens in my life." Whether that means dreaming up more best-sellers or seeing the impact of his ideas playing out in the real world, we can be sure of one thing. He'll soon be in his favorite un-gurulike pose, lying on his couch with his laptop on his belly, typing away.

THE LAST WORD

Although the accidental guru offers interesting approaches and ideas in Blink, *I believe there is a fundamental flaw in the argument. I agree that by putting the right people in place, companies can liberate themselves from their obsession with data-driven decisions. But I don't agree that you can achieve this by teaching people to change the way they formulate first reactions and go about decision making. Organizations are obsessed with data-driven decision making because human-resource departments focus on hiring individuals who make such decisions.*

Only when the organization changes to a more balanced approach will it hire and retain individuals who complement data analyzers. Let's not try to change the innate abilities of people. Rather, let's create a team of individuals and allow people to focus on their different abilities to come up with the best decision for the company.

Alan Schatten
Founder and president
The Schatten Group LLC
Oyster Bay, New York

The 10 Lives of George Stalk

From: Issue 91 | February 2005 | By: Jennifer Reingold

George Stalk is one of the preeminent business strategists of the last 30 years, and the price he paid for that lofty reputation was working himself to death. Three times, in fact. Jennifer Reingold brings Stalk to life—just as his doctors did—with a story so deeply reported that she even gives readers access to Stalk's dreams while he was in a coma. Even as Stalk grapples with how to slow down to keep from killing himself for good, he's advocating the exact opposite for global companies. Businesses need to play "hardball," unapologetically, if they want to gain the kind of massive competitive advantage needed to win.

It wasn't until the third time George Stalk Jr. was declared dead that his family agreed to turn off the life support. Just 52 years old, the peripatetic strategy consultant from Boston Consulting Group lay strapped to a hospital bed, a virtual skeleton with a ventilator tube protruding from his mouth. Stalk had been comatose for nearly three months, after the rupture of a blood vessel in his abdomen started a cataclysmic chain reaction of internal bleeding in February 2003. And although he'd fought back from the brink twice before, it was time, the doctors said, to let him go.

The physical contrast between the vital man of a few months earlier and the shell of a man lying motionless on the gurney could not have been starker. Stalk had been a crackling wire, one of the most energetic and intellectually curious people ever to roam the halls of corporate America. Intrigued by—or obsessed with—the X factor that makes one company more successful than another, the star consultant would eagerly jet anyplace, anytime, for the chance to nose around a company's manufacturing process, attack a byzantine cost structure, or convince a CEO that now was the time for change.

In Stalk's 26 years at BCG, he had gone to so many places and coined so many new ideas that his colleagues dubbed him Johnny Appleseed. In a world in which every dime-a-dozen consultant gets anointed a guru, Stalk was the real deal. He was the father of time-based competition, the concept that explained how Japanese factories were able to make better products more quickly. The most prominent name at one of the most elite strategy firms, he worked with some of the world's most powerful companies, including General Electric and Ford Motor Co., and had staked out a legacy as someone able to find solutions to vexing business problems before anyone else even figured out that there were problems. Whip-smart and ultracompetitive, he had little patience for those who didn't share his passion for helping companies figure out how to win. "He is brutally smart, and I choose those words carefully," says Michael O'Leary, former executive vice president at CIBC, which was a client. "He can be intimidating. But he is an absolute joy to work with. He is a verb, not a noun."

But while Stalk excelled at detecting toxic situations in his clients' organizations, he ignored the same warning signs when it came to his own well-being. As his wife, C. Henri, and six children whispered their good-byes, and his colleagues at BCG, meeting in Paris a few weeks later, bowed their heads for a moment of silence, the consensus was clear: George Stalk had literally worked himself to death.

Except that he wasn't gone yet. Deep inside his coma, trapped in the netherworld between life and death, Stalk's remarkable mind worked through a series of 18 intense hallucinations bursting with vivid characters, scenes, and dialogue. In them, Stalk was doing what he does best: solving problems.

Lying in a hospital bed at Johns Hopkins Medical Center, Stalk knew he was going to die, although not from the nuclear strike he imagined Japan had launched against England. Stalk and his wife had helped rescue survivors. Now he understood that he wouldn't recover from the mysterious illness he'd contracted but that he would be going to Heaven. His first thought was that this meant he'd have a chance to see Jim Abegglen, a former mentor at BCG who had been killed in the war.

But how to locate him? "I spent a lot of time trying to figure out how Heaven was organized," he says. "How would you find someone? Was it by geography? Was it by ethnic origin? Was it by where the person was currently living?" Stalk began an analysis of Heaven's internal structure, but it soon became clear that it wasn't needed; the two men would somehow eventually connect. Heaven, it turns out, has no org chart.

Faced with imminent death, some people's unconscious might have journeyed backward through life. Others might have dreamed of exotic places, or lived out fantasies that their conscious minds would never have permitted. But Stalk's brain just doesn't work that way. "I remember waking up saying, 'Jesus Christ, I just went for three months and didn't have a single sexual dream,'" he laughs. "It was about work."

An engineer by training, Stalk accepted the scenario he was given and then began to analyze his way through it. His deconstruction of Heaven was typical. "That's him!" exclaims Thomas Hout, a senior adviser at BCG. "George is tireless. Even as he imagines himself dying, he still asks these questions."

Somehow, some way, Stalk, now 54, confounded the experts, emerging from his coma to make a full recovery. No one would have begrudged him for retiring to grow vegetables on his Toronto-area farm or fly the radar-controlled planes he loves with his children. But not only is Stalk back to work, he's also on the road again, promoting a new book written with Rob Lachenauer, *Hardball: Are You Playing to Play or Playing to Win?* (Harvard Business School Press, 2004).

The book, a controversial reaction to the glut of squishy, culturally focused business books that have dominated the last decade, is about gaining an unassailable advantage over rivals. Written in a clear, no-nonsense style, it lists six strategies ranging from "unleash massive and overwhelming force" to "threaten your competitor's profit sanctuaries" to "entice your competitor into retreat." Each is illustrated with corporate examples, from the obvious (Toyota and Southwest Airlines) to the obscure (Wausau Paper and Federal-Mogul). The lesson is simple and harsh: Hardball players do what it takes to win.

Some people have interpreted *Hardball* as a business version of America's "go it alone" political strategy in the world, or as a total rejection of the idea that a company's culture and people are an important part of its edge. Although neither is true, BCG, fearing a political storm, altered some of *Hardball*'s chapter titles to make them sound less aggressive. But the changes didn't do much to soothe those who think business should be a kinder, gentler pursuit and that Stalk's testosterone-fueled emphasis on crushing your competitor is a Stone Age throwback. "[Stalk and Lachenauer] are on a brutal, macho trip," wrote one reviewer for the *Financial Times*.

Although *Hardball* was in the works before Stalk's illness, its publication serves another purpose, too. It's a powerful announcement that Stalk is back—and that he's as focused and as serious as ever. "When I got out of the hospital, I had less interest in finding a middle ground," he says. And *Hardball* is hardly the work of a man softened by his brush with mortality. "You want to be home by 5 P.M.? You want to clip coupons? You want to retire before China becomes a problem for your business?" Stalk writes. "Nuh-uh. To play hardball, you and your organization have to go to the 'heart of the matter' and stay there. You have to live by the rock face. You have to be willing to put your competitors through pain. You have to have a high energy level and the ability to sustain it."

> *The phone call came from BCG's Washington office, asking Stalk to go to London and give a speech in place of a U.S. Air Force general who had canceled. But first he had to meet the general at Andrews Air Force Base and pass muster. "We found the study you did for us years ago," said the general, voice full of disgust. He pushed it across the table. "I think this is a piece of crap." Stalk defended himself. "Of course I expected you to say this was a piece of crap," he said, "because you didn't have the guts to implement it."*
>
> *Standing up to the general was, it turned out, the right move: He loved this answer and gave Stalk the go-ahead to make the speech. To get him there on time, the Air Force sent him an F-16. Stalk landed just in time to see the horrible aftermath of that nuclear war between Japan and England.*

The vision of nuclear hell, like many of Stalk's hallucinations, has some basis in reality. An Air Force brat who moved 27 times as a child, Stalk actually watched the detonation of atomic bombs in Nevada as an 8-year-old. "My mother would get us up, and we'd look out of the motel window and watch the clouds go up," he says.

Stalk studied engineering at Michigan, then married C. Henri, whom he'd met during a summer working in Washington, and completed a master's at MIT. After graduating, he went to work as a consultant for the Air Force and then at Exxon. Along the way, he became interested not just in how a product worked but in how it could give a company a decisive advantage. He decided to go to Harvard Business School, mostly because it had a reputation for being a boot camp. "This place sounded like pure hell," he remembers with masochistic relish.

Stalk survived HBS, graduating in 1978, and had planned to join a high-tech start-up until he heard about BCG, the new-fangled consultancy with a tough reputation and a scientific approach to management. Stalk quickly became a star at figuring out a competitor's costs, but got pigeonholed as a cost expert and planned to quit. Instead, someone suggested he try a foreign office. Stalk chose Japan, something of a backwater at the time.

Shortly after Stalk arrived in 1979, Bruce Henderson, BCG's founder, posed a challenge: Why are the Japanese able to achieve higher levels of productivity and quality with smaller, more-capital-intensive factories? Because fat, happy American companies still worshipped the idea of scale, they didn't really understand the power of the Japanese factory, and Stalk had trouble getting them to fund his research. Instead, he did a series of stealth projects for such existing clients as Clark Equipment and John Deere, spending months at a time inside the factories of their joint-venture partners in Asia. He reached the radical conclusion that while quality and cost were important, time itself—or the ability to organize a factory or a business so as to get more done in less time—was the killer app. Stalk named the theory "time-based competition" and resolved to bring this just-in-time manufacturing system back home.

Becoming the chief evangelist for this new idea meant that Stalk's already taxing life turned into months, then years, of constant around-the-globe travel. A typical schedule: 10 days in Japan, 10 days in Europe, 10 days back in Japan, 10 days in the United States. He became a regular on Pan American Flight 01, the famous globe-hopping flight. Stalk figures he flew as many as 500,000 miles a year for a decade, appearing in exotic locales wearing a fly-fishing vest over a suit jacket (more pockets) and lugging an enormous, beat-up old briefcase full of Diet Coke.

In 1985, he came back to the States, yet he had trouble getting people to believe his theory. Frustrated, he decided to take a year's leave of absence from BCG and prove his ideas himself with a real factory in the United States. He landed at Hillenbrand Industries, a conglomerate with a struggling hospital-bed factory. Stalk took two years instead of one, but turned the factory around. The book that followed in 1990, *Competing Against Time: How Time-Based Competition Is Reshaping Global Markets*, written with Tom Hout, made him a star and gained him entree into the most elite companies.

At GE, for example, Stalk spent about 18 months answering Jack Welch's challenge to help him find companies that were improving continuously while still delivering higher profits. "He stood out as a guy who was the sharpest leading-edge thinker but also one who was so down-to-earth and so operational," says Mike Fraizer, now CEO of Genworth Financial and then a GE executive who traveled with Stalk. Welch and his team eventually brought Stalk's case studies to GE's executive learning center, where they were taught to thousands of executives.

Stalk gained a reputation as a brilliant thinker, but one who didn't suffer fools gladly. He sometimes abandoned projects if he felt that his clients didn't share his passion or commitment to change. And when he stopped learning, it was time to move on. Implementation wasn't his thing. "One of the things I learned early on was I always have to pair myself with someone who has patience with a client," he says. "I'm not going to be the guy that's there to get it done."

In the midst of this chaos, Stalk's family was growing as well, now consisting of six kids, four of whom were special-needs children adopted from Korea, Japan, and Russia. They lived on an island off the coast of Maryland while Stalk's home office was in Chicago. And while, unlike most work-obsessed sorts, he speaks constantly of his family, he's the first to admit he missed a lot of homework sessions and birthday parties. In 1992, Stalk moved the family to Toronto and took over BCG's practice there, figuring he wouldn't have to travel as much.

Yet Stalk simply couldn't downshift. There was the development of

BCG's worldwide innovation group, the revamping of the firm's marketing and communications arm, and in 1997, an e-commerce unit, which grew into a $450 million business. "His limits were just beyond [the norm]," says Lachenauer, Stalk's coauthor on *Hardball* and now CEO of GEO2 Technologies. "Some partner in Auckland would say, 'George, we really need you doing something with the Dairy Board,' something with no self-interest whatsoever. He'd go there at the drop of a hat." Tom Andruskevich, CEO of Canadian luxury company Henry Birks & Sons, remembers his first meeting with Stalk. "I spoke to him on the phone, and he literally got on a plane the same day and arrived at about 6 P.M. We talked until 11 P.M.," he says.

> *As he contemplated his own death, Stalk suddenly had an idea for a management story: Where have all the gurus gone? He consoled himself with the fact that he wasn't the only one about to disappear; many of the management strategists who had been big names throughout Stalk's career were dead or no longer adding new ideas to the field. But Stalk couldn't write the story because he was going to die. So how could he communicate it to someone on the ground? There was no way, he discovered, to send faxes or e-mail from Heaven. "I have to come up with something better here," he thought.*

It had been almost five years since Stalk had really felt healthy. As BCG went into warp speed during the New Economy boom, Stalk did too. In 1998, he contracted hepatitis in Thailand. In 2000, he came down with pneumonia, spending a month in bed unable to work. That same year, he decided to take a life-insurance physical. He didn't pass it.

Then 2001 hit, bringing with it the dual blow of the dot-com collapse and September 11. BCG's executive committee issued an all-hands-on-deck call, and Stalk, ever the good soldier, responded. He became interested in pricing as a competitive strategy and built up a pricing group within the company to $50 million in revenue. He also began work on *Hardball*. "The common theme is that [all my ideas] are about taking advantage to the point where competitors are left astounded by what's happened. And that's actually how I get through the day. I'm constantly looking at what's the opportunity to create advantage here. This is the lens I use over and over."

But Stalk's hardball approach to life was taking its toll, and his colleagues and clients could see it happening. "To a fault, he would show up when he was ill," says Marvin Adams, senior vice president at Ford, who worked with Stalk on a project around that time. "You could tell he was really starting to wear down." Stalk felt it, too, but thought that if he could just make it to the following spring, things would get better. "One doctor asked, 'What did you think was going to be different in the spring?' I said, 'I don't know, but it was far enough out there in the future that something had to be different.'"

He was right. One cold February day in 2003, he was in a Boston hotel room when he began to vomit blood. He decided to go back to Toronto, and by the time he got there, he had lost so much blood that he went straight to the emergency room. In a total system failure, a series of blood vessels ruptured in his stomach. Then, after a few weeks in the hospital, he lost consciousness and found himself trapped in limbo. Making matters worse, the SARS epidemic had hit Toronto just before he went into the hospital, which was placed under strict quarantine. His friends were unable to visit, and his wife and children were allowed in only sporadically, when it seemed most likely that Stalk was going to die.

At some point during Stalk's coma, his hallucinations changed from those of a man who knew he was dying to those of someone with a chance of survival. He launched into a series of rehabilitation dreams, all of which involved arduous tasks he had no choice but to complete.

Sent to an island in the Caribbean, Stalk realized that in order to survive, he had to go through an obstacle course while scuba diving. But he was unable to move and to breathe, so he was always the last to finish what he called the "mobility challenge." Suddenly, Stalk was on a mountain outside Las Vegas along with a group of invalids. Caught in a snowstorm, they had to fly a helicopter with a heavy hospital bed attached to it up the mountain. If they didn't make it, none of them would survive.

Next came a version of Survivor, *set in the 1700s. A random group of people had to work together to create everything from food to guns to fire. As Stalk had often observed with clients, the group quickly degenerated into a bunch of separate groups, all flailing away at the same time. It fell to Stalk to figure out the proper sequence of events, creating fire first, then, with the ashes, making gunpowder and finally steel for a gun to use for hunting.*

"Who are you?"

"What's the date?"

"Where are you?"

Every morning, Stalk dreamed that the doctors would ask him the same three questions, and every morning he would get one of the three wrong. "I'm George Stalk. I'm in England. It's February 21." His only chance at getting better was to answer all three questions correctly.

On May 5, the same day his BCG partners were praying for him in Paris, Stalk came out of his coma.

"Where are you?" a nurse asked him.

"England," he said.

"No," said the nurse, "you're in Toronto."

Stalk didn't believe her. He insisted she wheel in a television set. A few days later, when he regained the ability to speak and was able to call his wife, he realized that he was alive.

On May 28, 2003, Stalk was released from the hospital, with no sense of whether he would live another month or another decade. Typically, he immediately planned to return to work. But he soon realized that his expectations were a hallucination of their own. First, he was so weak that he could barely stand. Then there were the memory problems. "It took me several weeks before I could read a newspaper," he says. "I couldn't get to the bottom of the page without forgetting what was at the top."

He kept pushing himself—until things reached a head just over a month after he came home. "In the space of 24 hours," he says, "C. Henri caught me driving my car and making plans to fly to Hong Kong. Then Carl Stern [then managing partner of BCG] called to complain about me because I was calling too many people. [C. Henri] came in and said, 'Look, if you want to kill yourself, kill yourself. I'm here to help you [survive].' "

Chastened, Stalk pulled back, but it wasn't easy, as a memo he wrote to his staff in July made clear: "While the doctors are happy with the pace of my recovery, I am disappointed. I hoped to have this wrapped up and behind me by the end of August." Stalk returned to work full time in June 2004 but says he has sharply curtailed travel and a lot of on-the-ground client work. He makes a point of being home with his family and admits to feeling exhaustion as the day stretches on.

But you'd never know it to sit with Stalk 20 months after his ordeal began. Dressed in a tweed sports coat, beard neatly trimmed, oozing vitality, he has regained the 55 pounds he lost and more, thanks to his four-times-a-day chocolate ice cream fix. He leaps from one huge subject to another, nimbly segueing from the growing power of China to the freight logjam threatening the supply chain in this country. Although he sits calmly, the words spill out like water.

If this is what Stalk calls the "new George," it's scary to imagine the old one. But Stalk is now living his own form of time-based competition: Just like the Japanese factory managers he studied, his life is now about getting as much done as possible with maximum efficiency. The projects he takes on these days must have the potential to bear fruit in three to four years. And what was his planning horizon before? "Infinite," he says softly. One has the sense that he's mourning his life, even as it continues. He feels healthy again and the doctors don't see why he can't live a normal life span, but it's not the same. The guru of time is now a slave to it.

Stalk was dead, or at least everyone thought so. He lay in a closed casket at an English church, funereal chords echoing through the rafters, about to be buried after succumbing, finally, to his mysterious illness.

But he wasn't dead yet, although no one knew that because he couldn't speak or rap on the casket. Suddenly, his cell phone rang inside his coffin. It was his assistant, Bronwyn, calling to tell him that a colleague at BCG had just heard that he'd been sick and was sending a plane to pick him up and take him to the Mayo Clinic. "He said to put you on ice," Bronwyn said.

To come to terms with death and then to emerge to talk about it is the type of experience that flows a lot more smoothly on *Oprah* than it does in the halls of BCG. Perhaps that's why Stalk, when asked what he has learned from the ordeal, shifts uncomfortably in his seat. Later, he e-mails a list of "ah-has" from the hallucinations: "I have a lot of friends," he writes. "There are no voice mails, e-mails, or faxes in emergency rooms."

This is not the quality of analysis one expects from Stalk, the ultimate research geek. Particularly for an engineer, it may be much easier to remain in the world of the rational, where theories can be proven. "I am not an expert in this," he says dismissively, "nor have I been sufficiently interested enough to crowd out other things to become interested in this topic."

Stalk is much more interested in the rough-and-tumble rules of *Hardball*, the culmination of several decades of observing how companies win and lose in the real world. According to the "Hardball Manifesto" that opens the book, "the leaders of the world's most successful companies—the hardball winners—believe it is their obligation . . . to see and exploit their competitive advantage to the fullest. And, when possible, the hardball leaders will push that advantage to the point where competitors are squeezed and even feel pain." One particularly well-told example of "unleashing massive and overwhelming force" is Frito-Lay's move against the surging Eagle Snacks unit of Anheuser-Busch, which had made alarming inroads into Frito-Lay's core salty-snacks business. Using a combination of improved quality, price cuts, and better distribution under the inspired direction of then-CEO Roger Enrico, writes Stalk, Frito-Lay fought back—and put Eagle Snacks out of business.

But while Stalk enjoys playing the role of provocateur, it is not true that his book ignores the role of culture or leadership. Both are vital parts of strategy, he says, but many companies wrongly assume that culture itself is the strategy. The book is a resounding riposte to the notion "that it's somehow crude to talk about yourself as being a winner and by definition, that someone's losing," he says. "Excuse me, strategy matters."

Outside of *Hardball*, Stalk has limited his work to two other intellectual "buckets" (the BCG bigs took pricing away from him, although he is secretly trying to figure out a way back in). One is developing strategies for competing with the rising power of Chinese companies, which he says are fast becoming America's true rivals rather than simply low-cost sources. In order to survive, companies will have to pursue the Chinese market, and they'll have to improve their supply chains dramatically. Stalk is also working on "strategic dislocation," which means developing a methodology for anticipating the next technologies or concepts that will fundamentally change the world, much as the telegraph, the credit card, and the railroad have.

Sadly for Stalk, dividing his time into buckets makes it hard to do the free association that gets him his best ideas. And China, it turns out, is too big a subject for Stalk to study from the outside. "I've gotten to the point where I realize that if I don't go to China and spend time on the ground, I don't have much more to say," he says. But that is exactly the kind of work he's sworn off doing. "Four years ago, I would have said, 'Hot damn, I'm on my way!' Now I think the issue is either fish or cut bait. I haven't decided what to do."

It's the ultimate Hobson's choice. Stay healthy—but miss out on one of the great intellectual challenges of our time—or go and risk losing it all. "He talks about a new life, but it's a veneer," says O'Leary, his friend and former client. "He's still 90% the old George. He's doing it to the limit that he thinks he possibly can and get away with it."

While Stalk was in the hospital, a doctor told him he'd used up nine of his nine lives. But it's only cats that have nine lives. Consultants, George Stalk would like all of us to think, have 10.

THE LAST WORD

I just finished reading your article on George Stalk and wanted to commend you on a job well done. Not only was it well written, it made me both admire Mr. Stalk's drive and contributions and mourn for his family as they watch him drive headlong out of their lives and into an early grave.

As a consultant and executive coach, I've observed this type of behavior in a number of clients and on occasion have visited their hospital beds after heart attacks or pneumonia resulted from the stress brought about by their drive. The fortunate ones at some point realize there is more to life and regain some balance. I hope this happens with Mr. Stalk; I greatly enjoyed Hardball: Are You Playing to Play or Playing to Win? *and would hate to think it's his last book.*

> *Mario Sikora*
> *Executive director*
> *Enneagram Consulting & Training Center*
> *Philadelphia, Pennsylvania*

Gospels of Failure

From: Issue 91 | February 2005 | By: Jena McGregor

It's human nature to rubberneck at a wreck. But all too often, when faced with failure, we don't study it so much as gawk at it and then try to keep moving. The results of three colossal organizational failures—the 9/11 terrorist attacks, the *Columbia* space shuttle explosion, and the fabrications of *New York Times* reporter Jayson Blair—caused prominent organizations to step back and put their own failures under the microscope. Consider them together and some universal themes emerge. Imaginations, cultures, and lines of communication get clogged in an organization. Inevitably, individuals see what's happening and try to warn the higher-ups, but their messages get lost and go unheeded. Only after it's too late are their words rediscovered, serving as bitter reminders that disaster could have been averted. The lessons of these massive failures can help any organization avert a catastrophe of its own.

Here's a riddle. What is the only business book ever to spend more than 19 weeks on the *New York Times* best-seller list, sell more than a million copies, and be nominated for the prestigious National Book Award?

Give up? It's *The 9/11 Commission Report,* which is shaping up to become the surprise hit of the last year. It's a trick question, granted: The 9/11 study isn't a traditional business book; at least, it's not the overhyped, how-to, warmed-over fluff that all too often dominates the genre. But the commission's report is a careful analysis of flawed organizations, and of the devastating effects of siloed cultures and ineffective management.

So it's finding fans in pockets across the business world. Felix Barber, a Zurich-based senior adviser to the Boston Consulting Group, says he thought the report was "one of the best books on organization I've read." Ian Mitroff, a professor at the Marshall School of Business at the University of Southern California, observes, "virtually every page is about flawed organizations."

And Jamie Gorelick, one of the 9/11 commissioners, says she has spent a "tremendous" amount of time talking to business groups and senior management teams since the book's release. Their intense response to the commission's 567-page volume, already in its sixth printing, has startled her. "There are bunches of people I've come across who have read the whole thing cover to cover and carry it around with them," she says. "For some people, it's the *Little Red Book*. It's weird. I expected people to read it. I didn't expect people to inhale it."

Really, the fervor isn't so surprising. We live and work in a world where organizational failure is endemic—but where frank, comprehensive dissections of those failures are still woefully infrequent; where success is too easily celebrated and failures are too quickly forgotten; where short-term earnings and publicity concerns block us from confronting—much less, learning from—our stumbles and our blunders.

Now we have an opportunity to buck the tide—in the form of three brutally honest anatomies of catastrophe, none of them directly from the business world, published in the last year and a half. The 9/11 Commission's gripping book, the *Columbia* Accident Investigation Board's thorough report of the space-shuttle tragedy, and *The New York Times*'s reflective account of the scandal involving the fabrications by reporter Jayson Blair are windows on our own organizations' vulnerabilities. With the glaring clarity of hindsight, all of these tragedies are striking reminders that while individuals can be quite adept at picking up on hints of failure in the making, organizations typically fail to process and act on their warnings.

The FBI field agent warning about terrorists in flight schools; the engineers requesting better photos of the space shuttle's wing after it was struck by debris; the department editor who wrote a memo warning that Blair shouldn't be writing for the paper—all these individuals were sending signals of impending disaster. "The biggest screaming headline is that all the knowledge needed was already inside," says Jeffrey Sonnenfeld, associate dean of executive programs at the Yale School of Management. Or as George Tenet, the former director of central intelligence, told the 9/11 Commission, "The system was blinking red."

Reacting to those weak signals—to the information trapped within the system—may or may not have prevented these catastrophes. Indeed, we cannot begin to sift through every cause that led to what are unthinkable disasters. But each report stresses one of three factors—imagination, culture, or communication—as the greatest culprit in ignoring, trapping, or suppressing crucial warning signs. These were the factors that made the blinking red signals so hard to see.

Imagination

INSTITUTIONALIZING DISRUPTIVE INTELLIGENCE

On September 4, 2001, just before a meeting of cabinet-level officials called the Principals Committee—the first such gathering under the Bush administration to address Al Qaeda—Richard Clarke sent a fervent personal letter to Condoleezza Rice, then the national security adviser. The real question, the former counterterrorist coordinator insisted, was "Are we serious about dealing with the al Qida [sic] threat? . . . Is al Qida a big deal?" It seems preposterous in hindsight, but it's a breathtaking illustration of how, even seven days before September 11, government leaders still were underestimating the severity of the threat Al Qaeda posed.

The 9/11 Commission calls this lack of imagination "the most important failure" of leaders in the September 11 tragedy. A sort of "cultural asymmetry" had taken hold, blinding leaders to the gravity of the danger. "To us, Afghanistan seemed very far away," the commission members wrote. "To members of Al Qaeda, America seemed very close. In a sense, they were more globalized than we were."

Here, then, was the world's only superpower being threatened by a fanatical, remote, bootstrapped organization. Forgive the analogy, but that sounds remarkably like the innovative start-ups we know from the business world. Think Napster and the recording industry, or Linux and Microsoft. The 9/11 Commission report may call this "cultural asymmetry"; it also sounds a lot like the concept of disruptive innovation.

Yet cultural asymmetry is just one of the commission's powerful ideas about the failure of imagination. Perhaps the most startling is the concept of "institutionalizing imagination": "It is therefore crucial," the commission writes, "to find a way of routinizing, even bureaucratizing, the exercise of imagination."

Bureaucratize imagination? Could this be the most oxymoronic statement ever made? Not really. "We don't mean, 'Okay, guys, let's all join hands
and be more imaginative,' " says Gorelick, the former 9/11 commissioner.
"You don't really institutionalize imagination." Rather, she says, "you put in
place systems that allow the imagination that's naturally occurring to actually break through."

The commission's report proposes a process for doing so. It sounds a lot
like scenario planning, a common business process that provides a framework for imagining multiple potential futures. Although the intelligence
community had analyzed possible surprise attacks for years, these methods
were not used consistently. The Counterterrorist Center did not perform
"red team" analyses from the enemy's perspective that likely would have
predicted the use of airplanes in suicide attacks. Nor did it develop indicators for monitoring this kind of attack—or potential defenses against it.

Even if your organization is already using scenario planning, leaders
tend to focus on the probable rather than the disruptive. "Every president
wants one scenario," says Peter Schwartz, whose firm, Global Business Network, has done scenario planning with everyone from Ford Motor Co. to,
well, the CIA. "In every situation, it's tell me what will happen. When you
ask that question, it forces the intelligence community to come up with one
most likely scenario. And the most likely scenario in every situation is more
of the same." To get top management to listen to more than one outcome,
Schwartz psychologically tricks them by presenting the most credible outcome first. "If you don't give them that scenario first, then they will reject
everything until they hear the scenario they already believe in," he says.

Trying to imagine future scenarios—without the right framework or
expertise—can, of course, turn bewildering. A more manageable approach,
says Karl Weick, a professor at the University of Michigan Business School
and the author of *Managing the Unexpected* (Jossey-Bass, 2001), is to think
backward from a potential outcome, which will surface the events that
could create it. Weick suggests using the future perfect tense ("By next quarter, we will have lost our biggest customer") as a simple but disciplined way
of imagining what could happen. "It anchors you in the future," he says.

That exercise is exactly what Clarke urged Rice, with eerie prescience, to
do in his September 4 missive. "Decision makers should imagine themselves

on a future day when the [Counterterrorism Security Group] has not succeeded in stopping al Qida attacks and hundreds of Americans lay dead in several countries, including the U.S.," Clarke wrote. "What would those decision makers wish that they had done earlier?"

Culture

DISTURBING THE PERFECT PLACE

The National Aeronautics and Space Administration (NASA) spent the 1960s, quite literally, shooting for the moon. The seemingly impossible successes it achieved during the Apollo era made it a symbol of human accomplishment, establishing a remarkable "can do" culture. But even as the mission of NASA changed, and its goals shifted from man-on-the-moon triumphs to routine shuttle operations, the early glories held fast. NASA had become a "perfect place," wrote Yale professor Garry Brewer back in 1989. In such cultures, he wrote, the ability to listen to dissent requires "the shock of heavy cannon."

Somehow, even the *Challenger* disaster of 1986 was not heavy enough. Then, early on the morning of February 1, 2003, the *Columbia* shuttle exploded over the piney woods of East Texas. The physical cause for the accident may have been a piece of foam debris that struck the shuttle's left wing just seconds after launch, but that wasn't the only problem. "In our view," writes the *Columbia* Accident Investigation Board (CAIB) in its report, "the NASA organizational culture had as much to do with this accident as the foam."

NASA, in a nutshell, remained conditioned by its past success. Even after *Challenger*, the CAIB authors write, NASA suffered from the symptoms of the perfect place. Its decision making was still marked by unwarranted optimism and overconfidence. NASA was still a place where lessons-learned programs were voluntary, where frontline engineers feared ridicule for expressing their concerns, where, writes the CAIB, "the intellectual curiosity and skepticism that a solid safety culture requires was almost entirely absent."

How do we eliminate perfect-place arrogance in our own organizations? First, don't be straitjacketed by traditional perspectives. After the foam strike was discovered, engineers called it almost an "in family" event. This meant it was treated in the same way as well-known, traditionally "accepted" risks and therefore was wrongly written off as posing no harm. Although top shuttle management quickly dismissed the threat, lower-level engineers were concerned and asked for better photos in order to more accurately assess the damage. Though they tried three different bureaucratic channels, all of their requests were denied.

"Take your labels lightly, don't hold them dogmatically," says Karl Weick, who has studied high-risk organizations extensively. In addition to the in-family label, Weick notes, NASA had long thought of the shuttle as being "operational" when it had really never left the experimental phase. "Once you attach that kind of label to it, you seal yourself off from any likelihood that you're going to learn anything."

NASA's perfect-place culture also led to a warped outlook on safety. After the engineers' requests for photos were denied because there was no "requirement" for them, they found themselves "in the unusual position of having to prove that the situation was unsafe," write the CAIB authors, "a reversal of the usual requirement that a situation is safe." This may sound like mere semantics, but it meant NASA exhibited an overconfident, prove-it-wrong attitude rather than one that demanded engineers prove it right.

To help break down such attitudes, Weick suggests a similar semantic reversal. By restating a close call as a near hit, you turn the event on its head. You almost failed, rather than barely succeeded. It's simple, but it can be a great reminder that the system is all too capable of big mistakes. "In general, it just breeds a kind of wariness, a kind of attentiveness," says Weick. "Complacency is what you're worried about."

So does all this mean we don't shoot for the moon? That we dwell on our failures rather than taking pride in our triumphs? Not at all. But there's a fine line to walk between a proud culture and a prideful one, between celebrating a healthy history of success and resting on your laurels. "I call it delusions of a dream company," says Sydney Finkelstein, a professor of management at Dartmouth's Tuck School of Business and the author of *Why Smart Executives Fail* (Portfolio, 2003). "It creeps up on you. That honest pride starts going toward self-confidence, overconfidence, complacency, and arrogance. It's just a natural progression."

Communication

DISSOLVING ENVIRONMENTS OF SEPARATION

At its core, the newsroom of *The New York Times* traffics in information. Its products are stories, its suppliers are diverse voices, and its mission is to ferret out the truth. So it's hard to miss the irony spelled out by the authors of the report investigating the Blair scandal. "A failure to communicate—to tell other editors what some people in the newsroom knew—emerges as the single most consistent cause, after Jayson Blair's own behavior, of this catastrophe." The newsroom of *The New York Times*, the report's authors write, was "an environment of separation."

Add to this environment the imperious, hard-driving leadership of executive editor Howell Raines, a self-declared "change agent" bent on outdoing other papers, and you have a recipe for communication disaster. Raines's reputation for playing favorites and pushing his ideas of what should be in the paper only worsened the situation. "There was no sense that he was on [the newsroom's] side, that he respected them, that he listened to them," says USC business school professor Warren Bennis. "There's a marvelous Middle Eastern phrase about leaders who've stopped listening. They say, 'He has tired ears.' That's arrogance."

Under Raines's leadership, communication also deteriorated in an increasingly centralized hierarchy. Department heads had traditionally been crucial communication links; they were key to information flow between frontline editors and masthead-level editors, or top management. But as much of their power shifted upward, these key links in the communication chain suffered a loss of authority. With that, surely, went a decline in communication.

Yet the report's recommendations make clear that the *Times*'s problems were bigger than just Raines. Rather, they plead for strengthening the social network at the *Times* in order to share information more effectively. "Too much information about matters large and small," the report laments, "is locked in too few brains." The report's authors, many of them reporters and editors themselves, called for meetings that were more inclusive of all levels of the organization, intranet tools for seeking out resident experts, and office hours for management, similar to those of university professors, in order to open communication pathways. Members requested more informal brainstorming among reporters and editors in different departments, more cross-departmental meetings, and temporary assignments on different desks.

These seem like simple things, but they're actually tough to pull off. "I think people often underestimate the amount of resourcefulness that's required to proactively shape new communication patterns," says Niko Canner, a cofounder of management-consulting firm Katzenbach Partners. "Do people understand the way to communicate information so that they will get value from an exchange with a conversational partner they're not used to talking with? Can they build those new behaviors into the day-to-day of how they do their work?"

Valdis Krebs, a developer of software that maps social networks, agrees. "If there's not a network connecting two departments, then one can bring the best data in the world to the other and it won't be trusted." Krebs uses his software to help clients map out who knows whom within an organization—he calls the maps "organizational X-rays"—and then does something decidedly less high-tech. He introduces people on the borders of the networks, creating opportunities for them to work together. Over time, "through day-to-day work, we learn to trust each other," he says. "And when you get upset, I learn to trust that, too."

It's an intriguing, potentially important, exercise. But in real life, at times of real failure, those social networks won't work unless leaders let them. When people bypass the organization's hierarchy, the manager's instinctual response can be to thwart them, even punish them for breaking the chain of command.

In the face of failure, however, leaders must embrace the unconventional. They have to allow communications at the periphery—and have the discipline and humility to listen for notes that sound off-key. They must shape cultures that are open both to the possibility of failure and to the need to learn when problems do occur. And they, like all of us, have to imagine the unimaginable. And they should start now. Because, as Richard Clarke warned in his 2001 memo, "That future day could happen at any time."

THE LAST WORD

I loved this article!! As a business coach and strategist, I work with many fast-growing companies and their leaders all the time. I see overconfidence and arrogance creep into the best of companies.

Denise Corcoran
Burlingame, California

Making Change

From: Issue 94 | May 2005 | By: Alan Deutschman

"I can change. Really." It's become one of the great clichés in life. The sad fact is that most people do not change, although they can. This has huge repercussions in the personal realm, most notably on our health, as well as in business, where competing in the increasingly volatile global marketplace requires us to break out of established routines that no longer work. Alan Deutschman takes us on a fascinating journey into the latest insights from the worlds of cognitive science, linguistics, and neuroscience that explain how people can change if they're nurtured to do so psychologically, emotionally, and spiritually. Some of these skills run counter to what comes naturally to the quant jocks who often end up in charge in business. But if we want to benefit from all that will come from change, these insights from science will take root.

Change or die. What if you were given that choice? For real. What if it weren't just the hyperbolic rhetoric that conflates corporate performance with life and death? Not the overblown exhortations of a rabid boss, or a slick motivational speaker, or a self-dramatizing CEO. We're talking actual life or death now. Your own life or death. What if a well-informed, trusted authority figure said you had to make difficult and enduring changes in the way you think and act? If you didn't, your time would end soon—a lot sooner than it had to. Could you change when change really mattered? When it mattered most?

Yes, you say?

Try again.

Yes?

You're probably deluding yourself.

You wouldn't change.

Don't believe it? You want odds? Here are the odds, the scientifically studied odds: nine to one. That's nine to one against you. How do you like those odds?

This revelation unnerved many people in the audience last November at IBM's "Global Innovation Outlook" conference. The company's top executives had invited the most farsighted thinkers they knew from around the world to come together in New York and propose solutions to some really big problems. They started with the crisis in health care, an industry that consumes an astonishing $1.8 trillion a year in the United States alone, or 15% of gross domestic product. A dream team of experts took the stage, and you might have expected them to proclaim that breathtaking advances in science and technology—mapping the human genome and all that—held the long-awaited answers. That's not what they said. They said that the root cause of the health crisis hasn't changed for decades, and the medical establishment still couldn't figure out what to do about it.

Dr. Raphael "Ray" Levey, founder of the Global Medical Forum, an annual summit meeting of leaders from every constituency in the health system, told the audience, "A relatively small percentage of the population consumes the vast majority of the health-care budget for diseases that are very well known and by and large behavioral." That is, they're sick because of how they choose to live their lives, not because of environmental or genetic factors beyond their control. Continued Levey: "Even as far back as when I was in medical school"—he enrolled at Harvard in 1955—"many articles demonstrated that 80% of the health-care budget was consumed by five behavioral issues." Levey didn't bother to name them, but you don't need an MD to guess what he was talking about: too much smoking, drinking, eating, and stress, and not enough exercise.

Then the knockout blow was delivered by Dr. Edward Miller, the dean of the medical school and CEO of the hospital at Johns Hopkins University. He turned the discussion to patients whose heart disease is so severe that they undergo bypass surgery, a traumatic and expensive procedure that can cost more than $100,000 if complications arise. About 600,000 people have bypasses every year in the United States, and 1.3 million heart patients have angioplasties—all at a total cost of around $30 billion. The procedures temporarily relieve chest pains but rarely prevent heart attacks or prolong lives.

Around half of the time, the bypass grafts clog up in a few years; the angioplasties, in a few months. The causes of this so-called restenosis are complex. It's sometimes a reaction to the trauma of the surgery itself. But many patients could avoid the return of pain and the need to repeat the surgery—not to mention arrest the course of their disease before it kills them—by switching to healthier lifestyles. Yet very few do. "If you look at people after coronary-artery bypass grafting two years later, 90% of them have not changed their lifestyle," Miller said. "And that's been studied over and over and over again. And so we're missing some link in there. Even though they know they have a very bad disease and they know they should change their lifestyle, for whatever reason, they can't."

Changing the behavior of people isn't just the biggest challenge in health care. It's the most important challenge for businesses trying to compete in a turbulent world, says John Kotter, a Harvard Business School professor who has studied dozens of organizations in the midst of upheaval: "The central issue is never strategy, structure, culture, or systems. The core of the matter is always about changing the behavior of people." Those people may be called upon to respond to profound upheavals in marketplace dynamics—the rise of a new global competitor, say, or a shift from a regulated to a deregulated environment—or to a corporate reorganization, merger, or entry into a new business. And as individuals, we may want to change our own styles of work—how we mentor subordinates, for example, or how we react to criticism. Yet more often than not, we can't.

CEOs are supposedly the prime change agents for their companies, but they're often as resistant to change as anyone—and as prone to backsliding. The most notorious recent example is Michael Eisner. After he nearly died from heart problems, Eisner finally heeded his wife's plea and brought in a high-profile number-two exec, Michael Ovitz, to alleviate the stress of running Disney. But Eisner proved incapable of seeing through the idea, essentially refusing to share any real power with Ovitz from the start.

The conventional wisdom says that crisis is a powerful motivator for change. But severe heart disease is among the most serious of personal crises, and it doesn't motivate—at least not nearly enough. Nor does giving people accurate analyses and factual information about their situations. What works? Why, in general, is change so incredibly difficult for people?

What is it about how our brains are wired that resists change so tenaciously? Why do we fight even what we know to be in our own vital interests?

Kotter has hit on a crucial insight. "Behavior change happens mostly by speaking to people's feelings," he says. "This is true even in organizations that are very focused on analysis and quantitative measurement, even among people who think of themselves as smart in an MBA sense. In highly successful change efforts, people find ways to help others see the problems or solutions in ways that influence emotions, not just thought."

Unfortunately, that kind of emotional persuasion isn't taught in business schools, and it doesn't come naturally to the technocrats who run things—the engineers, scientists, lawyers, doctors, accountants, and managers who pride themselves on disciplined, analytical thinking. There's compelling science behind the psychology of change—it draws on discoveries from emerging fields such as cognitive science, linguistics, and neuroscience—but its insights and techniques often seem paradoxical or irrational.

Look again at the case of heart patients. The best minds at Johns Hopkins and the Global Medical Forum might not know how to get them to change, but someone does: Dr. Dean Ornish, a professor of medicine at the University of California at San Francisco and founder of the Preventative Medicine Research Institute, in Sausalito, California. Ornish, like Kotter, realizes the importance of going beyond the facts. "Providing health information is important but not always sufficient," he says. "We also need to bring in the psychological, emotional, and spiritual dimensions that are so often ignored." Ornish published studies in leading peer-reviewed scientific journals, showing that his holistic program, focused around a vegetarian diet with less than 10% of the calories from fat, can actually reverse heart disease without surgery or drugs. Still, the medical establishment remained skeptical that people could sustain the lifestyle changes. In 1993, Ornish persuaded Mutual of Omaha to pay for a trial. Researchers took 333 patients with severely clogged arteries. They helped them quit smoking and go on Ornish's diet. The patients attended twice-weekly group support sessions led by a psychologist and took instruction in meditation, relaxation, yoga, and aerobic exercise. The program lasted for only a year. But after three years, the study found, 77% of the patients had stuck with their lifestyle changes—and safely avoided the bypass or angioplasty surgeries that they were eligible for under their insurance coverage. And Mutual of Omaha saved around $30,000 per patient.

Framing Change

Why does the Ornish program succeed while the conventional approach has failed? For starters, Ornish recasts the reasons for change. Doctors had been trying to motivate patients mainly with the fear of death, he says, and that simply wasn't working. For a few weeks after a heart attack, patients were scared enough to do whatever their doctors said. But death was just too frightening to think about, so their denial would return, and they'd go back to their old ways.

The patients lived the way they did as a day-to-day strategy for coping with their emotional troubles. "Telling people who are lonely and depressed that they're going to live longer if they quit smoking or change their diet and lifestyle is not that motivating," Ornish says. "Who wants to live longer when you're in chronic emotional pain?"

So instead of trying to motivate them with the "fear of dying," Ornish reframes the issue. He inspires a new vision of the "joy of living"—convincing them they can feel better, not just live longer. That means enjoying the things that make daily life pleasurable, like making love or even taking long walks without the pain caused by their disease. "Joy is a more powerful motivator than fear," he says.

Pioneering research in cognitive science and linguistics has pointed to the paramount importance of framing. George Lakoff, a professor of those two disciplines at the University of California at Berkeley, defines frames as the "mental structures that shape the way we see the world." Lakoff says that frames are part of the "cognitive unconscious," but the way we know what our frames are, or evoke new ones, springs from language. For example, we typically think of a company as being like an army—everyone has a rank and a codified role in a hierarchical chain of command with orders coming down from high to low. Of course, that's only one way of organizing a group effort. If we had the frame of the company as a family or a commune, people would know very different ways of working together.

The big challenge in trying to change how people think is that their minds rely on frames, not facts. "Neuroscience tells us that each of the concepts we have—the long-term concepts that structure how we think—is instantiated in the synapses of the brain," Lakoff says. "Concepts are not things that can be changed just by someone telling us a fact. We may be presented with facts, but for us to make sense of them, they have to fit what is already in the synapses of the brain. Otherwise, facts go in and then they go right back out. They are not heard, or they are not accepted as facts, or they mystify us: Why would anyone have said that? Then we label the fact as irrational, crazy, or stupid." Lakoff says that's one reason why political conservatives and liberals each think that the other side is nuts. They don't understand each other because their brains are working within different frames.

The frame that dominates our thinking about how work should be organized—the military chain-of-command model—is extremely hard to break. When new employees start at W. L. Gore & Associates, the maker of Gore-Tex fabrics, they often refuse to believe that the company doesn't have a hierarchy with job titles and bosses. It just doesn't fit their frame. They can't accept it. It usually takes at least several months for new hires to begin to understand Gore's reframed notion of the workplace, which relies on self-directed employees making their own choices about joining one another in egalitarian small teams.

Getting people to exchange one frame for another is tough even when you're working one-on-one, but it's especially hard to do for large groups of people. Howard Gardner, a cognitive scientist, MacArthur Fellow "genius" award winner, and professor at Harvard's Graduate School of Education, has looked at what works most effectively for heads of state and corporate CEOs. "When one is addressing a diverse or heterogeneous audience," he says, "the story must be simple, easy to identify with, emotionally resonant, and evocative of positive experiences."

In Louis V. Gerstner Jr.'s successful turnaround of IBM in the 1990s, he learned the surprising importance of this kind of emotional persuasion. When he took over as CEO, Gerstner was fixated on what had worked for him throughout his career as a McKinsey & Co. consultant: coolheaded analysis and strategy. He thought he could revive the company through maneuvers such as selling assets and cutting costs. He quickly found that those tools weren't nearly enough. He needed to transform the entrenched corporate culture, which had become hidebound and overly bureaucratic. That meant changing the attitudes and behaviors of hundreds of thousands of employees. In his memoir, Gerstner writes that he realized he needed to make a powerful emotional appeal to them, to "shake them out of their depressed stupor, remind them of who they were—you're IBM, damn it!" Rather than sitting in a corner office negotiating deals and analyzing spreadsheets, he needed to convey passion through thousands of hours of personal appearances. Gerstner, who's often brittle and imperious in private, nonetheless responded admirably to the challenge. He proved to be an engaging and emotional public speaker when he took his campaign to his huge workforce.

Steve Jobs's turnaround at Apple shows the impact of reframing and telling a new narrative that's simple, positive, and emotional. When he returned to the company after a long exile, he recast its image among employees and customers alike from a marginalized player vanquished in the battle for market share to the home of a small but enviable elite: the creative innovators who dared to "Think different."

When leaders are addressing a small group of people who have a similar mind-set and shared values, the reframed message can be more nuanced and complex, Harvard's Gardner says. But it still needs to be positive, inspiring, and emotionally resonant. A good example is how chairman and publisher Arthur Sulzberger Jr. rescued *The New York Times* from crisis. Former editor Howell Raines had alienated much of the newsroom's staff, undermining its communal spirit with a new culture of favoritism. Raines fell when a star reporter he had shielded from criticism was exposed for fabricating news stories. The scandal threatened the famed paper's credibility. Gardner says that Sulzberger successfully reframed the narrative this way: We are a great newspaper. We temporarily went astray and risked sacrificing the community spirit that made this an outstanding place to work. We can retain our excellence and regain our sense of community by admitting our errors, making sure that they don't happen again, and being a more transparent and self-reflecting organization. To achieve these goals, Sulzberger replaced Raines with a new top editor, Bill Keller—a respected veteran who reflected the lost communal culture—and he appointed a "public editor" to critique the paper in an unedited column. Now, Gardner says, "the *Times* is a much happier place and the news coverage and journalistic empire are in reasonable shape."

Radical Change

Reframing alone isn't enough, of course. That's where Dr. Ornish's other astonishing insight comes in. Paradoxically, he found that radical, sweeping, comprehensive changes are often easier for people than small, incremental ones. For example, he says that people who make moderate changes in their diets get the worst of both worlds: They feel deprived and hungry because they aren't eating everything they want, but they aren't making big enough changes to quickly see an improvement in how they feel, or in measurements such as weight, blood pressure, and cholesterol. But the heart patients who went on Ornish's tough, radical program saw quick, dramatic results, reporting a 91% decrease in frequency of chest pain in the first month. "These rapid improvements are a powerful motivator," he says. "When people who have had so much chest pain that they can't work, or make love, or even walk across the street without intense suffering find that they are able to do all of those things without pain in only a few weeks, then they often say, 'These are choices worth making.' "

While it's astonishing that most patients in Ornish's demanding program stick with it, studies show that two-thirds of patients who are prescribed statin drugs (which are highly effective at cutting cholesterol) stop taking them within one year. What could possibly be a smaller or easier lifestyle change than popping a pill every day? But Ornish says patients stop taking the drug because it doesn't actually make them feel any better. It doesn't deal with causes of high cholesterol, such as obesity, that make people feel unhealthy. The paradox holds that big changes are easier than small ones.

Research shows that this idea applies to the business realm as well. Bain & Co., the management consulting firm, studied 21 recent corporate transformations and found that most were "substantially completed" in only two years or less while none took more than three years. The means were drastic: In almost every case, the CEOs fired most of the top management. Almost always, the companies enjoyed quick, tangible results, and their stock prices rose 250% a year on average as they revived.

IBM's turnaround hinged on a radical shift in focus from selling computer hardware to providing "services," which meant helping customers build and run their information-technology operations. This required a momentous cultural switch—IBMers would have to recommend that a client buy from competitors such as Hewlett-Packard and Microsoft when it was in the client's interest. But the radical shift worked: Services have grown into IBM's core business and the key to its success.

Of course, radical change often isn't possible in business situations. Still, it's always important to identify, achieve, and celebrate some quick, positive results for the vital emotional lifts that they provide. Harvard's Kotter believes in the importance of "short-term wins" for companies, meaning "victories that nourish faith in the change effort, emotionally reward the hard workers, keep the critics at bay, and build momentum. Without sufficient wins that are visible, timely, unambiguous, and meaningful to others, change efforts invariably run into serious problems."

Supporting Change

Even when leaders have reframed the issues brilliantly, it's still vital to give people the multifaceted support they need. That's a big reason why 90% of heart patients can't change their lifestyles but 77% of Ornish's patients could—because he buttressed them with weekly support groups with other patients, as well as attention from dieticians, psychologists, nurses, and yoga and meditation instructors.

Xerox's executives learned this lesson well. Four years ago, when the company was in crisis, they came up with a new vision that required salespeople to change the way they had always worked. "Their whole careers, salespeople had done one thing," says James Firestone, president of Xerox North America, who leads a sales force of 5,400. "They would knock on doors, look for copiers, see how old they were, and sell a refresh. They knew how to do that." The salespeople had such predictable routines that they could plan their days, weeks, even years. It was comforting. But it just wasn't succeeding any longer.

Under the new strategy, the salespeople were supposed to really engage with customers so they could understand the complexities of how their offices operated and find opportunities to sell other products, such as scanners and printers. Maybe they would find that the customer actually needed fewer machines that could do more than the old ones had. Learning about the client's needs meant that the sales reps had to take a lot more time and talk to more people about broader issues. It undermined the cozy predictability of their routines. The reps became anxious, Firestone recalls. "They'd say, 'I know how to sell and make a living the old way, but not the new way.'"

Their anxiety was compounded by the fact that Xerox lagged in giving them the support they needed. It often took a couple of months before the salespeople received their scheduled training in the new approach. And it took two years before the company changed its incentive pay system to fit better with the new model, in which the reps had to invest a lot more time and effort before they signed deals. Eventually, though, the change effort, by expanding the sales focus to a larger range of products, helped Xerox avoid bankruptcy and return to profitability. "People need a sense of confidence that the processes will be aligned internally," Firestone says. "For large companies, this is where change usually fails." Even if change starts at the top, it can easily die somewhere in the middle. That's why Xerox now holds "alignment workshops" that ask middle managers—the people who make processes work—to outline the ways its systems could inhibit its agendas for change.

This Is Your Brain on Change

Are most of us like the fearful copier salespeople who dread disruption to their routines? Neuroscience, a field that has exploded with insight, has a lot more to say about changing people's behavior—and its findings are guardedly optimistic. Scientists used to believe that the brain became "hardwired" early in life and couldn't change later on. Now researchers such as Dr. Michael Merzenich, a professor at the University of California at San Francisco, say that the brain's ability to change—its "plasticity"—is lifelong. If we can change, then why don't we? Merzenich has perspective on the issue since he's not only a leading neuroscientist but also an entrepreneur, the founder of two Bay Area start-ups. Both use PC software to train people to overcome mental disabilities or diseases: Scientific Learning Corp. focuses on children who have trouble learning to read, and Posit Science Corp. is working on ways to prevent, stop, or reverse cognitive decline in older adults.

Merzenich starts by talking about rats. You can train a rat to have a new skill. The rat solves a puzzle, and you give it a food reward. After 100 times, the rat can solve the puzzle flawlessly. After 200 times, it can remember how to solve it for nearly its lifetime. The rat has developed a habit. It can perform the task automatically because its brain has changed. Similarly, a person has thousands of habits—such as how to use a pen—that drive lasting changes in the brain. For highly trained specialists, such as professional musicians, the changes actually show up on MRI scans. Flute players, for instance, have especially large representations in their brains in the areas that control the fingers, tongue, and lips, Merzenich says. "They've distorted their brains."

Businesspeople, like flutists, are highly trained specialists, and they've distorted their brains, too. An older executive "has powers that a young person walking in the door doesn't have," says Merzenich. He has lots of specialized skills and abilities. A specialist is a hard thing to create, and is valuable for a corporation, obviously, but specialization also instills an inherent "rigidity." The cumulative weight of experience makes it harder to change.

How, then, to overcome these factors? Merzenich says the key is keeping up the brain's machinery for learning. "When you're young, almost everything you do is behavior-based learning—it's an incredibly powerful, plastic period," he says. "What happens that becomes stultifying is you stop learning and you stop the machinery, so it starts dying." Unless you work on it, brain fitness often begins declining at around age 30 for men, a bit later for women. "People mistake being active for continuous learning," Merzenich says. "The machinery is only activated by learning. People think they're leading an interesting life when they haven't learned anything in 20 or 30 years. My suggestion is learn Spanish or the oboe."

Meanwhile, the leaders of a company need "a business strategy for continuous mental rejuvenation and new learning," he says. Posit Science has a "fifth-day strategy," meaning that everyone spends one day a week working in a different discipline. Software engineers try their hand at marketing.

Designers get involved in business functions. "Everyone needs a new project instead of always being in a bin," Merzenich says. "A fifth-day strategy doesn't sacrifice your core ability but keeps you rejuvenated. In a company, you have to worry about rejuvenation at every level. So ideally you deliberately construct new challenges. For every individual, you need complex new learning. Innovation comes about when people are enabled to use their full brains and intelligence instead of being put in boxes and controlled."

What happens if you don't work at mental rejuvenation? Merzenich says that people who live to 85 have a 50-50 chance of being senile. While the issue for heart patients is "change or die," the issue for everyone is "change or lose your mind." Mastering the ability to change isn't just a crucial strategy for business. It's a necessity for health. And it's possibly the one thing that's most worth learning.

THE LAST WORD

"Making Change" is spot on. My cardiologist telling me "You won't survive a heart attack; you need bypass surgery right now" still echoes in my ears 13 years later. Dr. Ornish's approach to change not only had an impact on my life, it also altered the way I work with clients. I've learned four things from my experience. Even when you know your life depends on it, change is hard, half-measures don't work, no one can make the choice to change for you, and finally, you can't make significant change alone. I wouldn't be here if not for the support of my friends, my family, and especially my wife, Emily.

Dick Axelrod
Wilmette, Illinois

Join the Circus

From: Issue 96 | July 2005 | By: Linda Tischler

The circus is an unlikely place to find a paragon of innovation, but Cirque du Soleil isn't your garden-variety circus. And that's the point. The Montreal-based performing arts group reinvented the circus as a popular entertainment, and reinvents itself with each daring new stage show. Its approaches to finding, training, and retraining talent, unleashing creativity, and building a beloved brand look like elaborate tricks right out of one of Cirque's shows. But they're calculated risks, the result of intense planning. Are you pushing yourself to do triple somersaults? If not, why not?

Inch by inch, the aerialist in the red flamenco outfit edges her way up a tightrope stretched at a 45-degree angle from the main wire, 20 feet above the stage. Curling her toes downward to steady her grip, she clutches a fan for balance. There is no net. Snare drums strike up an ominous patter that warns the audience this is a trick with real danger. Suddenly, as the young woman nears the summit of the tent, her foot slips, and she struggles, desperately, to secure her footing. The crowd holds its breath, as if one errant sigh could send her plummeting. For a long second she hovers, perilously. Then, regaining her balance, she scampers the last few feet to safety, to thunderous applause.

It is a classic circus trick, performed flawlessly—down to the expertly executed "slip"—served up in a show that is unconventional, even by the bizarre standards of the big top. Sure, there are tumblers, but they are bouncing on beds, not trampolines; there are trapeze artists, but they twirl in the center of giant chandeliers, not between platforms. And what garden-variety circus is likely to begin with a death-bed scene starring a midget and a dying clown, with a band of acrobat angels hovering overhead? It could only be Cirque du Soleil.

The surreal new production, "Corteo," currently touring Canada, is the latest extravaganza produced by the privately held, Montreal-based entertainment company. It opened in late April, two months after the debut of "Ka," the company's $165 million martial-arts-themed production at the MGM Grand in Las Vegas. This fall, in partnership with Clear Channel Communications, Cirque will mount a 100-date North American arena tour featuring the music of Cirque. Next year, it will premiere its much-anticipated collaboration with Apple Corps, the Beatles' record company, bringing the total number of Cirque shows in Vegas to five. A deal is in the works with Disney to mount Japan's first permanent show in Tokyo in 2008.

At a time when audiences for all performing arts are declining, Cirque du Soleil has taken a particularly moribund segment of the market—the circus—and created an entertainment juggernaut, with a burgeoning record label, a retail operation, and a deal with Carnival Cruise Lines. And we're not talking circus peanuts here. The company's Las Vegas shows regularly play to sold-out audiences of "kids of all ages"—as long as those tykes are willing to shell out as much as $150 per ticket—for a daily gross of a cool million. Can't get to Sin City? Then it's likely one of the company's six touring shows will cycle through your town, whether it be Barcelona, Minneapolis, or Sydney, sometime soon. Throw in the additional resident show, "La Nouba" at Disney World in Orlando, and the company's ticket sales top 7 million a year—that's about 135,000 per week—for annual revenues estimated at between $550 million and $600 million.

Pretty impressive for an operation that began as a band of Quebec street performers 21 years ago. And even more impressive than the dollars is the way Cirque du Soleil has captured the public's heart: In Interbrand's 2004 poll of brands with the most global impact, Cirque ranked No. 22—ahead of the likes of McDonald's, Microsoft, Volkswagen, and (ouch) Disney.

Clearly, we all have something to learn from these clowns (and acrobats and tumblers and dancers). You don't have to be a fan of the big top— though, really, who doesn't love a circus?—to understand that Cirque du Soleil is an impressive high-wire innovation act. Offbeat and wild it may be, but Cirque could still teach most businesses a thing or two about recruiting and retaining supremely talented specialists, coaxing extreme creativity from a diverse band of employees, and building a powerhouse global brand. But above all, it's a study in the virtues of taking big but controlled chances, as you'd probably expect in a business that's all about using skill and training to skirt death and disaster for the sake of beauty and laughs. "We like to take risks," says Daniel Lamarre, Cirque's president and COO, from a cafe in Barcelona, where he's visiting the road show "Dralion." "It's part of who we are. Every time we come in a comfort zone, we will find a way to get out, because being comfortable in our business is very, very dangerous."

The appetite for discomfort begins with the company's fundamental operating philosophy. Cirque has steadfastly refused to employ the impresario's favorite trick: Take a hit show (think *Mamma Mia* or *Phantom of the Opera*), clone it with a touring company, and send it on the road. Each Cirque du Soleil show is unique, one of a kind, despite stunningly high production costs. Even a traveling show, which doesn't require the enormous capital investment of a permanent theater, can cost upward of $25 million to mount and require three years to conceive, cast, design, train, and produce. And, as the backers of expensive Broadway stinkers like *Taboo* will tell you, even a fat wallet doesn't inoculate producers from the occasional bomb.

It's this willingness to take creative risk that is Cirque's original genius and the key to its competitive success, says Renée Mauborgne, coauthor of *Blue Ocean Strategy: How to Create Uncontested Market Space and Make the Competition Irrelevant* (Harvard Business School Press, 2005) and professor of strategy and management at INSEAD. Cirque combined the thrill of the circus with the high production values and intellectual sophistication of the theater or ballet to create a new art form and, along with it, a new "blue ocean" market. The company's future, she says, will depend on its ability to sustain that culture of risk taking, particularly as competitors enter the market. "The danger is that when you begin to be imitated, you start entering into red-ocean competition, where your focus is on outcompeting rivals rather than on creating the next blue ocean," says Mauborgne. "Then the competition, and not the marketplace, sets your agenda."

Already the sharks are in the water. A rival clowncentric production called "Slava's Snowshow" is drawing raves for its "breathtaking images."

The Canadian Cirque Eloize has been lauded as "a new generation of circus performers focusing on innovation, imagination, and show-stopping panache." Even venerable Ringling Brothers has added more theatrical elements to its show. And in late April, literally across the street from Cirque's original Vegas outpost, Steve Wynn debuted "Le Reve," a Cirque-style show, at his posh new $2.7 billion Wynn Las Vegas. Ironically, Wynn is the very guy who gave Cirque's founder, CEO, and creative guru, Guy Laliberte, his biggest break, by installing the company's first permanent show, "Mystere," at his Treasure Island hotel in 1993.

In Montreal, Cirque acknowledges the mounting competition but refuses to let it distract from the main mission. It must focus on the challenge of producing 11 blockbuster shows, often as much as 10 times a week, 52 weeks a year. That requires the ability to recruit, train, and replace injured or retiring performers, to continually find and develop fresh acts, and to maintain constant vigilance over the productions, from their costumes to their often daunting technical complexity. It has taken Cirque two decades to build an infrastructure—what director of creation Gilles Ste-Croix calls Cirque's "machine"—that can consistently deliver that level of support and innovation. Most important, however, is the company's ability to reinvent the brand with each new production. That, he says, is the toughest bar for competitors to overcome.

Lamarre agrees, pointing to the willingness of Cirque's Laliberte to put creativity before profits: "I haven't yet met anyone willing to invest as much money as Guy does in production, infrastructure, and risk taking." Cirque plows more than 70% of its profits back into new initiatives, R&D, and new shows every year, he says. "We built our brand on creativity, and if we don't respect this first value of our brand, it would be counterproductive for us long term." It can all make for a chaotic, stressful, demanding—or, if your DNA is up to it—exhilarating work environment. Says Lamarre: "A typical day at the office for me begins by asking: What is impossible that I'm going to do today?"

The saga of Cirque du Soleil is, if not impossible, then pretty improbable. In the early 1980s, in a small town near Quebec, a street performer named Gilles Ste-Croix and some friends formed a theatrical troupe called Le Club des Talons Hauts (the High Heels Club), specializing in circus arts: juggling, acrobatics, stiltwalking, music. One of the members was a fire breather and accordion player named Guy Laliberte. In 1982, the troupe organized a street performers' festival, which was so successful it inspired Laliberte to approach the city of Quebec with a proposal for a show called Cirque du Soleil (Circus of the Sun) to help celebrate Canada's 450th anniversary.

From the start, the show was hardly a conventional circus. It had outrageous costumes, original music, and clever performers—but no animals. Despite the dearth of beasts, it was a rousing success. Those initial decisions were brilliant, says Mauborgne, since they essentially redefined the game. By not featuring animals, Cirque eliminated one of the most costly and controversial parts of any circus. And by shifting the focus from an event geared to kids to one designed for adults, it could reinvent the pricing model as well. By combining the best of circus and theater, Cirque pulled in an audience the traditional circus had never seen: adult theatergoers accustomed to paying steeper ticket prices. In 1987, the troupe made its first visit south of the border, premiering at the Los Angeles Arts Festival. It was also Cirque's first big risk. Had the show bombed, the company was too broke to get the equipment back to Canada. Fortunately, it was a smash.

Cirque soon embarked on what would become a close and synergistic relationship with an industry that shares its coolheaded approach to risk: gambling. At the beginning of the 1990s, Steve Wynn saw a Cirque touring show and persuaded Laliberte to bring a big top to Vegas. The show sold out. With a gambler's eye for a potential big score, Wynn offered to build a permanent home for the company in his new hotel. "Mystere" opened in December 1993 and was sold out for a year. Wynn upped the ante in 1998, building a spectacular theater for "O" in the Bellagio. It was an instant sensation, and seven years later continues to sell out three months in advance. In 2000, shortly after Wynn sold his Mirage Resorts to MGM, Laliberte got a call from Terry Lanni, CEO of the new MGM Mirage and a Cirque fan from his days at Caesars Palace. Lanni was eager to field more shows in Vegas, so Cirque developed "Zumanity" and "Ka."

The partnership has been a blockbuster for both sides. For Cirque, the deal has brought a partner willing to sink hundreds of millions into creating unique venues for its shows. As for the MGM Mirage, "Ka" alone troops

4,000 folks a night past the MGM Grand's array of upscale restaurants, shops, and roulette wheels.

Half an hour outside of Montreal, in the scruffy suburb of Saint-Michel, sits the world headquarters of Cirque du Soleil, overlooking a former dump. The 100,000-square-foot complex, fronted with corrugated steel, looks less like the home of a circus than of a food-processing plant. Inside, there are three training studios, a costume shop, and a props workshop, as well as the casting team and corporate staff. This is the Cirque "machine"— the infrastructure on which the company's innovation process depends.

Cirque creators say that innovation, for them, always begins with a story. For example, Laliberte instructed "Ka" creator Robert Lepage to craft an epic tale that included martial arts, an art form no other Cirque show had yet explored. Then, to feed the shows' voracious appetite for hugely skilled performers, Cirque's innovation process shifts to the attraction, training, and retention of talent. Teams of new recruits are in constant training in Montreal before being dispatched to replace artists in existing shows, or to appear in new productions. With more than 700 artists (out of 3,000 total employees), culled from 40 different countries, and speaking 25 languages, the Cirque operation is like a mini United Nations, complete with translators.

At the moment, Florence Pot, head talent scout, is a woman on a mission: She's searching the globe for a quartet of wild and crazy guys for the company's next big show. The marriage of Cirque's performing arts and the Beatles' music will debut at the Mirage next summer in the space vacated by Siegfried and Roy. "The show will re-create the atmosphere of the Beatles before they were stars, when they were just young guys with no fear of trying new things," Pot says. For Cirque, that translates into a job spec that reads like a description of an L.A. skate punk: Wanted—four rebels who can run, jump, and do somersaults on Rollerblades. Must be compact, powerful, and bouncy. Fondness for "She Loves You" a plus.

Once the Beatles show is cast, it's not as if the casting team can go home. First there's the company's annual attrition of 20% of injured or retiring performers. Then there's Ste-Croix's pledge to produce four more shows over the next four years. And Cirque doesn't want standard-issue acrobats, jugglers, or trapeze artists. Cast members must also meet demanding artistic qualifications and, depending on the particular show, unusual performance requirements. In "O," for example, performers must be scuba certified. In "Zumanity," the R-rated show at Vegas's New York, New York hotel, gymnasts may be asked to perform topless.

Those requirements can be a challenge, even to experienced performers. Michelle Cassidy, an elegant blond dancer from South Africa, initially auditioned for "Zumanity." The Cirque casting team thought she was perfect en pointe, but a nonstarter for the company's bawdy cabaret-style show. "I just wasn't out there enough," she says. She was eventually cast as La Belle, a beautiful queen, in the tamer "Mystere."

Craig Paul Smith, a world-championship-level tumbler for Great Britain, was fine with the acrobatic tricks in "O," but, he says, "I got to the point where I was scared to put my head under the water because I was panicking so much." In "O," cast members must go underwater to change costumes or pick up props. "My breakthrough came when I told myself, 'You learn how to breathe, or you go back to England and learn a trade,'" he says.

The task of finding a constant supply of such versatile performers falls to Cirque's 12-member casting team. They show up at the Olympics and world championships to sign athletes. Others canvass the globe looking for fire jugglers, pole climbers, martial artists, bungee jumpers, Wheel of Death spinners, and artistically inclined midgets. To satisfy its ongoing need for slithery-limbed girls, Cirque supports a school for contortionists in Mongolia. Meanwhile, to staff the cast of "Varekai," Cirque scouts recruited traditional toe-knuckle dancers from a company in the Republic of Georgia that has a lock on the world supply.

Once cast, performers report to Montreal for six or eight weeks of basic-training boot camp, run by a Russian coach, Boris Verkhovsky. His assignment is tricky: to turn athletes into artists. It's not an easy transition, he says. The artistic process requires spontaneity, imagination, and creative risk taking—qualities that could get an elite athlete bounced off the team. "A lot of athletes come from an environment where they are literally told when to inhale and when to exhale," Verkhovsky says. "A side effect is that they're not very independent thinkers."

Besides teaching athletes how to unleash their inner thespians, Verkhovsky sometimes has to turn a class of raging divas into a cohesive band of brothers. To that end, he often prefers the also-ran to the medalist. "Somebody who almost made the team probably has the same repertoire of tricks, but is still hungry," he says. "The expectation of recognition is much less, so the prima donna syndrome is much lower."

And then he has to push the performer to achieve feats never attempted in an Olympic arena. That, he says, is Cirque's differentiator, and a requirement the boss insists upon. "Guy Laliberte consistently asks, 'Where's my f—ing triple somersault?' " Verkhovsky says, "even when he's watching a contortion act. If he feels we're getting too comfortable and too artsy, he will remind us that this is a circus and it is about performance at the maximum level. That is the great challenge."

I've just settled into my seat in the theater in Las Vegas when a lounge lizard in tight black vinyl pants and a greasy pompadour grabs my hand and pulls me up to the stage. The gigolo says he has my ticket, "M-69." He wants me to retrieve it . . . from the belt buckle above his crotch. The audience seems to think this is a fine idea. My husband thinks otherwise. It's my job.

Welcome to Sleazy Cirque, a.k.a. "Zumanity," where full-frontal Pilgrims, obese vixens in fishnets and thongs, and guys clad only in codpieces cavort, much to the joy of bachelorette parties, gay cabaret hounds, and nice married couples alike. This is not your father's Cirque. Until 1999, Cirque shows had a relatively consistent look, since many were the vision of a single creator, Franco Dragone (who left to form his own company, ultimately creating Wynn's "Le Reve").

Dragone's departure forced Cirque to take one of its biggest risks ever: to open its doors to other creators. The results have given the company new creative juice, spawning productions as diverse as frisky "Zumanity," epic "Ka," and soon, the musically driven Beatles show. It is the creative equivalent of the gymnast's triple somersault.

That commitment to constant innovation may help Cirque avoid the biggest hazard facing creative companies: a focus on defending their turf, rather than creating the next blue ocean. It's a nerve-racking way to do business, and Lamarre concedes he never stops being anxious before a new show. But he and his team, he says, are dedicated to always seeking the next big wave. "If there's a pattern that exists, we're going to break the mold," he says. "We want to reinvent ourselves all the time."

THE LAST WORD

On June 18, 24 of Saatchi & Saatchi's most imaginative, creative minds came together for two days in the library of the Soho House in New York. Their purpose? To reinvent Saatchi & Saatchi. Exactly 35 years on in Saatchi & Saatchi's history, it was time to transform the company into a new, velocity-driven ideas hothouse that could create sustainable growth for clients in a new marketing era—an era where mass marketing was dead, power has switched from brands through retailers to consumers, new platforms and new media were emerging daily, and nothing in the old playbook worked anymore.

These lucky people were greeted with one piece of preparation when they arrived in New York: Linda Tischler's article on Cirque du Soleil, its reinvention, and the bare bones of Blue Ocean Strategy. At 9:00 A.M. next morning, we waded in by looking at a DVD of Cirque du Soleil in action and delving into what they had eliminated, reduced, raised, and created. A circus without animals, high-priced talent, three rings; a circus with high pricing, a theater, and multiple shows. Two days later a blueprint for a new industry model had emerged. Now all we have to do is bring it to life and execute it. Thanks to Linda for providing us with the inspiration, the process, and the tool to get started.

Kevin Roberts
Worldwide CEO
Saatchi & Saatchi
New York, NY

INDEX